BURSTING THE WINESKINS

MICHAEL CASSIDY

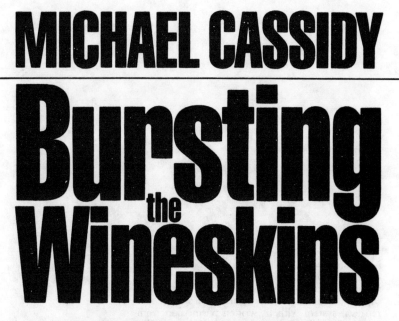

Bursting the Wineskins

The Holy Spirit's Transforming Work
in a Peacemaker and His World

Harold Shaw Publishers
Wheaton, Illinois

Cover photo courtesy of the Wine Institute of California

Unless otherwise indicated, all Scripture quotations are from *The Revised Standard Version of the Bible (RSV)*. References in footnotes may refer to the British edition of a title.

Library of Congress Cataloging in Publication Data

Cassidy, Michael, 1936-
    Bursting the wineskins.

    1. Cassidy, Michael, 1936-   2. Pentecostals—
Biography. 3. Holy Spirit. 4. Pentecostalism.
I. Title.
BX8762.Z8C383 1983 269'.4'0924 [B] 83-12585
ISBN 0-87788-094-8

Printed in the United States of America

93 92 91 90 89 88 87 86 85 84 83

10 9 8 7 6 5 4 3 2 1

For Olave
who has
tasted new wine
and helps others to
do likewise

No one puts new wine into old wineskins; if he does, the wine will burst the skins, and the wine is lost, and so are the skins; but new wine is for fresh skins.

Mark 2:22

The new wine is there. But the old wineskins of rigidity, inflexible denominationalism, hidebound traditionalism, and Christian factionalism often block its flow. The new wine being created by the work of the Spirit in the old wineskins must be released. God will provide his own fresh wineskins. But first the old wineskins must burst. Only then will a thirsty world be able to drink.

Michael Cassidy

Contents

Contents

Foreword

In this book my brother Michael witnesses to the inner work of the Holy Spirit as it affects daily relationships among God's people. His book is a personal witness rather than a theological thesis.

In evangelism and in the daily living of God's people, the Holy Spirit is not only the initiator and the effective power, but he also is the author. This is why it is always difficult for those who are compelled, inspired, and guided by the Holy Spirit to write about his work.

Michael, however, writes from his practical experience, and that is the strength of this volume. It is a faithful witness to the power, guidance, and balancing of the Spirit's ministry in us.

It is always difficult to keep a balance between the tremendous and unusual manifestations of the Holy Spirit in the lives of those who open up to him, and his work in keeping things in

order among brothers and sisters. One group takes one extreme
and another group takes another. Still others are afraid to write
about the work of the Spirit because they fear the potential mis-
understandings that this can bring. Of course, misunderstanding has nothing to do with the intentions of the Spirit
himself. But it does have a lot to do with how we react to the
impact of the Spirit in our own experience. So, in most cases, the
confusion lies not only with how people whom God blesses react,
but also with how they explain what they have felt and experienced.

The balancing factor in this book on the Holy Spirit, as
Michael writes, is the Lordship of Jesus Christ. He is the center.
It is he whom the Spirit glorifies. The Spirit takes the profound
and thrilling things of Christ and applies them in the lives of
ordinary people like ourselves. In glorifying Christ, the Holy
Spirit then shows his power. It is not power for self-demonstra-
tion but it is power to enlighten, to prompt, and to make the
community of believers move forward, giving glory to God.

If I change and simplify the image, I would say that the
Spirit's work is to bring out the radiant character of God's love
through Jesus Christ for us all to see and experience in fullness.

I have, therefore, been much impressed, blessed, and
inspired by this excellent discussion of the Holy Spirit. I pray
that those who read it will likewise be helped in many ways. For
instance, those who on the one hand tend to go to extremes by
pushing one particular experience will discover the balancing
power of the Holy Spirit in the person of the Lord Jesus Christ.
On the other hand, those who fear the workings of the Spirit will
understand that without him the Lord Jesus stays a stranger. In
their case, his work remains a mere story to be read about,
rather than a dynamic experience of God himself through that
Spirit who brings power into all believers' lives. Such people will
take courage from this book as they discover that the Holy Spirit
is the only one who can make the things of Christ a living reality
daily.

Another category of persons will be helped by this book. I am thinking of those who see the Spirit's work as affecting only our emotional life and feelings, so that one seems always in the triumph of heaven! These people will discover that the Holy Spirit is absolutely down to earth in the living of each day, so that when things go wrong in relationships they can be disentangled by his power.

The cross is central in the work of the Spirit. It wasn't until the Holy Spirit came and filled the hearts and minds of the disciples that the cross was lit up and became the center of the Good News. Before that it was a tragic event. So I pray that as the Spirit of God fills the hearts of those who read, we will discover together the depth of that great work that Jesus Christ did on the cross, out of which heaven opened and blessing came flooding into the hearts of men and women.

May God bless you as you read this tremendous account of grace, Michael's witness to the work of the blessed Spirit of God.

Festo Kivengere
Bishop of Kigezi, Uganda,
and East African Team Leader
of African Enterprise

Author's Preface

This is the story of one person's quest relating to the person and work of the Holy Spirit. It is a testimony, really. I share it because many others are caught up in a similar quest. Perhaps my own struggles may shed a little light on someone else's path of progress. If that happens, I will feel rewarded indeed.

I am thinking especially of those who live in that theological twilight between a rather rigid evangelicalism and a full-blown Pentecostalism. I am thinking of those who long to know more of the Spirit's fullness but who for one reason or another have not been able to identify unequivocally with the charismatic renewal in its present stage of development.

I am also writing for charismatics who know they have much to teach the rest of Christendom but who are not always aware of how much there is to learn from other sections of the body of Christ.

Put differently, I could say that my intention is to address, on the one hand, those whose fears of charismatics have paralyzed them into an unhappy and perhaps frustrating isolation from the fresh winds of the Spirit—and, on the other hand, those whose enthusiastic involvement in the charismatic renewal or in Pentecostalism has isolated them from the wider body of Christ with its important insights and correctives.

I hope also that the book will encourage many who may not be in any so-called camps, or bear any of Christendom's labels, but who simply want to move forward in the faith and in their discovery of the Spirit's blessings.

Let me also say that I write as a layman rather than a theologian. My hope, therefore, is that this volume will be an encouragement not only to many clergy but to many lay people as well. I have tried to stay reasonably down to earth, and personal, while at the same time not avoiding a modest measure of theological reflection. Because the issues around the work of the Holy Spirit have a strong theological component, some degree of theologizing cannot be avoided. The heavier parts, however, I have put in Appendices, where they may be explored by the more theologically motivated readers.

My appreciation goes to Derek Crumpton, David Bosch, Philip and Charmian Le Feuvre, and to my colleagues in African Enterprise, especially John Tooke and Bill Winter, for extensive counsel and suggestions relating to different sections of the book. Their wisdom has meant much. I am also much indebted to Rob Warner and Edward England of London who have helped me pilot the book through its final stages into published form. Enormous secretarial labors were performed by Bertha Graham, Pat Stockdale, and Hazel Hodgson. Malcolm Graham put in many hours of proofreading. Myrtle Beck, Brenda Peterson, and Colleen Smith helped me in many miscellaneous ways, especially with the finishing touches. I also owe much to many other friends and writers whose thinking has been absorbed almost unconsciously into my own. In this I think especially of Bishop Stephen Neill. Above all, I want to thank my dear wife, Carol, who constantly prays for me, supports me, and also helps me keep my feet on the ground. She also makes many sacrifices in order for me to give myself to projects such as this book.

My prayer in sending forth this book is that it will constitute a contribution to that wonderful Pauline process of "maintaining the unity of the Spirit in the bond of peace."

Michael Cassidy
Pietermaritzburg, Natal
July 1982

1
A Walk in the Fields

First be reconciled to your brother, and then
come and offer your gift.
Jesus, Matthew 5:24

THE LATE AFTERNOON SUN had not yet set over the majestic Drakensberg mountains when I set off on a walk through the fields of the Fyvie farm near Bergville. It was one of those lovely South African evenings when all nature seems to beckon through the gentle light to one's heart, saying that God is real and alive.

Carol and I had escaped to John and Beth Fyvie's farm for a quiet weekend. John and Beth were playing tennis and Carol was giving the children their baths, so I escaped into what in South Africa we call "mealie" fields ("corn fields" to the rest of the world).

Cows were drifting up to the sheds for milking and some ducks were winging their way home as I got down into the fields. Here and there I disturbed little groups of partridges flapping away with great commotion from almost under my feet. In the distance the jagged silhouette of the mountains rose to nearly twelve thousand feet against the glowing evening.

All was peaceful and quiet. It was good to be away from the bustle of town life and the constant pressures of ministry and travel. As I meditated and prayed, a distinct thought entered my mind seemingly out of the blue, but with the force of a breath from on high: "Before that conference next August, you must get right with Jim and Mary."

That was the first inkling I was to have that the South African conference on the Holy Spirit—dubbed the Renewal Conference—was to be of special importance to me. In fact I was hardly sure I even wanted to be there; I was not quite convinced that renewal gatherings were part of my "scene." But I had tentatively decided to go simply because I didn't want to contribute to further dividedness in the South African body of Christ.

Now came this word about something I had to do before that conference. I had to resolve a relationship that had gone wrong.

Jim and Mary had been close and dear friends. But as can happen even among Christians, we had become alienated seven years before. The reasons were complex; not even we ourselves fully comprehended them. It had been a source of great pain and grief to me. It had stuck in the landscape of my soul like a great rock that refused to move even with the eroding processes of time. "Here I am," I often thought, "preaching reconciliation, yet a relationship in my own life needs reconciliation."

The curious thing is that back in 1971 I felt I had received twofold guidance in this respect—first, to abandon the relationship for the time being and not to try to restart it, and second, to "forgive *from the heart*," as in Matthew 18:35. It was not that I didn't need forgiveness myself. I did, perhaps more than I could admit. But I had to forgive from the heart those wrongs, real or imagined, that I felt had been done to me. It's easy to verbalize our forgiveness of others, but truly to forgive *from the heart* is another matter. Unless forgiveness is heartfelt it is like burying a hatchet but leaving the handle exposed so it can be seized again at a later stage.

Another curious phenomenon was that ever since that sad rupture, I had repeatedly dreamed about Jim and Mary, always in the warm embrace of reconciliation, healing, and love. Those dreams had gone on regularly over the years.

Then one night, sometime in mid-1976, I had another vivid dream. I woke realizing that in some way those nocturnal experiences had already been bringing healing to my wounds. The forgiveness I now felt was not just verbal but from the heart. I had no explanation for that, no theological category for it, yet I knew it was so. God was doing something, saying something, to me—*in my sleep.* Beyond that, I recognized a new flow of the love I had previously felt for my two friends. Perhaps I should make contact again.

But now, in the mealie field nearly a year later, I realized I had done nothing about it. As for this conference, who knows what it would be about? And what was the link between my two friends in the States and a Christian gathering in faraway Johannesburg?

2
Signed,
Sealed,
Delivered

No one can say "Jesus is Lord" except by
the Holy Spirit.
St. Paul, 1 Corinthians 12:3

IN THE WEEKS THAT FOLLOWED, I had to give much thought to
my attitude to that coming charismatic conference on the Holy
Spirit. (The adjective *charismatic*, derived from the Greek word
charismata, meaning "gifts of grace" and referring specifically to
supernaturally given spiritual gifts, is widely used to describe
those movements in the church that stress the work of the Holy
Spirit.)

I also needed to think through the position of African Enterprise, the missionary organization I had started in 1961 to do
evangelism in the cities of Africa. We all stood firmly in what one
might call the evangelical camp. (The term *evangelical* describes
the broad spectrum of Christians who limit religious authority to
the Bible and who stress the New Testament doctrines of conversion, new birth, and justification by grace through faith alone.
Evangelicals hold to the full inspiration of the Bible as the Word
of God.)

Our views on the work of the Holy Spirit were straightforward and orthodox. We believed in the co-equality of the Holy Spirit, the Third Person in the Trinity, with God the Father and God the Son, and that the Spirit "proceeds," as the creed says, "from the Father and the Son." We knew that the Trinitarian formula had developed out of both Jesus' teaching and the disciples' experience. Before Jesus had come they had known "God *above* them," with the heavens declaring his glory and the firmament showing his handiwork. When Jesus came they knew "God *with* them"—"He who has seen me has seen the Father" (John 14:9). After Jesus' resurrection and ascension, they had known "God *in* them," in the person of the Holy Spirit. God was a Trinity of persons yet a unity of substance.

Then, as a team of evangelists, we had not only read our Bibles but observed the spiritual processes of hundreds of people coming to Christ over the years. We knew of the Holy Spirit's clear ministry not only before and at, but after conversion.

Before Conversion
Before conversion, it is the Holy Spirit who illuminates seeking minds and draws questing souls. One of the key scriptures in the whole evangelistic enterprise says that no one can say that Jesus is Lord, except by the Holy Spirit (1 Cor. 12:3). The process of revealing Christ as Lord to the inquiring mind is superintended by the Holy Spirit of God. Revelation is a supernatural thing. The natural man by himself cannot recognize that Jesus is Lord because, as St. Paul says in Corinthians, these things are "spiritually discerned" (1 Cor. 2:14).

Those ideas came home powerfully to me in one of our evangelistic missions in the city of Ladysmith in 1965. A businessman traveling from Rhodesia (now Zimbabwe) had stopped in Ladysmith on business and was detained there during our mission. (I did not know then that his Christian wife back in Rhodesia had been praying fervently for his conversion.) Now he found himself stuck for a week in this quaint little town with nothing going on in the evenings, except of all things, an evangelistic campaign. "Just my luck," he must have thought.

For want of anything better to do, poor man, he came to the town hall night after night. Halfway through the week he asked to talk with me and we went out for coffee after the meeting to a small roadside café. The sleepy little town had become the scene of an urgent quest. In those few days a deep desire had developed in him to find Christ for himself. But there was a fog over his mind. Nothing I said, no illustration, Scripture, or explanation seemed able to pierce the fog.

I realized there was nothing more I could say. The Holy Spirit would have to do his illuminating work. God the Father would have to draw him by his Spirit to the Son. I remembered Jesus' words: "No man can come to me unless the Father who sent me draws him" (John 6:44). Likewise Jesus had said it was the job of the Holy Spirit to convince the world of sin, of righteousness, and of judgment (John 16:8). And even the Old Testament contained the reminder that it is "not by might, nor by power, but by my Spirit, says the Lord" (Zech. 4:6). My perplexed friend, with his praying wife, would have to keep seeking until the Spirit brought that final illumination without which "no man can say that Jesus is Lord."

The last night the town hall was packed. As the service ended, I saw my friend barrelling down the hall toward me, his face aglow, his eyes radiant, his smile like Alice in Wonderland's Cheshire Cat.

"I see," he said. "I see. It's all so clear. How could I have been so blind? It's as if scales have been removed from my eyes. Praise God, I see!" I had said nothing new or fresh that night in my sermon, but his seeking heart had finally experienced that illumination which is the Spirit's special work in us *before* conversion.

At Conversion
From the time of my own conversion to Christ as a university

student in England in 1955, I had been convinced that the Holy
Spirit is the agent in new birth and that at the time of new birth
the Holy Spirit himself indwells the believer.

I remembered that gentle English morning in a little student
apartment in Cambridge when, with the help of my friend
Robert Footner, I had said Yes to Jesus Christ and invited him
into my heart by faith. Life was never the same again. I had no
theology to tell me what had happened except that I had
responded to God's promise in Revelation 3:20, and so had he.
"Behold, I stand at the door and knock; if any one hears my
voice and opens the door, I will come in." I had opened. He had
come in.

My journal records the feelings that gripped me that October.
"As I realized the true wonder of that promise, things began
happening with a wonderful and almost alarming rapidity. It
was as though I was having a radio wave of joy filtered into
me—a new surge of wonderful life, and a new and hitherto
unexperienced feeling of God's presence—all this in a few
hours. That evening I heard a sermon that for once *meant* something to me. For the first time I understood what it meant to
'have' Christ. I understood the meaning of the words, 'the
peace of God, which passes all understanding,' because for the
first time in my life I was experiencing true fellowship with God.
After the service I jumped onto my bike and tore round to tell
another of my friends all about it."

A week later I went to church and saw on a big poster at the
gate: "If any one is in Christ, he is a new creation; the old has
passed away, behold, the new has come" (2 Cor. 5:17). "Goodness," I said to myself, "even St. Paul found what I've found!"
I was almost as excited to read the testimony of Temple
Gairdner, a great Anglican missionary to Cairo. Shortly after
his conversion, he wrote: "That sense of newness is simply delicious. It makes new the Bible and friends and all mankind and
love and spiritual things and Sunday and church and God himself. So I've found." Now I myself was tasting that delicious
sense of newness.

But what had in fact happened? I mean, theologically and biblically, what had taken place in my life? Luckily, the Cambridge Inter-Collegiate Christian Union (CICCU) had weekly Bible studies. At one of those, Dr. Basil Atkinson, one of England's most formidable Greek scholars and one of Cambridge's great characters, spoke on the experience of new birth as Jesus explained it to Nicodemus. As he expounded John 3, his entire face lit up in a sort of celebration.

"The Holy Spirit is the agent of the new birth," he said. "Just look at verses 5 and 6: Jesus said, 'I say to you, unless one is born of water (John the Baptist's "baptism of repentance," which Nicodemus would have known about) and *the Spirit*, he cannot enter the kingdom of God. That which is born of the flesh is flesh, and that which is born of the Spirit is Spirit.' "

"When you open your heart to Jesus," Basil said, "he enters in the person of the Holy Spirit and indwells you." Flipping in his Greek New Testament to 1 Corinthians 3:16, he read: "Don't you know that you are God's temple and that God's Spirit dwells in you?" And 2 Corinthians 1:22: "He has put his seal upon us and given us his Spirit *in our hearts* as a guarantee."

"When we are born again by the agency of the Holy Spirit," Basil continued, "he enters our hearts and is there as a seal or guarantee that we belong to God. That word *seal* in the Greek, refers to the seal that oriental traders would put on their products as a sign of purchase. The trader would buy some merchandise at the beginning of his day's business. Without a supermarket cart to carry it all around with him, he needed to put his own mark on the merchandise, returning at the end of the day to collect it and take it home as his own."

"So you see," beamed Basil, as he could see truth coming home to us on the wings of illustration, "that is why St. Paul used this Greek word for 'seal' to describe what God does by his Holy Spirit at the time of our conversion. He seals us 'with the promised Holy Spirit, which is the guarantee of our inheritance, until we acquire possession of it, to the praise of His glory' " (Eph. 1:14).

That all made sense to me. It fitted my experience. I knew that Christ had come into my heart in the person of the Holy Spirit at my conversion. I believed then, and now, that this is the experience of every true believer at new birth, whether he or she is aware of it or not. This seemed even clearer when I discovered Titus 3:5: "He saved us, not because of deeds done by us in righteousness, but in virtue of his own mercy, by the washing of *regeneration* and *renewal in the Holy Spirit,* which he poured out upon us richly through Jesus Christ our Savior." If the Holy Spirit entered our hearts at the time of conversion, no wonder Paul prayed for the Ephesians that "the eyes of their hearts" should be enlightened to know "what is the immeasurable greatness of his power in us who believe" (Eph. 1:19). We, too, need both prayer and teaching so that the eyes of our hearts will be opened (a beautiful, suggestive little phrase) to grasp the overwhelming power at work in us from our conversion on.

After Conversion
I was so enamored with Basil's first Bible study on Nicodemus that I kept going to the CICCU Bible studies each Wednesday. Members of the Cambridge Inter-Collegiate Christian Union had got their loving clutches on me within hours of my arrival in Cambridge. Their notices all over the college boards, and via the college mailboxes, alerted every Cambridge student to the weekly Bible studies. Those studies soon took us into the book of Romans. (My interpretations often left much to be desired. For example, when I read "no human being will be justified in his sight by works of the law" (Rom. 3:20), I took this as divine confirmation that I had been right to change my degree course from Law to Languages!) Soon we were in Romans 8, which among other things spoke again about the work of the Spirit, especially after conversion.

First of all, "the Spirit of life in Christ Jesus" (Rom. 8:2), has set us free from the law of sin and death. Second, we are to "live according to the Spirit" (verse 5) and set our minds "on the things of the Spirit." To do this is "life and peace" (verse 6) in contrast to the "death" that results from setting one's mind on "the flesh," or the old nature (verse 6). Third, Paul tells us that we are "in the Spirit," if the Spirit is in us. "You are in the Spirit, if in fact the Spirit of God *dwells in you*" (verse 9). More than that, "Any one who does not have the Spirit of Christ does not belong to him" (verse 9b). In other words, the mark of belonging to Christ at all is the indwelling Spirit.

I saw that principle underlined further in the very next verse (verse 11). "If the Spirit of him who raised Jesus from the dead *dwells in you,* he who raised Christ Jesus from the dead will give life to your mortal bodies, also through his Spirit which *dwells in you.*" Three times in three verses—"the Spirit dwells in you." This was written to all the Roman believers.

Receiving the Spirit?

I emphasize those ideas because it was against the backdrop of that kind of scriptural teaching that I was later to find myself very confused by the phrase "receiving the Holy Spirit" which constantly recurs in charismatic writings. Had I not received the Holy Spirit? How then could I or any believer be challenged or prayed for to receive the Holy Spirit again?

For example, when I later read Dennis Bennett's book *Nine O'Clock in the Morning* I found him constantly speaking of praying for believers to receive the Holy Spirit. Then suddenly on page 115 there was a footnote: "Receiving the Holy Spirit or being 'baptized in the Holy Spirit' does not mean getting the Holy Spirit, but 'receiving' or 'making welcome,' permitting the Holy Spirit to fill more areas of our lives and to flow out from us to the world." My thought then was this: "If receiving the Spirit subsequent to conversion does not mean getting him in one's life for the first time, it is probably better not to use the phrase."

Then again on page 138, Bennett reports on a meeting in England: "After making sure that all present had personally accepted Christ as their Savior, I began to pray for those who asked—a few for healing or other needs, but mostly praying for them to receive the Holy Spirit. Once again the miracle began to happen as Christians, *already indwelt by the Holy Spirit,* began to trust Jesus to inundate them with his power of freedom so that the riches stored in them could break forth to the world" (italics mine).

Reading that paragraph I wondered to myself again, if they were "already indwelt by the Holy Spirit," does the phrase "receiving the Spirit" really clarify or does it confuse the issue?

Of course, back in 1955 hardly anyone in the mainline churches had even heard the word "charismatic" or been exposed to any such writings. All we knew was that we had received the Holy Spirit at our conversion and that he was the decisive factor in growth and progress after conversion.

I quickly discovered several other dimensions of the Spirit's post-conversion ministry. One of those, the granting of assurance of salvation, is very clear in Romans 8. No one had had to tell me I was a child of God and that I belonged to Christ as his son. That realization had been communicated to my theologically untutored heart spiritually rather than intellectually. I couldn't understand it. Then I heard Romans 8:16 in a Bible study and it all clicked. "It is the Spirit himself bearing witness with our spirit that we *are* children of God." Some weeks later when Billy Graham visited Cambridge for a mission, I sang for the first time "Blessed assurance, Jesus is mine." I knew that through the Holy Spirit.

The Word of God
There was something else. The Holy Spirit communicated to me (it must have been he—it was such a forceful conviction) that the Bible was in some special sense "the Word of God." In the first weeks and months after my conversion I used to ascribe divine authority only to the Gospels and to Jesus' own words, but not to the epistles. Then suddenly one day I knew, I just *knew,* that the whole Bible was the Word of God.

Late in 1955, a great controversy erupted in England with letters flowing fast and furiously to *The Times* on the issue of biblical authority and inspiration. It all stemmed from the visit of Billy Graham, a so-called "fundamentalist," to the intellectual corridors of Cambridge. (Whenever Englishmen get mad at each other *The Times* has to take up the slack and yield itself as battlefield.) I followed the interchange closely and devoured Gabriel Hebert's book, *Fundamentalism and the Church of God,* and then James Packer's reply, *Fundamentalism and the Word of God,* along with many others. I certainly didn't want the fundamentalist label, but I did want to hold on to the Spirit-given conviction that the Bible is the Word of God.

In another of those college Bible studies I discovered 2 Timothy 3:16—"All scripture is inspired by God." I believed it. Then I found 2 Peter 1:20—"No prophecy of scripture is a matter of one's own interpretation, because no prophecy ever came by the impulse of man, but men moved by the Holy Spirit spoke from God." I believed it. Then there were Jesus' words in John 16:13-14—"When the Spirit of truth comes, he will guide you into all truth . . . He will glorify me, for he will take what is mine and declare it to you." John 14:25 likewise quoted Jesus' own words: "But the Counselor, the Holy Spirit, whom the Father will send in my name, he will teach you all things, and bring to your remembrance all that I have said to you." I saw this as referring to the apostle's recognition of Jesus' words as God's truth. I believed it.

One other point. In those far-off days we undergraduates were taught many things about the work of the Spirit after conversion—in setting us apart for God, in guiding us, in helping us grow, in strengthening us, in bringing freedom from bondage, in exalting Christ, in enabling others to respond to Christ, and in bringing forth the fruit of the Spirit (as in Galatians 5:22). But no one ever mentioned the gifts of the Spirit described in 1 Corinthians 12 and 14. Evangelicals avoided that subject; at least no one ever spoke about it to me. Eight years later, as a student at Fuller Theological Seminary in California, I began to wonder why.

3
First Inklings

We must in no way hinder the Spirit of God.
Charles Troutman

WHEN THE RENEWAL CONFERENCE (mentioned in Chapter 1) loomed on the horizon for August 1977, I was not only given a personal priority of dealing with a broken relationship but was also presented with the challenge of what stand to take, both personally and as leader of an evangelical agency.

As I have indicated, our stance in African Enterprise had been pretty straightforward, conservative, mainline, true-blue evangelical. But it was inevitable, as members of an interdenominational ministry committed to the whole body of Christ, that both individually and corporately we already should have had some exposure to the charismatic renewal. One of the special privileges of interdenominational ministries is that one is constantly exposed to a wide range of viewpoints. Often these creatively disturb one's own theological status quo as they penetrate one's own ecclesiastical ghettos.

I have always personally resisted "Christian ghetto living" as both stultifying and suffocating. Though I have always thanked God for my conservative evangelical heritage through CICCU and Inter-Varsity and Fuller Seminary and so on, for some reason of either perversity or adventurousness I have never wanted to close myself off from other influences, whether ecumenical, charismatic, or Catholic. If a thing is true, it's true, whoever has found it. Bishop Don Jacobs once said to me in Nairobi: "Michael, let every Christian be both your brother and your teacher."

Perhaps that is why I responded so positively to another bishop friend, Stephen Neill (one of my special patron saints), when on numerous occasions he said to me: "Now, here's a book I want you to read. You won't agree with all of it, but then why should you?"—teaching me the importance of reading books with which one disagrees. "We can't be one-channel viewers," he would stress.

Of course that kind of outlook is very much in the English academic tradition in which I was raised. It is also part of the lifestyle of the Anglican church of which I am a member. Anglicans, of whatever theological persuasion, evangelical ones not excluded, live in a theological marketplace within their own denomination which has never been theologically homogeneous. Each member, and especially those who have clear or definite theological convictions, has to work these out or proclaim them or defend them, according to inclination. So theological pluralism doesn't frighten Anglicans, and it has never frightened me; in fact I enjoy it. Perhaps it is this which has opened Anglican and Episcopalian hearts across the world so readily to the renewing winds of the Holy Spirit.

Truth Matters
Yet my strong evangelical instincts and deep commitments to biblical truth, as I understand it, have always checked me from quickly embracing new Christian fads or from an easy acceptance of the slogan that "doctrine divides and love unites."

"Why," I thought, "does the New Testament contain so much doctrine if doctrine is unimportant?" To me, right theology and doctrine were vital. Another dear friend down the years, Francis Schaeffer, had taught me "Truth matters." At the Berlin Congress on Evangelism in 1966 I had rejoiced in his affirmation: "Historic Christianity rests on truth—not truth as an abstract concept, nor even what twentieth-century man regards as 'religious' truth, but on objective truth...Historic Christianity rests on the truth of what today is called 'brute facts' and not just upon unknown experiences of human beings in past ages...Behind the truth of such history is the great truth that the personal, infinite God is objectively 'there.' He actually exists (in contrast to his not being there): and Christ's redemptive and finished work actually took place at a point of time in real space-time history (in contrast to this not being the case). Historic Christianity rests on the truth of these things in absolute antithesis to their not being true."[1]

That certainly is just as true of the work of the Holy Spirit as of the resurrection, the ascension, or the new birth, so I wasn't willing to be swept off my theological feet by any Tom, Dick, or Harry who claimed some special new experience of the Holy Spirit.

What Happened at Yale
Even so, I couldn't honestly close my mind or my eyes to what was happening around me and across the world. The first inklings I received of something beyond my rather orthodox evangelical understanding of the Holy Spirit was when David Fisher, a friend who had been at Yale University in the early 1960s, came to Fuller Seminary and told us about revival going on among the students in the Inter-Varsity group there (Yale's counterpart to the CICCU at Cambridge). David said numbers of the students were also "speaking in tongues," whatever that meant. I knew it was in the Bible somewhere, among passages I had skipped over.

He reported that some sort of infilling of the Holy Spirit had

taken place in several students and that not only were certain
spiritual gifts being manifested but there was a new love and joy
among them, and a new evangelistic zeal. Beyond that, they had
held a twenty-four-hour prayer vigil for one of their startled
chaplains who had been taken to the hospital with a serious illness. An even more startled chaplain had been released by the
hospital the next day.

With those happenings a seismic shock went through the
ranks of Inter-Varsity's national leadership. What were they to
do, as a respectable evangelical group?

On January 22, 1963, Dr. Charles Hummel, one of the
national leaders of the Inter-Varsity Christian Fellowship
(IVCF), arrived nervously on campus to investigate the whole
business. He had been taught that the gifts of the Spirit were
given only in the first century to establish the church. Now that
view was being challenged, not by some theologian with another
interpretation, but by *events*.

He later wrote: "From all I could see, both the exercise of
these spiritual gifts and their results were quite biblical, although
contrary to my own theological convictions. . . I left the campus
with praise for the Lord's work in the Yale Christian Fellowship
and its broadening influence on the campus. I also went away
with the questions which were to pursue me for years."[2]

My own reaction to David Fisher's story was similar. My
stance was exactly that of the IVCF leadership, who then witnessed other campuses being similarly touched. Hummel said:
"Most IVCF leaders had a theological bias against the movement, yet we wanted to welcome any new work God might be
doing. How could we deny the significance of the fact that many
were exercising these unusual gifts according to biblical teaching
and with beneficial results to student lives?"[3]

Charles Troutman, general director of IVCF, sent a memo-
randum to all IVCF field workers. A summary paragraph
stated:

If this is a movement of God for all his children—even though it may be abused—then we want to be part of it. If this is not a movement of God, we want to help those of our brethren who have become enmeshed. If there is a misplaced emphasis, we want to bring a balance. We must in no way hinder the Spirit of God from working in individuals as he wills.[4]

Summer 1963

That cautious but gentle openness encouraged my friend David to go off the next summer to Latin America to learn more about some of the reported happenings there, but not before he had introduced me to Harald Bredesen, a Lutheran pastor who was a friend of his. Bredesen startled me further with a story of a personal experience: he testified to a new release of the Holy Spirit which had apparently transformed his life and ministry. Flowing out of that experience had come some very remarkable happenings, one of which has stuck vividly in my mind ever since he told it.

He had been at a breakfast meeting in a New York hotel. There he had met a young woman who testified to dryness in her spiritual life. Bredesen responded by saying that his own devotional life had taken on a new depth through "speaking in tongues." She was totally mystified and asked what that was.

"It means speaking in a language that God gives you," Harald had replied. The young woman asked whether he could do it whenever he wanted to and Bredesen replied in the affirmative.

"Would you like me to pray for you this way now? I won't embarrass you," he promised.

The story fascinated me. "What happened?" I asked. "How did she respond?"

"Well," said Harald, "I'd no sooner asked her the question than I began to feel a prayer language welling up in my heart for her and I began to pray out the sounds with my head bowed. When I had finished I opened my eyes. The girl was almost ashen in color.

"Why...why...I understood you," she gasped. 'You were praising God and speaking a very old form of Arabic.' " I listened goggle-eyed as Harald reported how she then told him that she was the daughter of an Egyptologist and that she herself spoke several forms of Arabic—she had in fact studied archaic Arabic. She even complimented him on his accent. "You spoke it like a Bedouin! Where on earth did you learn old Arabic?"

Harald told her he had never learned it. It was the language God had given him for that moment to confront her as a needy and perhaps slightly skeptical human being. God had done it in a manner that would be incontrovertible to her mind. It was certainly astounding to mine. I had never heard anything quite like it. Did God still do that sort of thing in the twentieth century?

I decided I would have to reserve judgment. In the meantime I signed up as a summer worker with the Billy Graham Los Angeles Crusade. Billy Graham had already exercised a massive influence on my life. For one thing, my friend Robert Footner, who had led me to Christ, had himself been won under Graham's ministry at Harringay in 1954, so I was a second-generation Graham convert. Then, a few weeks after my own conversion, Dr. Graham's controversial mission had come to Cambridge. That had really set me on my feet. On top of that, my own call to evangelism had taken place in Madison Square Garden after one of the New York Crusade meetings in summer 1957. So Billy Graham was a special hero to me. And the Los Angeles Crusade, closing with 200,000 people present at the final meeting in the Coliseum, was another unforgettable experience.

But the charismatic question wouldn't go away. Another of my close friends, Edward, who had been active with both Inter-Varsity and the Billy Graham Association, suddenly got caught up in the charismatic renewal. One smoggy afternoon, a good friend from the Billy Graham Crusade headquarters called me into his office.

"Mike, what's going on with Edward?"

"What do you mean?" I responded with some apprehension (I could see he was a bit put out).

"Well, we have had a complaint. Someone phoned his house about crusade business and was told he couldn't come to the phone as they were all in a prayer meeting and there had just been a prophecy in tongues which someone was busy interpreting. What do you make of that?" He looked mystified.

"Oh, brother, don't ask me," I replied. "I'm just as much in the dark as you."

Some weeks later Edward resigned from his associations with both Inter-Varsity and the Graham Association. That shook me. Seems like this whole thing is some kind of dynamite, I thought. Better take it easy.

4
The Lesson
of the Lion

We must insist from the beginning that
we believe... in a spirit world which
can and does invade the natural
or phenomenal universe.
C.S. Lewis

WHEN DAVE FISHER CAME BACK from Colombia, he reported
that the whole place down there was popping with strange happenings of the Holy Spirit. One story he told in a newsletter
focused on Victor Landero, a one-time bartender who had also
managed a group of prostitutes.

An uneducated ruffian, Landero had been converted in 1957
through reading a Bible that someone gave him. He immediately rid himself of both bar and brothel and began to share
Christ with all who would listen in a remote unevangelized area
upriver to which he had moved. There were no missionaries
around to tell him or his converts what could or couldn't happen
in the twentieth century. They just read and learned from Victor's Bible and believed what they read there. And the book of
Acts began to be reenacted. The miraculous became an
accepted, expected part of their daily lives.

David's newsletter told of one incident related to an extraordinary dream of Victor's. Years later I read the same story in a book by professor Peter Wagner of Fuller Theological Seminary, one of the world's senior missiologists. I'll let Peter tell the story.

One night Victor Landero had a vivid dream of a certain hut in the woods which he had never seen before. A clear voice said to him, "The people in that hut are dying without Christ because no one ever told them of Him." It took some time to do it, but months later Victor started out through the woods with no idea where he was going. After only two days, he came into a clearing and saw the hut of which he had dreamed. He knocked on the door, met the family, and told them why he had come.

The woman of the house was speechless. Only three nights previously, she had dreamed a strange dream. She saw her house full of people with a stranger talking to them out of a book. The word "gospel" came to her in her dream, although she had never heard the word before.[5]

David Fisher then told how the woman had gathered her family and friends that evening to listen to the message from this mysterious stranger. Virtually all responded by committing their lives to the Jesus of whom Victor spoke. Staying with them for some days, Victor got them grounded in the first principles of their new-found faith. In due time this little group became a thriving New Testament church, typical of many others springing up in extraordinary ways.

Wagner went on to report how Landero had spent many hours with the believers in this area praying to God.

One day something unusual happened. They were overcome with a sense of joy that they could not explain. They prayed through the night, and read the book of Acts to each other. After they had done this several times, spontaneously one of them spoke in tongues! Others soon began to do the same.

A type of charismatic movement had started in the Colombian forest, but it was a "spontaneous combustion" process. Obviously, this particular manifestation of the Spirit had come down from heaven. It was not something that had been taught to them by other Christians.[6]

It didn't end there. Soon after the gift of tongues, the gift of interpretation came.

One of the first messages received through tongues and interpretation was a clear command to persevere in what they were doing. They received it as the voice of God. Then they started praying for the sick and many were healed. A blind man received his sight. A paralytic began to walk for the first time. Young men saw visions, and old men dreamed dreams. Everyone was praising the Lord.[7]

That kind of thing challenged the directors of the Latin American Mission (L.A.M.) to their boots. Like the Inter-Varsity directors, they were facing not abstract theological arguments but facts. What were they to do?

David Howard, director of the Colombian field of L.A.M., a man with no Pentecostal inclinations, later wrote:

Slowly, God removed our skepticism, confirming the gifts of the Spirit by showing the fruit of the Spirit in the lives of the believers who received these gifts . . . They showed more love, joy, peace, and other Christian attributes than many Christians who had known the Lord for years.[8]

Peter Wagner concludes his section on Landero and his Colombian friends by noting that

Howard and his colleagues exercised Christian patience and tolerance in what was for them an unusual and difficult situation. They have never regretted it, for the Spirit has continued to work in many extraordinary ways, and most of all, the Lord is adding daily to the church such as should be saved.[9]

Kenneth Strachan

As far as I was concerned, Dave Fisher's stories, especially
about Landero, were very interesting, especially because they
were connecting in my mind with what I had heard in my last
term at Fuller Seminary from Dr. Kenneth Strachan, then general director of L.A.M. L.A.M. certainly was, and is, one of
the twentieth-century's great missionary agencies and Ken
Strachan was one of its great missionary statesmen and leaders.
He knew he had cancer and was in the homestretch of his life.
How privileged we felt when we students heard he was coming
to lecture on missions for a term at Fuller. I listened avidly to
everything he said, drank in the lessons he had learned, and
cultivated his friendship at a personal level.

Few visiting professors who came to Fuller Seminary in those
years made such an impact on the students as did Strachan. His
dedication, his humanity, and the godliness of his character
struck all of us. But what impressed me most was his spiritual,
intellectual, and theological integrity in the face of some of the
unusual spiritual phenomena breaking out in these infant Latin
American churches, especially in Colombia. After all, visions,
tongues, prophecies, and healings had hardly been an integral
part of his frame of reference up to that point.

If I remember rightly, his own view up to then had been that
these phenomena occurred as an authenticating witness to the
first-century church, but they had all stopped with the end of the
apostolic period. Yet now he heard of them in his own missionary area, and in churches over which he had, in at least some
degree, a measure of jurisdiction and responsibility. Strachan
reported to us how he had had these miraculous phenomena
rigorously investigated by trusted colleagues. The result was
that he had been forced to alter his presuppositions about what
God was doing in the twentieth century. That is never easy.
Most of us would rather cling to our views of the possible than
allow ourselves to be shaken, even by hard evidence to the contrary.

A friend of mine in Durban, South Africa, was once leaving a little restaurant after a party with a group of friends. As he put his hand to the door, prior to opening it and stepping out into the street, he heard a lion roar. He knew it had been a good party, but not that good. He also knew he was not hearing things. And beyond that he knew by definition and rational presupposition that there *are* no lions in city-centers, not even in South Africa. So, although slightly mystified, he stepped boldly out into the street and almost into the jaws of—you guessed it—a real, live, large-as-life African lion. His presuppositional world did a 360° turn in a thousandth of a second. He pulled off a gymnastic feat that would have been the envy of an Olympic gold medalist, launching himself backward through the door of the restaurant, where he fell at the feet of his astonished friends. Of course, he didn't know about the circus in town or the frenzied lion-tamer struggling frantically to locate the whereabouts of his wayward star performer.

One does sometimes have to change one's presuppositions in the face of facts. Victor Landero's story, plus the honest testimony and conclusions of Ken Strachan, changed mine, even as, in another sense, a lion in a Durban street had interrupted the ordinary life of my friend.

5
Stirrings among the Bones

So I prophesied as I was commanded; and
as I prophesied, there was a noise, and
behold, a rattling; and the bones
came together, bone to its bone.
Ezekiel 37:7

THE LATTER PART OF 1964 saw four of us from Fuller Seminary set out for Africa as the newly formed African Enterprise team. Our burden for urban evangelism in Africa was compelling; we couldn't wait to get started. Our views on the work of the Holy Spirit were safely and soundly evangelical, as I have said, although our hearts were open to learn more of God's mysterious ways.

After some eighteen months of hectic campaigning in Natal and in Lesotho (formerly Basutoland), where we conducted a nationwide evangelistic endeavor just prior to that country's independence, the door opened for me to attend the World Congress on Evangelism in Berlin in late 1966. That gathering called together evangelical leaders from all over the world for reflection on the imperative of world evangelization; the theme: "One Race, one Gospel, one Task." No one there would have doubted the importance of the Holy Spirit in the task of world evangelization, yet, novice though I was to the world evangelical scene, it struck me as curious that so few Pentecostals were present (although much ado was made over the presence of the controversial Oral Roberts). Either evangelicals weren't too interested in Pentecostals, or Pentecostals weren't too interested in world evangelization. I wasn't sure which.

In any event, I was preoccupied with the uproar caused in the South African delegation, and beyond it, by my treatment of the topic assigned me, "Political Nationalism as an Obstacle to Evangelism." I had showed how both white and black nationalism impeded evangelism. Illustrating this from my South African experience, I stepped so squarely on the theological toes of certain Dutch Reformed South Africans present that they demanded that the Congress authorities expunge my paper from the Congress record. My only consolation lay in the fact that the more they thundered, the more friends I gathered from all over the world.

Then, when Dick Halverson of Fourth Presbyterian Church in Washington, D.C., spoke on evangelism and the release of the Holy Spirit as an overflow of fellowship, as in Acts chapter two, I found myself under conviction by that Spirit to apologize to my two Dutch Reformed friends for reciprocating the hostility in their volcanic reaction to my paper. My apology was received by one and rejected by the other. "I want to vomit and go home," was the latter's reply.

Perplexing though all that was, equally perplexing on a different front was my being cautioned by one evangelical leader "not to touch the charismatic renewal with a barge-pole," while another took me to breakfast and told me how his whole life and ministry had been revolutionized by an experience that he called "the baptism in the Holy Spirit."

I left Berlin wondering more than ever why a deep commitment to evangelism, a Pentecostal fullness of the Holy Spirit, and an authentic social concern should not come together. Hadn't the Bible put all those ingredients into one package and marked them "mix well"? Yet the mixing didn't seem to be happening.

Flying on to the States, I met at least two or three other friends from Fuller Seminary days who not only professed a new experience of the Holy Spirit, but who were manifestly changed as a result. One of them, now a relaxed, free, and loving person, had been one of the most rigid, unbending, uptight spiritual automatons I had ever known. To see him so radically altered kept the cogs of my searching soul turning.

Shrine Auditorium
One day soon after that a friend invited me to one of Kathryn Kuhlman's services in the Shrine Auditorium in Los Angeles. He wanted to reinforce in me the belief that God could still heal in the twentieth century. He got us two tickets so we could sit on the platform. Clearly he expected that seeing would be believing.

Of course there were the inevitable subcultural hurdles to negotiate. First of all, the organ prelude seemed more appropriate to the spins and whirls of a roller-skating rink than a religious service. Miss Kuhlman's entry onto the stage with a Lawrence Welk-type spotlight and organ crescendo was almost more than I could handle. Her peroxided hair and evening gown at 2:30 in the afternoon threatened to be the last straw. My stiff upper lip got stiffer.

But then something began to happen. The presence of God became real. It seemed he could handle all those accouterments better than I. Warm and worshipful singing uplifted Jesus, the Son of God. Heartfelt praying called on the Spirit of God to manifest himself. Miss Kuhlman preached a clear gospel message with no frills. Many people committed themselves to Christ.

Then came the healing section of the service. Keep in mind that my mood was still set on sniffing out the phony. My spirit was skeptical. Yet testimony after testimony was given of healings right there in the service, often to the individual's obvious astonishment. A variety of people testified to seeing from eyes that had not seen in years, or hearing from ears that had not heard.

Through all of this my spirit remained on the alert for the faintest trace of anything staged, preplanned, or contrived. I did not see it. I simply saw person after person, young men and women, older people and children, reacting with what one could conceive of as an almost New Testament spontaneity to the mighty works of God in their lives.

The Lame Walk

I was most vividly impressed by an incident involving a seven-year-old boy whose legs had been deformed from birth. According to his mother, he had never walked in his life without braces and crutches. He had seen Kathryn Kuhlman on television and had said to his mother: "Mommy, take me to that lady. Jesus is going to heal me through her." The mother, never a churchgoer, was reluctant but at the child's insistence finally agreed. They had joined the line-up early that morning and had been given good seats near the front.

During the healing service Kuhlman suddenly said: "There is a crippled child somewhere down on my left whom Jesus is healing right now. Please come out from wherever you are and take your leg-braces off." There was a stir over in the left front section and people began to lift a severely handicapped little boy over the seats.

"That's right," urged Kuhlman. "Now bring him down here and get those braces off." I was astounded. What if this didn't work? What if he fell down and damaged his already inadequate limbs further? I quaked almost as much for the evangelist as for the child and his trembling mother.

I was hardly prepared for what happened in the next moment. The braces removed, the child was lifted to his feet and helped up the steps to the stage by the mother.

"Now let him go, ma'am," Miss Kuhlman said. "Let him walk on his own." Still apprehensive, the mother obeyed. The little fellow stepped gingerly forward, at first shakily, then more confidently. Across the stage from one side to the other he went, then turned around and walked back, a spellbound incredulity etched on his little face. The mother stood frozen, ashen, her hands clutched over her cheeks while her tears welled up and overflowed.

"Now," urged Kuhlman, "I want you to run—over to the other side of the stage and back again. Come on. Off you go." The child raced across the stage, not seeing his mother faint behind him. He spun on his heels, turned around, and raced back.

With a seat on the stage, I had a grandstand view of all this. Laurence Olivier himself could not have pulled off an act like that. Indeed it was no act, at least, not a human act. It was, I recognized, an act of God. I could not deny it, nor did I have any desire to do so.

"I have never seen him walk before," his mother, now recovered, said through her tears.

That was how I came to believe that God still heals today. My mind went back to the first time I had been faced with this sort of phenomenon.

Lawrence Hammond

I had been in the New York area some years previously visiting Mrs. Marion Johnson, a leader in what was then known as International Christian Leadership, a ministry to civic and political leadership founded by Abraham Vereide. That group was in back of the annual Presidential Prayer Breakfast. I had gotten to know Vereide in 1960 and by attending the Presidential Prayer Breakfast in 1961 had been introduced to many others in that outreach.

Marion was one of these new-found friends. She had urged me to visit her on one of my vacations. She was always full of the Spirit's latest happenings in her life and in the lives of her friends.

"Oh! Michael, dear," she expostulated in her effervescent and grandmotherly way, "I must tell you about how the Lord has healed my dear friend Lawrence Hammond who lives in

Chicago." The story was so extraordinary that I resolved to go to Chicago on my way back to seminary in California and hear it firsthand. So, when I finally got to Chicago some weeks later, Lawrence Hammond greeted me warmly and told me what had happened to him. It went something like this. He had been taken terribly ill with some kind of intestinal obstruction and other problems. This landed him in the hospital, where his condition deteriorated horribly. His abdomen was grotesquely swollen. The surgery which was decided upon was apparently not calculated to give much ground for hope. Having insisted on knowing his true condition, he had been told his chances were marginal.

"I think they were mainly interested in me as a guinea pig for medical science," he laughed.

Two or three days before the scheduled operation he decided to call his Episcopal minister to come to his bedside, to anoint him with oil, and to pray for him. He waited patiently, but his desperation mounted as no minister appeared. Finally, on the day of the operation, the church's new curate entered his hospital room in a state of jitters.

"I'm terribly sorry," he apologized as he put his hat down on the bed. "Rector is out of town and can't come, so they asked me to come over. But I don't know what to do. They never taught us about healing at seminary. I've never anointed anyone with oil."

"My heart absolutely sank," Lawrence said to me. "I had been depending so much on a visit from our minister because I knew he believed in healing. Now here I was with this poor young fellow, who was totally helpless in the situation." Knowing he had me transfixed, he went on. "I simply asked the curate if he believed God could heal, to which he replied in the affirmative. Then I asked him to lay hands on me and pray. The young man, still pale, reached out his hands toward my bulging stomach. As he touched me, and before he could pray, it was as if a 3,000-volt electric current went through me. The curate got such a fright he rebounded from the bedside and fell to the ground, knocking his hat off my bed as he did so. There and then the physical swelling of my stomach visibly subsided, like air coming out of a balloon or a soccer ball." Lawrence's face glowed as he told the story.

"So I pulled all the plastic tubes out of myself and leaped from my bed shouting, 'I've been healed, I've been healed!' By this time the curate was up off the floor and we sort of danced a jig around the ward. All this noise attracted the attention of a Jewish rabbi who just then was passing through the ward. He had often seen me and knew the seriousness of my condition. As he saw my normal-sized stomach and gathered basically what had happened, he rushed out the door and down the passage shouting, 'It's just like the Red Sea! It's just like the Red Sea!' "

There they all were—the whooping patient, the dancing curate, and the ecstatic rabbi—when several horrified nurses rushed in, calling for order, calm, and sanity.

"But he's been healed!" beamed the curate, grinning like the Cheshire Cat.

"Yes, he has, he has, indeed he has!" bubbled the rabbi. The nurses, now joined by a doctor or two, got Lawrence back into bed.

"I told them," Lawrence reported, "that I was not going to have the operation. After many protestations I agreed with them that they could take me upstairs for some further tests, but that was all. Their tests revealed my condition as 75 percent normal; surgery was no longer necessary." Hammond went on to relate how his condition improved 5 percent a day in the next five days. He was then discharged as normal.

"What are you going to put on my medical report?" Lawrence asked the doctor as he stood at the door of the ward. The doctor paused, and then with a quizzical look replied: "I will put 'Healed—source unknown.' " And that was that. Lawrence left the doctor and nurses to their agnosticism and stepped out hale and hearty into the world to tell one and all that Jesus Christ still heals today.

Lack of Faith

The question I began to wonder about was, why don't we see

48   *Bursting the Wineskins*

more healing in today's church? Perhaps it is because there are
so few who have the faith of children. Jesus said, "According to
your faith be it done to you" (Matt. 9:29).

If that is the requirement, then churchgoers who have been
conditioned by twentieth-century naturalistic presuppositions
presumably see very little of the overtly miraculous simply
because they believe in it so little.

Dr. Rodman Williams, a Presbyterian writer, puts it this way:

> We are having to learn much...in matters of the Spirit. We
> now know that the world of extraordinary healing, mighty
> works of deliverance, and so on, ought never to have become
> alien to us. It surely was not thus to the primitive Christians.
> We now realize that we have been blinded by a modern world
> view that intellectually and empirically views all that happens
> or may happen as belonging to the realms of natural forces.[10]

That was just how I felt I had been. Blinded. I was far more a
creature of my time than I realized. I had been limiting God as
to what he could and couldn't do.

Williams articulates the understanding that began to dawn on
me in the months following the Shrine Auditorium experience:

> Despite at times its slow process and our frequent falling
> back, we are beginning to move ahead in this world reopen-
> ing before our eyes. It *was* true after all, what we read in the
> New Testament. By the Spirit of God, people really were
> healed of all manner of diseases and ailments: they *actually*
> were delivered from forces of evil beyond the reach of natural
> means. For such is happening again in our midst.[11]

What struck me increasingly was the realization that perhaps
there really is so much more available for the Christian community as a whole to appropriate. The power of God is there, but
our little faith does not release it. The situation is laden with vast
potential, but limited by our lack of expectation. Was that what
Karl Barth recognized when he wrote of the Christian community as the place where "astonishing" and "extraordinary"

things may happen? "The Christian community can and must be the scene of many human activities which are new and supremely astonishing to many of its own members as well as to the world around because they rest on an endowment with extraordinary capacities."[12]

Emil Brunner, another theological giant, in *The Misunderstanding of the Church* put it this way: "We ought to face the New Testament witness with sufficient candor to admit that in this...Spirit which the Church was conscious of possessing, there lie forces of an extra-rational kind mostly lacking among us Christians today."[13] Brunner was recognizing that the modern church's problem is basically a lack. The powers stemming from the Holy Spirit seem to be in short supply. When they do appear, as they did in that Shrine Auditorium, they seem strange to us. But they were not strange to the New Testament.

This is not to say that most of us are unfamiliar with the power of the Spirit working through the spoken word to convict and convert and transform. My personal experience and evangelistic ministry bore testimony in modest measure to that. But manifestations like the healing of the crippled child I had not seen before.

Perhaps that is what Brunner also felt when he observed from the New Testament that

Word and Spirit are certainly very closely connected... There exists even in the New Testament a certain tension between Word and Spirit. 'The Kingdom of God does not consist in talk but in power' (1 Cor. 4:20). The apostle Paul freely admitted that he won the Corinthians not through words of wisdom but through demonstrations of the Spirit and of power. Here he indicated a reality that can reveal itself apart from words, like that power of the Spirit that struck down Ananias and Sapphira and killed them as though it had been a powerful electric current...We shall never understand the essential being of the New Testament Church if we do not take fully into account these revelations of the

Spirit. . . The Spirit operates with overwhelming, revolutionary, transforming results. It manifests itself in such a way as to leave one wondering why and how.

Here the mighty energies of the Spirit are more important than any word, although these energies, insofar as they are those of the Holy Spirit, owe their origin to the Word of God. Present day evangelists and missionaries usually realize this fact far better than we theologians who not only undervalue the dynamic power of the Holy Ghost, but often know nothing of it.[14]

An astonishing confession. Perhaps we missionaries and evangelists should not exempt ourselves any more than the theologians.

Before leaving for South Africa at the end of that 1966 trip in the U.S., I heard the reactions of several senior church leaders and academics who were looking at some of the same data facing me. Dr. John Mackay, former president of Princeton Seminary, commented: "The uncouth life of Pentecostalism is often preferable to the aesthetic death of the main line churches."

Dr. Henry Van Dusen, one-time president of Union Theological Seminary in New York, voiced his conclusion after a world tour when he saw many aspects of the worldwide church: "I have come to feel that the Pentecostal movement, with its emphasis on the Holy Spirit, is more than just another revival. It is a revolution in our day. It is a revolution comparable in importance with the establishment of the original Apostolic Church and with the Protestant Reformation."

Dr. Sam Shoemaker, a well-known Episcopalian leader from Pittsburgh, went on record to conclude that "God is trying to get through into the church, staid and stuffy and self-centered as it often is, with a kind of power which will make it radiant and exciting and self-giving."

Dr. Philip Hughes, a British leader, and then editor of the Anglican magazine, *The Churchman,* came away after a visit to California saying, "The breath of the living God is stirring among the dry bones of the major, respectable and old-established denominations.''

If such men were coming to such conclusions, who was I to stand aloof? I returned to South Africa with my mind somewhat "blown," as the expression is, and with the intensified realization that I, along with all thoughtful Christians, needed to come to terms more fully with what was going on around us.

6
Rebekah and a Word of Knowledge

Let her be the one whom thou hast appointed.
Abraham's servant, Genesis 24:14

BACK IN THE FULL SWING of evangelistic ministry in South and East Africa in the late sixties, I had moved toward a position of openness and goodwill toward the new Pentecostalism. My stance was much like one more recently articulated by the Canadian evangelical scholar Clark Pinnock:

The new Pentecostalism seems to this observer to be a genuine movement of the Spirit of God renewing His church. I speak as an observer, who though standing outside the new Pentecostalism proper, has learned to appreciate it from personal involvement in charismatic groups... From these experiences I have emerged a stronger and better Christian... I agree with Karl Barth that there may often be too little of the pneumatic in the church (i.e., that which relates to the Holy Spirit) but never too *much*. Therefore it thrills my soul to see multitudes of people allowing the Spirit to operate freely in their midst.[15]

So wherever I went I encouraged openness to these fresh breezes of the Spirit. Though I could not help people in any dramatic fashion into new discoveries of the Spirit's fullness, I could encourage them to be open to a new release of the Spirit within. I could help alter their presuppositions about the operations of the Spirit, as mine had been altered.

For me one momentous nudge in this direction came from the curious direction of my romantic life. Like most young single men, even Christian ones, I had had my share of heartaches and made my share of blunders. Relationships of promise seemed to grind to a frustrating halt—either with a check in my own spirit, or in the young woman's, or in both of ours.

Toward the end of 1964, shortly before leaving Fuller Seminary to return to South Africa, I was caught up in a particularly complex tangle. I was at a loss to know which way to turn. Driving along a side road in West Los Angeles, headed toward a speaking engagement in Bel Air Presbyterian Church, I pulled the car off the road. I had a few minutes to spare and felt a deep need of some word from God about this anguishing area of my life.

My mind turned to Genesis 24, the story of Isaac and Rebekah. The word of Abraham to his servant in verses 3 and 4 was immediately quickened to my needy heart. "You will not take a wife for my son from the daughters of the Canaanites, among whom I dwell, but will go to my country and to my kindred and take a wife for my son Isaac." What impressed itself on me out of this story was that God wanted me, like Isaac, to find my life partner in my own country and among my own kindred. That meant I was not to marry an American, but a South African.

Like Abraham's servant I prayed, "Let her be the one whom thou hast appointed" (Gen. 24:14). I also rejoiced in the obvious lesson of the story that God could circumstantially cope with this aspect of life and lead one to the right person. How touching the servant's words were in verse 48, when he realized that the maiden Rebekah was "the one appointed" for Isaac: "Then I bowed my head and worshipped the Lord and blessed the Lord, the God of my master Abraham, who had led me by the right way to take the daughter of my master's kinsman for his son." Rebekah's family, too, recognized that "the thing comes from the Lord." And so "Isaac...took Rebekah, and she became his wife; and he loved her" (verse 67).

From then on, the story of Isaac and Rebekah had special significance for me. It was a challenge to caution, faith, and dependence. After all, with one major mistake in this area of my life, my ministry would be over. I knew that. The point had been well made to me by Charles and Honey Fuller, who founded Fuller Seminary and who had prayed much for me about this. Whenever I saw Honey she would remind me, "It must be the right girl, Mike. The *right* girl." She even wrote me little notes from time to time to believe God and trust him. I was to wait for his provision.

Waiting

But that was in 1964. Waiting is always easier said than done. Headstrong and faithless as I often was, I floundered around in confusion, impatience, frustration, and in mistaken flights of fancy that hurt both others and myself. One old Dutch Reformed saint encouraged me that in the case of Adam and Eve "the Lord...brought the woman to the man" (Gen. 2:22). "If he did it for Adam, he can do it for you," said my friend with a great roar of Afrikaans laughter as we drove one day along the Cape coast. "Just relax, Mike, the Lord will bring her right across your path. You don't have to hunt as the Gentiles do!"

The five-year period from 1964 to 1969 was particularly difficult. Not only were they extremely demanding years of ministry, but almost all my friends were married. And no relationship would jell for me. It seemed that God had forgotten about me, and I was getting into my thirties. Over and beyond that, we were doing ministry on most of the university campuses of

South Africa and I inevitably met some of the choicest and love-
liest young Christian women in the country. In missions, too, we
saw the cream of the crop. Not surprisingly, my colleagues,
especially Chris Smith (an incorrigible matchmaker), were
always picking particular ones for me, trying vainly to get me
married and on my way.

Not Good to Be Alone

Things came to a head for me in our citywide mission to Nairobi
in the latter part of 1968 and early 1969. The pressures on every
front were enormous. Compounding it all, a tremendous sense
of loneliness gripped my life. Genesis tells us that in his created
order God saw that everything was "good," with one notable
exception. "It is not good that the man should be alone" (Gen.
2:18).

I can honestly say that most of the time through those bache-
lor years the sense of God's companionship was real and satisfy-
ing. But it would be dishonest not to admit to some awful
moments of loneliness, perhaps on weekends or right after an
exhausting and demanding mission. At such times I would
either fight a mighty spiritual battle or else drift back in confusion or disobedience into former relationships that were not
working out.

One Saturday afternoon in early 1969, when all the others on
the team were preoccupied, I went for a long walk under the
warm African sun. "Lord," I prayed, "this is the last major
mission I can go through without the companionship and help of
a wife. Please undertake and supply for me. May your Spirit
guide me to the right person." Our next major endeavor was to
Cape Town University in August 1969. A year of preparation
had gone into the campaign and things looked good. Excellent
cooperation between student groups, superb publicity, and
months of fervent prayer all suggested a great mission ahead.
My own spiritual and mental preparation had also been inten-
sive, but against the backdrop of a crisis in my personal life.
Struggling vainly to get a relationship with a long-standing

girlfriend to work, just before leaving for Cape Town I finally said, "Lord, if you want me to remain single and serve you as an unmarried man, so be it. I have failed too dismally in this matter and disappointed you and others too deeply and struggled too frantically. Won't you now just take over this whole area unconditionally? I give up. Nothing is working out. I am just failing you, myself, and others in trying to handle it my way. Over to you, Lord. Single or married, I am *yours*. Do with me as seems good to you."

The relief in coming to that point was great, although I felt deep regret that it had taken me until I was thirty-two before it really happened. Too cheaply and glibly I had said that sort of thing before. But within a couple of days of leaving for the Cape Town varsity mission, I prayed it and meant it more truly and sincerely than ever before.

The Matchmaker

One day, about five or six days before the mission, Chris Smith and I were busy with a mob of Christian students stuffing envelopes for a major publicity mailing. The door opened and in walked a very beautiful girl. Almost immediately she commanded the attention of the room. She was introduced as Carol Bam, a local schoolteacher, and one of the assistant missioners. One of the other woman missioners, designated as mission counselor to one of the women's residences, had come down with malaria, and the students had chosen Carol Bam as her substitute.

Chris, true to form, immediately gripped my arm and pulled me over to the side of the room. Speaking in a whisper and with one eye half-cocked in Carol's direction, he mumbled: "If you fumble the ball this time, old buddy, you've really had it."

"You rascal!" I replied. "Keep quiet and lick that envelope." And that was that, until a few nights later when Chris again spoke of Carol as we enjoyed a late night walk. It was Chris all over again; another backfiring mismatch in the offing, I thought.

The mission got under way with huge attendances in the lunch hour, up to 2000 students, with up to 700 or 800 in the evenings. The assistant missioners in the residences reported amazing openness and many conversions.

One evening, assistant missioner Carol Bam reported to me that she had two high-powered agnostic friends whom she had gotten to know when she was working part-time in the science labs at Cape Town University some years previously. They wanted to challenge me. Would I go out to coffee with them? So there we were—two missioners defending the faith against two ardent but inquiring agnostics. It was a good evening.

Then, on Saturday, the day after the mission ended, mission co-ordinator Mick Milligan of the student YMCA, the best Christian student group I have encountered anywhere, got us all out on a picnic. Carol Bam preoccupied herself with the Milligan children (that frustrated Chris Smith). She also talked about getting a new teaching job next year. Time and again Chris's scheming eye would catch mine. In the end, just to oblige Chris (without telling him, of course) I asked this elusive teacher how she would enjoy a game of tennis. We set it up for Tuesday afternoon.

Then came Sunday. Chris and I went out for a hike on Table Mountain starting at Constantia Nek and following the trails from the rear of the mountain. We were tired after a demanding week. Inevitably Chris brought up his now-favorite subject, Carol Bam, urging me to take her out. I refused. He implored me to pray about her. I looked blank. He finally said, "Won't you even *consider* her?"

"OK. If it'll make you feel better I'll consider her." ("When will this man lay off and give up?" I thought to myself.) We hiked for an hour or so, finally scrambling to a promontory from which a majestic view opened up—the southern suburbs down on the left flank of Constantia Nek and the ocean down near Hout Bay on our right. Our legs dangled over an impressive drop.

"Mike, why don't we have a word of prayer together here and now about Carol?"

What could I say? How could I decline prayer? Of course, it would be another in a long line of similar prayers with Chris, going back over many years. But I could not be a total cad. "Surely no harm in praying," I reflected. "All right, old buddy. You win. I'll pray." My enthusiasm was less than total. So, with a gentle Cape breeze ruffling our hair and with one of the most beautiful parts of South Africa spread out like a painter's canvas below us, we prayed, then clambered up from our perch, and set off across some rugged terrain to get back to the trail. I had gone about forty yards when it happened—the nearest thing to a telegram from God I ever received.

"This is the girl. Go ahead."

I almost stopped in my tracks. But I didn't doubt or query the message for a moment. It was unmistakable in its intensity, so clear, so simple, the voice of the Spirit. It was for me the "word of knowledge." It was God. I was being enabled supernaturally to know something I could not naturally know. Though I knew very little about Carol at that stage, here was one of those promised whispers from the God who had assured us: "And your ears shall hear a word behind you, saying, 'This is the way, walk in it'" (Isa. 30:21).

I didn't say a word to Chris. I was too overwhelmed. It was too momentous to share with anyone. I just pondered the whole extraordinary happening in my heart. But my spirit almost bounded down the mountain and we got back to the car with my secret intact.

Carol

That night I preached to a packed student service in the Mowbray Methodist Church. There she was—halfway back in the center aisle. And I loved her; I knew she was "the one appointed" for me. I suspect my sermon took wings!

After the service, I walked to the hall for the coffee time. Going up the path as I headed for the hall, all alone, was assistant missioner Carol Bam. We walked into the hall together and mingled with students. It was good to have her standing at my side. Later a student said to me, "When I saw you two side by

side, chatting to students, I thought you looked good together."
I said nothing to Carol, but I looked forward to that tennis date
on Tuesday.

Early the next morning, about four, I was suddenly wide
awake, almost as if shaken into consciousness by some unseen
hand. And again came the inner voice, just as clearly as before.

"You must stop Carol taking that job."

"Why Lord?" I responded in my heart.

"Because she will be with you in Johannesburg and the States
next year." Very direct. Very specific.

It was a strange word—but one whose meaning would later
become clear. For the moment I saw it only as further confirmation that we would by then be married. But the part about stop-
ping her from taking the job added urgency to my already
excited spirit.

I remained reflective till dawn, then rose, prayed with vigor,
and went to breakfast with only one thought. I must see Carol,
quickly and urgently. But when? Her whole day was occupied
with teaching. My evening was committed to a student bull session in one of the residences. Then my phone rang, my bull
session was cancelled; my evening was free.

I phoned Carol's home and left a message with her mother for
her to call me back. She did, late in the afternoon. Would she
have dinner with me that night? I asked.

"Yes, but I have to be in early. I have a lot of grading to do
tonight," she responded casually.

"Cool cat," I thought. "She's got a surprise coming."

We chatted casually over dinner, my excitement mounting. I
liked what I heard, and saw, and sensed. Yes, she was the one for
me.

"Let's drive down to Hout Bay," I suggested. On the way to
the car we passed Westerford High School. She chatted on
cheerfully and then stopped me dead in my tracks by saying,
"You know I had a funny experience today. I had to go for a job
interview here at Westerford School. They want me to teach
next year and have totally rearranged the teaching schedule to

give me the class and subject I want—matriculation level biology. They have gone to tremendous lengths to accommodate my preferences, but suddenly I had this strange feeling that I couldn't take the job. That's mystifying—when it's just what I want. So the principal has given me two days in which to make up my mind. Today is Monday. I must tell him on Wednesday.''

The job. That was the word—the spirit's word—at four A.M. "You must stop Carol taking that job." Everything clicked. It was further confirmation. I would propose marriage at the first suitable moment.

And I did, half an hour later, walking on the beach.

Carol was thunderstruck. She had recently been through a very distressing romance and had broken her engagement. She had resolved never to consider marrying anyone till she had known him at least two years. The whole scenario of her recent trauma and resolution raced through her mind in split seconds of bewildered reflection. Now along comes this crazy missioner who proposes not after two years but after two hours of the first date.

"Well," she said with total astonishment etched all over her face, "I can't say yes, but I can't say no." Then she kept me waiting a further forty-five seconds before saying Yes!

We were engaged to be married. Back in my room I headed right to Genesis 24. With overwhelming joy and gratitude I read verse 48: "Then I bowed my head and worshiped the Lord, and blessed the Lord. . . who had led me by the right way."

I also picked up *Daily Light*. I read the Scripture selections for that day. "What God is there in heaven or in earth, that can do according to thy works, and according to thy might?" (Deut. 3:24); "Who in the heaven can be compared unto the Lord? Who among the sons of the mighty can be likened unto the Lord? O Lord of hosts who is a stronghold like unto thee? or to thy faithfulness round about thee?" (Ps. 89: 6, 8); "Among the gods there is none like unto thee, O Lord; neither are there any works like unto thy works" (Ps. 86:8); "For thy word's sake, and according to thine own heart, hast thou done all these great things to make thy servant know them. Wherefore thou art great, O Lord God: for there is none like thee, neither is there any God beside thee, according to all that we have heard with our ears" (2 Sam. 7:21–22).

It was a great reading. Our God lives, speaks, acts, reveals by his Spirit. He is not silent. I went to sleep rejoicing.

7

Isaac
and the Word
of Prophecy

Make love your aim, and earnestly desire
the spiritual gifts, especially that
you may prophesy.
St. Paul, 1 Corinthians 14:1

Poor Chris. We kept him in the dark. Carol wanted this kept a complete secret until she was ready to tell her parents who might need, she felt, some preparation for the shock. All week long I kept up the act. How I acted! How I dissembled! I didn't know I had it in me to be such a capable deceiver. In the meantime, I lived in Genesis 24 in the Isaac and Rebekah story, reading it, rereading it, and savoring its import.

The following Saturday Chris and I were driving into the center of Cape Town to meet Elizabeth Whitsett, one of our African Enterprise Board members from the U.S. "Mike," he said, "I just wish you'd consider dating that girl, Carol. I've just had her on my mind so much for you. In fact I've even put a specific entry in my prayer diary, a request that 'God should join Michael and Carol Bam together in marriage.' "

"Chris," I responded with feigned exasperation, "you know

why I won't date her? I'll tell you. You're just putting too much pressure on me. Just don't talk to me about the girl again."

"Well," said Chris, with an audible groan of frustration as he prepared to play his final card, "there's just one thing I want you to do. Please. Just one thing. I want you in your devotions tomorrow to read Genesis 24, the story of Isaac and Rebekah. I've had it so much on my heart as somehow specially for you." Of course I almost burst inside with a combination of my own frustration at not being free to tell him until Carol gave me the green light, plus my own joy at this further confirmation.

"All right, brother," I replied, poker-faced. "Just for you, tomorrow I'll read Genesis 24 about Isaac and Rebekah. Now let's close the subject and think about this luncheon."

That afternoon Carol and I slipped away to a beautiful farm in Franschhoek, at the foot of the Hottentot's Holland mountains. Some dear friends who owned it had invited us to spend the weekend with them. It was virtually our first unhurried time together, and how wonderful it was. Just to be together, walking through the vineyards, thinking, talking, dreaming, praying. How good God had been.

The next morning, very early, I rose and went out on to the mountainside for prayer, reflection, and quiet. Then, just as strangely as some of these other things had happened, yet just as real, I suddenly felt the presence in a remarkable way of Charles and Honey Fuller. How they had exhorted me. How they had prayed for me. How they had held on in faith. And now it was as if the veil of heaven (they had both gone to be with the Lord) was being pulled back and we were all being permitted several mysterious moments of fellowship together. The sense of the experience lay in a communicated joy and relief and gratitude to God on their part that I had finally found the person of his choice for me—"the one appointed"—for whom they had prayed.

Disclosure
On Sunday evening at the end of that weekend Carol and I returned to Cape Town where I was scheduled to speak at a

students' follow-up meeting. Carol had agreed by now that I should share our secret with Chris. It was now six days since we had become engaged and we were getting used to the idea. Now I could confidentially tell our plans to Chris, although we decided not to make a public announcement until my ministry in Cape Town was over. Before going to the student service I dropped Carol off while I raced by Chris's room and captured his prayer diary. Finding the entry about Carol and me I simply wrote "Answered: Genesis 24:48" in bold red ink, scored it with a line above and below, pocketed the diary, and set off for the service.

When it was over, I suggested that Chris come out with me for a drive. I was tired and wanted to escape for a while. We drove up to the top of Signal Hill with its majestic view of Cape Town, parked the car, and surveyed the sparkling sea of lights, the marked semicircle of empty darkness delineating the gentle curve of the famous Table Bay. After a few moments I slipped my hand in my pocket, pulled his diary from it, and tossed it nonchalantly into his lap.

"What on earth is this?" he asked screwing up his eyes to see it in the dark. Then slowly, incredulously, he alternated his eyes from my grin to his little book and then fumbled through to the page that carried his special entry.

It was a moment we would never forget. Chris simply exploded, like a sort of Vesuvius suddenly deciding it had been quiescent too long and that the moment had arrived for a good old-fashioned eruption. With laughter and banter, with praise and prayer, we reflected on the extraordinary saga. Our God is truly an amazing God, worth following and serving to the ends of the earth.

Now comes the part of the story that constitutes the *raison d'être* for sharing this whole experience in such detail.

Elisse

The following weeks were rich and memorable. In a dozen different ways, especially from the Scriptures, the Lord confirmed the rightness of it all. We announced our engagement on my thirty-third birthday, September 24 (1969), and set the wedding date for December 16. Some weeks later I had to leave for a brief period of ministry and to report back in the United States. During that time I was taken one day by an old friend, Ed, for lunch with Paul and Elisse Larsen, a couple who lived in Pasadena and whom I had briefly met some three years previously.

Paul and Elisse had long been involved in the charismatic renewal. According to Ed, Elisse had "a well-matured prophetic gift." I wasn't quite sure what he meant, although back in 1966 in a prayertime following a meal at the Larsens', Elisse had burst forth in an extraordinary word of exhortation and revelation which was expressed in the first person singular as if God himself was speaking. At the time it seemed clearly that the word was for me, and later everyone was in accord with that conclusion. But how to integrate the happening into my current theological framework I wasn't sure. After all, I had not heard at any time in my growth and training of the Lord speaking directly, other than in the Scriptures. Indeed, I knew that this sort of thing was suspect in many circles. And of course, even if genuine it was open to dangerous abuse, such as I have seen often since then.

Prophecy in the Old Testament

Whether or not prophecy still happens outside the Scriptures, one surely sees plenty of it inside the Scriptures, especially in the Old Testament. Time and again we find the Old Testament telling how the Spirit of the Lord would "come *upon*" one of the prophets, who would then speak as from God.

Thus "the Spirit of the Lord came upon Jahaziel," and he said, "Hearken, all Judah and inhabitants of Jerusalem, and King Jehoshaphat: Thus says the Lord to you, 'Fear not, and be not dismayed at this great multitude; for the battle is not yours but God's' " (2 Chron. 20:14-15).

Likewise Ezekiel testified: "The Spirit of the Lord *fell upon me*, and he said to me, 'Say, Thus says the Lord'. . . ." and the message was communicated. As the servant of God he then proclaimed the Word and reported on it a few verses later saying, "I was prophesying" (Ezek. 11:5,13). Seemingly Ezekiel understood prophecy to take place when the mind and will of God were being conveyed through a human agent to God's people. The prophet heard or discerned the will and Word of God and declared it. At that moment he prophesied.

When we come to Isaiah and Jeremiah it is little short of astonishing how clearly they are able to reiterate "Thus says the Lord . . ." or to testify unequivocally, "Thus said the Lord to me" (Jer. 13:1, 14:1, 15:1, 16:1, 17:19, 18:1, 21:1, 25:1, etc.).

On the other hand, we also know the awesome responsibility of claiming to exercise such a gift and how the false use of it is an abomination to God and a fearful hazard to his people. "Thus says the Lord of hosts: 'Do not listen to the words of the prophets who prophesy to you, filling you with vain hopes; they speak visions of their own minds, not from the mouth of the Lord' " (Jer. 23:16). It is possible for people to make supposedly prophetic utterances that are nevertheless false, not authentically from God. "I did not send the prophets, yet they ran; I did not speak to them, yet they prophesied" (Jer. 23:21). Here is another picture of false prophecy and of wasted religious activity outside the will of God.

More frightening yet are these words: "I have heard," says the Lord, "what the prophets have said who prophesy lies in my name, saying, 'I have dreamed, I have dreamed!' How long shall there be lies in the heart of the prophets who prophesy lies, and who prophesy the deceit of their own heart . . . Behold I am against those who prophesy lying dreams, says the Lord, and who tell them and lead my people astray by their lies and their recklessness, when I did not send them or charge them; so they do not profit this people at all, says the Lord" (Jer. 23:25-26, 32).

By 1969 I was familiar with this passage, so the possibility of counterfeit, which I have recognized even more markedly since that time, was not lost on me even then. On the other hand, the question remained. Was there still in our day any genuine prophecy in any way comparable with that of which the Old Testament prophets spoke? What did the apostle Paul mean, for example, when in 1 Corinthians 14:1, he said, "Make love your aim, and earnestly desire the spiritual gifts, especially that you may prophesy"?

Did that refer only to preaching, as my orthodox evangelical teaching had always led me to believe? And could one truly say of preaching, as Paul said of prophecy in 1 Corinthians 14:22, "Prophecy is not for unbelievers but for believers"? If not, then perhaps prophecy may include preaching and can, on occasion, go beyond it.

And what about Paul's saying "Let two or three prophets speak, and let the others weigh what is said. If a revelation is made to another sitting by, let the first be silent. For you can all prophesy one by one, so that all may learn and all be encouraged" (1 Cor. 14:29-31). Paul ended this discussion as he began it—on the primacy of prophecy. "So, my brethren, earnestly desire to prophesy, and do not forbid speaking in tongues."

I had been perplexed with such queries ever since the first experience with Elisse in 1966. Now I was back with her again— full of the exciting developments with Carol which had so recently taken place.

After lunch we retired to the living room. Coffee over, Elisse said, "Tell us, Mike, how you met Carol."

I began to narrate the story in brief and had gotten only a few minutes into it when Elisse who had been listening in a relaxed way suddenly began to give an almost physical impression of someone being filled to the brim, like a spring or a bottle about to overflow. I didn't quite know what was happening. Quietly Ed said, "Mike, let's just be still for a moment before the Lord."

Then, with her eyes closed, Elisse began to speak out in a strong but deliberate voice:

Son of Abraham—
Son of Abraham—

Son of Abraham—
I have called you Isaac,
And I have brought a Rebekah unto you, Isaac, my son.
I have snatched her out of a snare
and a trap of Satan
and have given her unto you.

And as you heard me in this thing and were
obedient, so you will even again hear my voice,
and regularly in other things, like a bell.
I will cause you to ride on the highways of the earth.
Trust that which I am putting in your heart.

There are some shakings that shall come upon you,
Yea, everything around you that can be shaken will be shaken,
But what remains will be of my Spirit.
In the midst of the battle, stand still in quietness and peace,
For this day I have kindled my fire within you.

My reaction was first one of awe. I had said nothing at all to Elisse about the Isaac and Rebekah background. So I was greatly excited at yet more confirmation about Carol.

On the other hand, I was fearful over the word about shakings. Unknown to me, our team was due in the following two years to enter a set of convulsions that would leave the work almost destroyed. During that time of flux I had to hold onto these prophetic words, plus the accompanying assurance that God was somehow in it all for his purposes. But on November 23, 1969, in the Larsens' home, I knew none of that. My preoccupation was with the marvelous word of confirmation about Carol, and its being couched in the Isaac and Rebekah metaphor, with which I had been living so intensely throughout that time.

Later Elisse told me that every time I mentioned Carol's name in the post-lunch discussion the name Rebekah leaped overwhelmingly into her mind until finally she was compelled to burst forth with that prophetic word.

Theological Implications

I needed that sort of divine confirmation, given the speed with which my relationship with Carol had developed. How marvelous, therefore, that God granted that assurance with such clarity through his Spirit's working.

But inevitably, apart from the personal, my concern was with the theological. For here, incontrovertibly to my mind, was the operation of yet another supernatural, charismatic gift. And if it could happen once authentically, it could happen again. It not only could but *should*.

One of the intriguing things was that prophetic utterance was not something I expected. It was not part of my presuppositional world in any significant way. My exposure to such things had been modest, and I was not therefore spiritually programmed for that sort of thing at all. It was therefore another big surprise, one I could not ignore.

And so this thought pressed upon me even more deeply: Was the modern church often shortchanging itself by screening out (by presupposition, pride, and prejudice) aspects of the supernatural heritage that was not only part of its birthright but should be part of its normal life? After all, so many of these ideas are in our systematic theologies or in our lectures on the early church or the book of Acts. But is not our doctrine meant also to be operational and functional, not simply in the teaching and experience of the new birth, but in the outworking of the Spirit's daily power in us for life and ministry? Somehow we have talked ourselves, often quite eloquently, into accepting something less than what was the norm in the early church. Thus Charles Williams in his sensitive volume *The Descent of the Dove* can lament that "the languages and habits of heaven seemed for a few years, a few decades, to hover within the church after a manner hardly realized since, except occasionally and individually."[16]

But did God intend it to be like this? That is the question. It is undeniable that millions of believers today are beginning to give a negative answer to that question. God did not mean us to be deprived of his gifts, they say. John Taylor in his work on the Holy Spirit, *The Go-Between God,* concludes that

> the whole weight of New Testament evidence endorses the central affirmation of the Pentecostalists that the gift of the Holy Spirit transforms and intensifies the quality of human life and that this is a fact of experience in the lives of Christians. The longing of thousands of Christians to recover what they feel instinctively their faith promises them is what underlies the whole movement.[17]

My conclusion after this experience with Elisse was that something supernatural and divine had taken place. But was it prophecy?

Prophecy in the New Testament

Obviously the function of the Old Testament prophets will not be exactly duplicated in our day. After all, the Scriptures have been encoded and the canon of both Testaments is closed. On the other hand, prophecy and the prophets form an obvious line of continuity between Old and New Testaments, the Old Testament prophetic line ending not with Malachi, the last of the Old Testament writers, but with John the Baptist. As Jesus said: "All the prophets and the law prophesied until John" (Matt. 11:13).

What then do we see in John the Baptist? We see a combination of *proclamation* and *prediction.* He declared that there was both wrath to come (Luke 3:7) and grace to come through Jesus, the Baptizer in the Holy Spirit (Luke 3:16). John stands as the link between the two Testaments.

So how do we define the New Testament ministry of prophecy? For instance, if we are to desire to prophesy, what are we to desire? Perhaps the answer comes partly as we see the makeup or composition of the word and partly as we see how the Bible uses it (see Appendix A, p. 229).

The word *prophet* (Greek *prophetes*) is made up of *pro* (a prefix meaning "before" or "for") and *phemi* (meaning "to speak"). So the prophet is one who "speaks before," in the sense of proclaiming a message ahead of time, or the one who "speaks for," in the sense of speaking on behalf of God. Prophecy includes both the predictive element—"foretelling," and the proclamatory element—"forthtelling," declaring the will of God. Both of those elements are present in the words of the Old Testament prophets.

What about the New Testament? Bullinger's Greek lexicon says of the word *propheteia* (prophecy) that it means "speaking forth utterance inspired by the Spirit of God, referring either to the past, present, or future. Prediction is not the main feature, but a showing forth of God's will." Interestingly, in Elisse's word to me, both ingredients were present. The confirming of Carol as the partner of God's choice for me was primary, yet the predictive element was there also in the sense of a general word about my future ministry ("I will cause you to ride on the highways of the earth") as well as advance notice of an impending crisis ("Everything around you that can be shaken will be shaken").

In broad terms, my reflections on the New Testament data tell me that prophecy is that process by which a believer, under the inspiration or special anointing of the Holy Spirit, may declare forth or confirm the will of God, relating to either the past, present, or future in such a way as to edify Christians or, on occasion, convince outsiders. One friend summarized it for me saying, "Prophecy happens when someone who has listened for the word and will of God declares it." I think that comes closest to it for me.

The events of that morning in 1969, however, with all that had preceded it, were evidence enough for me that God not only spoke through his prophets of old but he still speaks today. The issue, in one sense, is: did God speak or does God speak? My conclusion is that He *does*.

8
Gather My People Together

One man's piety is another man's poison.
Richard Lovelace

Maintain the unity of the Spirit
in the bond of peace.
St. Paul, Ephesians 4:3

As a student at Fuller Seminary in the early 1960s I was challenged by a number of scripture verses. They became part of God's mandate to me for my life. One was Psalm 50, verse 5: "Gather my saints together unto me" (KJV). It was not that I felt that I by myself could do this, or that God was laying such a mighty injunction on me alone. I simply recognized that the Scriptures here revealed a deep desire in the divine heart that God's people should be *together,* together with him and with each other. And I felt in this psalm an injunction—no doubt to all God's people—at that moment quickening my heart. There and then I decided I would like to be part of that process of drawing Christian believers together.

The fragmentation of the church struck me as a scandal. What could the world possibly make of us as we tore each other down, competed, criticized, worked at cross purposes, and carried on a sort of trench warfare? We lob theological or other sorts of grenades at each other from the safety of our own religious trench, which is just another name for an extra deep rut. We then block our ears while the thing explodes with shattering consequences in the trench of other Christian soldiers just over the way. What kind of army is that? What sort of teamwork is that? What enemy would be impressed by that? Certainly no football, baseball, rugby, or cricket team could function that way. But the church often does. The tragic consequences are plain for all the world to see.

I remember as a child playing soccer one day during a break between classes. I was just about to score an easy goal, both the goal-keeper and backs being out of position, when I was knocked down from behind. I went flying. The ball went flying. My dramatic goal was never scored. Imagine my consternation when I found that the fellow who had knocked me over was on my own side. That is how it often is in the church. When one is about to attempt a goal for God—a campaign, a new outreach, a special endeavor—one is knocked over by one's own side, from behind. Never from the front. Christians tend to avoid frontal assault. They prefer the verbal dart, from the rear.

Whatever the hazards, and I was aware of them, we in African Enterprise would commit ourselves in our ministry to a cooperative approach with all who could sincerely subscribe to the historic creeds of the church. Our own message would remain unswervingly evangelical in its content and in its attempted faithfulness to biblical revelation, but we would also try to be catalysts and contributors to the process of "gathering the saints together" to their Lord. Not only would that strengthen our effectiveness and add new credibility to our witness, but it was also integrally related to the work of the Holy Spirit. The injunction of Scripture is to "maintain the *unity of the Spirit* in the bond of peace" (Eph. 4:3). In fact, Paul went further and said that "if there is...*any participation in the spirit*... complete my joy by being of the same mind, having the same love, being in full accord and of one mind" (Phil. 2:2).

Paul saw *any* participation at all in the Spirit as carrying with it the imperative of Christian accord, fellowship, and cooperation. "Only let your manner of life be worthy of the gospel of Christ, so that whether I come and see you or am absent, I may hear that you stand firm in one spirit, with one mind, striving side by side for the faith of the gospel" (Phil. 1:27). Clearly, Christian conduct worthy of the gospel is to be marked by unity and cooperation. We are to "stand firm" in the gospel as well as to strive side by side for it "in one Spirit" and "with one mind." There is to be true partnership in the gospel. The reason, as we see in Jesus' prayer in John 17, is "that the world may believe." Christian disunity, rivalry, and isolation from one another makes the gospel unbelievable to the world; it quenches the work of the Spirit. If we are "eager for manifestations of the Holy Spirit" (and who is not?), then according to Paul we are to "strive to excel in *building up* the church" (1 Cor. 14:12). Multitudes of Christians excel in tearing down the church. How many excel in building it up? But if we want to see the Holy Spirit manifested, that is where we are told to excel—"in building up the church." Specialists in construction, that's what we need. Not wrecking crews.

Diversity

In his book *The Dynamics of Spiritual Life,* Richard Lovelace writes:

> The instruments through which God works in the church are human beings. If our hearts and minds are not properly transformed we are like musicians playing untuned instruments or engineers working with broken and ill-programmed computers. The attunement of the heart is essential to the outflow of grace. . . [18]
>
> There are many lines of estrangement in the modern church which are readily dissolved by the application of a balanced understanding of spiritual dynamics. For one thing, different groups within the church are at odds with one

another because their models of the Christian life, its beginnings and its fullness, are so diverse. One group of genuine believers can never remember a conscious conversion to faith in Christ; another insists that a datable experience of being "born again" is essential; a third says that a second distinct experience of "the baptism of the Holy Spirit" is necessary for Christian maturity. When we "test the spirits" in the lives of representatives among these groups, we often find an equal level of spiritual vitality—or deadness—in each sector. The Christian life is being offered in diverse packages, but what is inside is the same—newness of life in Christ. Nonetheless, the different groups enjoying this life are readily offended by one another's packages. One man's piety is another man's poison. What is needed to reconcile these models is a "unified field theory" of spirituality.[19]

In other words, these different groups need to get together. Each has strengths and weaknesses, and each has something to give and something to learn from the other.

There is also the problem of language and vocabulary.

Remember that genuine experience of Christ has generated several different theological languages during the church's history. Because of human limitations and the grandeur of the subject, no single language has been adequate to convey this. Reporters on Christian experience who describe it in a language strange to us may only be viewing the same thing from another perspective. We need to listen with care and sensitivity for the distinctive notes of true Christianity expressed in unfamiliar patterns.[20]

One thing for which I have always been thankful in our style of cooperative evangelism in African Enterprise is that it has enabled us to meet almost all sections of the church of Christ and to discover that no one has all the truth or all the darkness. We all have some of each. Because our evangelism so often required that we talk to people who never talked to each other, we increasingly became persuaded in the early 1970s of the wonder it would be if we could organize an opportunity for some of these people to meet and relate and share in fellowship. Imagine if ecumenical social activists, evangelical pietists, and neo-evangelical evangelists could all confer. Imagine if Pentecostals and non-Pentecostals, charismatics and noncharismatics could share their riches. Wouldn't such an encounter bring all of us closer to the full-orbed truth of Christ and his word?

Durban '73

How delighted I was when toward the end of 1967 the Spirit of God placed in our hearts the vision for a South African Congress on Mission and Evangelism. This Congress would seek to draw together South African Christians from all backgrounds to look at the vital issues of mission and evangelism in our complex national crucible.

The Congress took over five years to bring to fruition; in March 1973 it finally happened.[21] But it was not fully representative. The Pentecostals for the most part were not there. Nor were there Dutch Reformed delegates. The involvement of both in a major ecumenical experience in South Africa had to wait until the giant South African Christian Leadership Assembly (SACLA) in July 1979. As for the charismatic renewal, in 1973 in South Africa it was only a trickle or a small stream, not the mighty river it has since become.

However, what we learned from the Durban Congress (which became a watershed in a number of ways for the South African church) was the sheer difficulty of getting Christians together. Yet what richness and spiritual blessing there were once this happened and once everyone got over their fears, hangups, and caricatures about each other. For example, as we moved into high gear in planning, one South African evangelical actually went to the Billy Graham headquarters in Minneapolis to try and dissuade senior aides there from encouraging Dr. Graham to come. Reason? Some ecumenicals were going to take part in the South African gathering.

Another North American leader phoned me about the ecclesiastical mix and said: "You can't do it this way. We won't have
it."

"What kind of theological imperialism is this?" I thought.

"Brother," I said calmly, "we *are doing it* this way."

Another leader, a prominent noncharismatic wrote, "You
can't include David du Plessis, the big Pentecostal, on your program."

That brought another polite contradiction: "Brother, we *are*
including David du Plessis. Sorry to disappoint you."

Social activists said, "You mustn't have Billy Graham."
Others objected to Hans-Ruedi Weber of the W.C.C. And so it
went. All the Peters were saying, "No, Lord, I won't meet with
Cornelius." Yet surprisingly, once they were all together, the
world did not cave in.

One evangelical went up to Hans-Ruedi Weber at the Durban Congress and said, "Does the World Council know that you
are giving such evangelical Bible studies?"

"They pay me to give such studies," replied Hans-Ruedi
with a twinkle.

I was near the North American leader who had opposed
David du Plessis's participation just after David had finished his
major talk. The opposer had been waiting defensively for a plug
on tongues. Instead came an evangelical address on forgiveness.
Nothing about tongues at all. "Wow!" he whispered to his
neighbor. "I didn't know Pentecostals could talk like that." His
damning had been based on distance. He was down on what he
was not up on—which is my wife's definition of prejudice.

Several very hot social gospelers and political activists gasped
when they heard both Billy Graham and his brother-in-law,
Leighton Ford, plead that the personal gospel be "fleshed out"
in compassionate social concern. As for Billy Graham's evangelistic rally, which took place with 50,000 people present midway
through the Congress, one Catholic priest who had never been
in on an evangelistic rally, let alone seen 4,000 inquirers respond

to an evangelistic invitation, burst out, "Oh, may it be a milestone for South Africa."

Yes, at every level—theological, social, political, evangelistic, and charismatic—Christians learned from each other.

Forgiveness

In the Congress when it came to the work of the Holy Spirit, there was great value in hearing a range of viewpoints. David du Plessis began by noting how for years the person and work of the Holy Spirit had been neglected, but now a great change had come, with many denominations giving prominence to this theme. Du Plessis stressed how he saw forgiveness as a key prerequisite to the fullness of the Holy Spirit.

> There came a day when God challenged me to go to my brethren in other churches. "But Lord, they are dead!" He said: "Yes, but I never sent any disciples to bury the dead. I sent them to raise the dead." "But they're enemies." God said: "I have given you an invincible weapon against your enemies. *Love* your enemies." I said: "How can I love people who do things of which I cannot approve?" God said: "Forgive them. Forgive them." I said: "Lord, I can't forgive them. How can I justify their teachings, their actions, their deeds?" He said: "I never gave you any authority to justify anybody. I gave Christians authority only to forgive everybody."[22]

David went on to tell how he also felt called, to the alarm of some of his friends, to minister to Catholics, but with the Lord's exhortation:

> Don't minister to Catholics if you cannot love them. As long as you condemn them you are not loving. You cannot love if you don't forgive. The more you love, the easier it is to forgive, and the more you forgive the easier it is to love. Love is a fruit of the Spirit, and an unforgiving spirit ruins your love. A

forgiving spirit increases the fruit of the Spirit . . . My friends,
my life was completely revolutionized from the day I began to
practice forgiveness.[23]

Fullness

When it came to the difference between receiving the Spirit and
being baptized in the Spirit, du Plessis noted that Jesus came
and said to a theologian, "You must be born of the Spirit." But
he didn't say how.

> When he came to the woman at the well, he didn't use that
> theological term at all. There he said: "I can give you a drink
> of living water which will satisfy you for ever. Everlasting life.
> You'll have a well *in* you." Then on the day of the feast he
> explained how this could happen: "If any one thirst, let him
> come to me and *drink*. He who believes in me . . . out of his
> heart shall flow rivers of living water" (John 7:37–38). Out of
> you, not into you. Note too, he did not say "out of your
> head," but "out of your heart." In other words, "out of your
> innermost being will flow rivers of living water," not out of
> your head. It's your heart he's talking about.

David then stressed his view that in the new birth and conversion we come to Christ and "drink," as it were, of "the water of
life, freely." That is when we become sons and daughters. That
is when the Spirit comes *into* a person. But when you come to
baptism, water is put not into us, but onto us or over us. No
baptized baby drinks the water. Therefore, David concluded:

> Baptism in the Spirit is the Spirit poured over you, but a drink
> is the Spirit within you. I'm so glad to tell you I know thou-
> sands of beautiful Christians who have indeed had a drink,
> and have a well within them, and are therefore sons and
> daughters of God, even though they claim no baptism in the
> Spirit. I don't call baptism in the Spirit the infilling. I call the
> drink the infilling. A baptism is not into you, it's over you. So
> today, if you want a drink, Jesus alone can give it to you. If
> you want the baptism, Jesus is the only baptizer. Nobody else.

That's where you get the blessing, and that's the Pentecostal message.

This fascinating, though controversial (and to many, unorthodox) understanding of that doctrine intrigued Congress delegates and paved the way for several testimonies, two of which interested me particularly.

Bill Burnett

First came Bill Burnett, then Anglican bishop of Grahamstown, and later Archbishop of Cape Town, until his early retirement from that post in 1981. He admitted an element of surprise at finding himself giving a "testimony." "It doesn't seem properly Anglican," he noted with a twinkle. "It doesn't sound quite British!"

Burnett then went on to relate that in his own experience it seemed to be more God's searching for him, than he for God. "If my search had been what counted, I think I'd still be crawling around on hands and knees," he said. He then told how he had been baptized "in a fit of absent-mindedness, sent to a church school, meaningfully confirmed, regularly dosed with injections of grace, and finally converted at seventeen while reading a book." A call to the ministry followed. However, whether in preaching, preparing theological statements, working for better race relations, or struggling for church unity, something always seemed to be missing—the power of the Spirit of God. He began to long for a fresh personal empowering through the Holy Spirit. On Sunday, March 13, 1972, it happened.

It was curious. I had no desire to be Pentecostal at any time. I knew nothing about it, in point of fact. I wasn't aware at the moment it happened even of a sense of need. I had just come from a retreat where I had had loving communion with God. But on Saturday, March 12, I was preaching in a church school in Grahamstown on the text from Romans 5:5: "The love of God is shed abroad in our hearts by the Holy Spirit who is given to us." I felt my heart warmed somehow or other. Then after Holy Eucharist next day in the same chapel, I retired home for a quiet Sunday. I was reading a Sunday newspaper, not very edifying literature. There was just a quarter of an hour before lunch. Somehow I felt a tug to go to my chapel and while I was there I began to pray in silence, as was my custom, and to sense the presence of God so that he could do with me whatever was in his will. On this occasion I simply offered to him every part of my body I could think of.

Before I could get through doing that, somehow, unexpectedly, the Holy Spirit fell on me. I didn't know quite what was happening. A quarter of an hour was up by then and I had to go to lunch. But after lunch I couldn't rest. I had to go back to the chapel where I was blessed anew and refreshed. I rejoiced and then found myself praising God in a wonderful new way. I didn't know what it was, I was simply praising God. I was also full of joy and delight and love. That was why I was praising God, because his love had simply filled me to overflowing in a way I'd never known before. Of course I knew before that God loved me. I knew that at my conversion, but somehow it hadn't been the same full blessing of his love.

Bishop Burnett told of the great difference that experience had made in his life and ministry.

It has brought a new freedom to love and a new joy in prayer. No longer is prayer talking to the wall or the foot of the bed. It really is a fellowship and a dialogue in prayer, a rejoicing and a delight. And, what's more you can go on and on and on. I find also a new power over sin, a new power in proclamation, a new ability to forgive.

His testimony intrigued me because Bill Burnett had been my chaplain at high school. I knew him from way back. And, no doubt about it now, he was a changed man. Indeed, his influence since that time has been mightily used under God to accelerate a major impetus of renewal in the Anglican church of South Africa.

Shortly after Burnett's experience, the Archbishopric of Cape Town became vacant. "Too bad about this Pentecostal thing he's into," many Anglicans said. "He would have made a good archbishop. But that's disqualified him." Others, more daringly, whispered, "Don't you think that, just possibly, he may have been given this new experience in the Holy Spirit to equip him for the job?" It was a wild idea. Almost unthinkable. A charismatic Archbishop? The thing seemed virtually a contradiction in terms. But Burnett was swept into the position by one of the quickest, easiest, and most uncontested archepiscopal votes in the history of the Anglican church in South Africa.

Tom Houston

A different sort of testimony came from British leader Tom Houston, a Baptist. He testified that his search for the fullness of God had been a "series of failures." In twenty years of searching, Tom said, he had tried the Hudson Taylor way, the George Müller way, the Charles Finney way, the John Wesley-Nazarene way, the East African revival way, the Keswick way, and for four years the Pentecostal way. He had even had what some termed the baptism in the Spirit. The important thing that emerged for Tom was not that he should have all of God, but that God should have all of him.

I suddenly realized I was after the wrong thing—that I couldn't have an experience that would make me God. As I searched for the fullness of God, I realized I was seeking to feed my pride. Tom Houston was to be God's gift to the church, God's gift to the pulpit. That had to go. Having tried all those ways I realized that what was important was not what I had of God but what God had of me. If I was to go back over my life, I could show again and again that the spiritually significant things in my life took place when he reached down and, unsought, did something remarkable. I was converted that way. Nobody spoke to me, nobody followed me up, nobody gave me literature. I had none of those things. God just reached down when I was a boy and grabbed me.

What does it all add up to? It adds up to the fact that the initiative was always his. There is never a time when God is not working in my life or in the work to which he has sent me. He doesn't go to sleep like the gods Elijah talked about. What is required of me is response in two basically simple ways: first of all, the response of an up-to-date repentance so that there is nothing in my life about which I am not in the open, with God and with others; and second, the response of faith to what I know of him—as Father, Son, and Holy Spirit.

Tom then underlined du Plessis's emphasis on forgiveness as it related to the Spirit's fullness. To Tom the greatest thing about the power of the Spirit was that he brought into the believer's life the capacity to forgive. "If you forgive, it opens things up. If you don't, it dams things up."

That surely, Tom said, was the heart of Pentecost.

This can be seen from so many angles. Here was Jesus, who had been judicially murdered. Fifty days later his men go onto the streets and say to the people, "You did it." They did not mince words. But they didn't go on to say, "Pilate should be put from office; we should impeach Caiaphas; something should be done about Herod." Instead, they preached forgiveness. What else could Peter do? When Jesus came back, he came back loving and forgiving. Peter, sick at heart with his sin, was reinstated with love and forgiveness by the Lord. How could he have any other message when he got up to preach at Pentecost? That was the miracle of Pentecost. It had never happened before, where a party whose leader had been judicially murdered went onto the streets and preached forgiveness to those who had done it. No wonder 3,000 were converted in one day.

We also know that we cannot have forgiveness in a cup for ourselves. We can have forgiveness only as in a channel or pipe, when the other end is open and forgiveness is flowing through us to others. When that is happening we will see evangelism that really works.[24]

Complementary Stories

What struck me most was not the difference in those three stories but their complementary nature. Du Plessis, Burnett, and Houston were all saying important things. Listening to the three, one had a powerful sense of the Spirit's deep work in all of them. All were testifying with different vocabularies to the Holy Spirit as the author of new life. All three were dynamic men of the Spirit, though their testimonies varied. All three are still being used by God. Works of grace and rivers of new life flow from all three.

As far as I was personally concerned, I found in the Durban '73 Congress one clue that became increasingly important: the life, vitality, fruit, and evidence of the Spirit's presence are more important than the labels, semantics, and vocabulary attached to the phenomena. On the other hand, I couldn't avoid struggling with the theology of it all, and that process continued for me long after the Durban Congress was over.

The Congress experience, with its multiplicity of Christian viewpoints, also persuaded me more than ever that true togetherness in the Christian church was worth striving for as the matrix out of which could come, not only the Spirit's greater manifestation, but also the greatest forward movement of mission and evangelism.

As David Watson, a prominent Anglican canon and evangelist has said:

Unless renewal precedes evangelism, the credibility gap between what the church preaches and what the church is will be too wide to be bridged. It is only when the world sees the living body of Christ on earth that it will be in any way convinced of the reality and relevance of Christ himself.[25]

9
Helps
on the Way

The eminently humble person, though he be
inflexible in his duty and in those things
wherein God's honour is concerned... yet in
other things he is of a pliable disposition...
ready to pay deference to other's opinions,
loves to comply with their inclinations, and
has a heart that is tender and flexible,
like a little child.
Jonathan Edwards

BY THE MID-SEVENTIES, I found myself caught in an interesting
and sometimes confusing web of currents and crosscurrents.
Plodding along in a rather pedestrian fashion, I found myself
pushed forward by one set of observations and held back by
another. Charismatic and Pentecostal positives seemed to be off-
set by almost as many negatives. Evangelical caution, conserva-
tism, and theologizing often proved more of a friend than a foe,
more of a balance than a negative restraint.

The insights and blind spots of each constituency contributed
in about equal measure as I sought to progress. It brought home
the fallibility of both, the rich discoveries of both, and the need of
each for the other. As I reflect back, the catalogue of helps and
hindrances fell out pretty much as follows in the next two chapters.

Life and Growth

First of all, against a backdrop of a culturalized and often over-cerebral evangelicalism and ecumenism, I saw tremendous vitality and growth in churches and people touched by the charismatic renewal. As David Watson has noted,

> Many Christians today are weary of reports, reforms, reunion schemes, discussions, dialogues and debates. We spend our time talking to ourselves while the world plunges headlong into suicide and despair. And it is in this context that the primary need for a dynamic spiritual renewal by the Holy Spirit of God becomes obvious and urgent. We lack the fire and passion which has always been the mark of the Spirit's presence.[26]

Over and against the dead formalism of many mainline churches is seen the spectacular growth of the Pentecostal movement worldwide. For example, in Latin America its growth has been prodigious. It is said that in Chile and Brazil the Pentecostal church is growing faster than any other church anywhere and possibly faster than any other church at any other period in church history. Chile has one million Pentecostals out of a population of over seven million; Chile's church membership in 1932 was only 10,000. That represents a hundredfold increase in fifty years. When Manuel Umana, a Chilean Pentecostal pastor, died, his funeral was attended by 100,000 people. In Brazil, one branch of the Pentecostal church established 227 congregations in nine years' work. In Sao Paulo one Pentecostal church building holds 25,000 people. In Colombia there are reportedly more than 10,000 Catholic charismatic prayer groups. In Seoul, Korea, the world's largest congregation, the 250,000 member Full Gospel Central Church, is pastored by the Pentecostal Dr. Paul Yonggi Cho. "Look for men and women who are Spirit-filled," he urges, when explaining the incredible phenomenon of his congregation.

In the United States, a Gallup Poll, conducted for *Christianity Today* (Jan-Feb 1980), reveals that 19 percent of all adult Americans (i.e., over 29 million) consider themselves to be Pentecostal or charismatic Christians.

These 29 million Pentecostal-charismatics are found at almost equal percentages (18-21) in the Roman Catholic, Baptist, Methodist, and Lutheran denominations, and are similarly scattered among many smaller denominations and independents, and, of course, the "classical" Pentecostal denominations formed since 1906...About one quarter of those who reckon themselves to be Pentecostal-charismatic are Roman Catholic and two-thirds are Protestants—corresponding approximately to the proportion of each in the American populace...[27]

The explanation for that surging growth is suggested by a noncharismatic theologian in the Church of Christ, Jack Cottrell: "The charismatic movement can be seen as the attempt to fill an emotional, experiential vacuum left in an American Christendom that has become more liberal and more rationalistic."[28]

Roman Catholic theologian Kilian McDonnell has stated: "Churches do not seem to be offering spiritual depth. People go where they can (1) be fed and (2) find community...People want to experience God, not simply to know he exists."[29]

In South Africa it was always a source of interest to me to observe how much certain churches have abominated the Pentecostals as "sheep-stealers." Yet sheep tend to go where there's food. The attractiveness of spiritual growth also became evident in the little parish church I attend in Hilton, Natal. Once it was almost lifeless and its membership very low. Now it is bursting at the seams. That did not come about through intense theological discussion (which I would welcome more than disparage). It came about through charismatic renewal. Nor is this to imply that there are no longer any problems. But at least they are the problems of life, not the problems of death.

Dr. James Packer of Regent College, Vancouver, has put it this way:

Though theologically uneven (and what spiritually significant movement has not been?) the charismatic renewal has drawn many people who are weary of that which only ministers to and appeals to the mind. After all, people have a heart too, and whoever bypasses that fact will in the end lose out. Even stiff upper lips can hanker to shout the occasional "Hallelujah."[30]

Underground Ecumenism

Some people see the charismatic renewal as the most unifying thing in Christendom today. I'm not sure I would go that far. In South Africa a wider and in my judgment more significant range of Christian leadership was brought together in SACLA (South African Christian Leadership Assembly) on the basis of an open evangelicalism. Perhaps that is a pointer to a new way ahead for the world church. Moreover, in other parts of the world I see people from a wide range of backgrounds clustering in charismatic renewal gatherings while cleavages in the overall body of Christ still remain deep and pervasive. Here and there the renewal has, in fact, even been more divisive than unifying. Even so, I would not want to minimize the gains and progress that have come in many parts of the world through allowing the Holy Spirit greater freedom among his people.

I recollect one interesting experience shortly before Mission '70 in Johannesburg, a very large interdenominational evangelistic endeavor led by African Enterprise in 1970. I was speaking in the leading congregation of a Pentecostal denomination that had thus far stayed out of the mission. At the end of my message I was startled by an outburst in tongues from one member of the congregation, one of my first experiences of such a thing. Moments later an interpretation was given. The message was a stern rebuke which included these words: "I am wanting to do a great work in this city, but I cannot because my people are setting one another at naught." The effect on the congregation was astonishing. A great spirit of repentance swept over the people. The following week the whole denomination entered the mission.

The Anglican church in South Africa provides another interesting case study. For years there has been a deep cleavage between this body (the Church of the Province of South Africa, CPSA) and another smaller, more self-consciously evangelical body (the Church of England in South Africa, CESA). The exchanges on everything from disputed properties to theology have, in the past, been bitter and acrimonious. CESA has for over a hundred years bewailed how unevangelical the more Anglo-Catholic CPSA is.

The charismatic renewal, however, has had such a dramatic effect on the Church of the Province as to make it almost unrecognizable as the denomination I knew fifteen years ago. Its movement in what I would call a more evangelical, biblical, and evangelistic direction has been dramatic and clear-cut. Whereas fifteen years ago it almost ostracized evangelicals, it now makes them bishops. As the Holy Spirit, who guides into all truth, has had greater control, he has in fact led the whole denomination back into the Bible in a new way and made it far easier for more traditionally evangelical bodies to relate in fellowship than before. What the Evangelical Fellowship of Anglican Churchmen (EFAC) failed to do, the charismatic renewal has done in a short time.

The situation with Roman Catholics is even more dramatic. It would have been almost unthinkable fifteen years ago for evangelicals and Roman Catholics to have true fellowship together, let alone cooperate in evangelistic endeavors. Yet in missions we have conducted in Latin America and Africa, Roman Catholics who have been mightily touched by the charismatic renewal have joyfully participated with us and have often been almost indistinguishable from other evangelicals.

Dr. Ralph Martin, a Catholic charismatic leader from the U.S., asserts that "literally millions of Catholics have been

renewed or converted to a significant relationship with Jesus as
Savior and Lord, and to a life of holiness and service empowered
by the Holy Spirit.''[31]

One of the fruits of the Catholic renewal, Martin feels, is

a heightened awareness of the evangelical heart of Roman
Catholic Christianity . . . I would say that the Catholic Charismatic Renewal is broadly characterized by a basic conversion
or reconversion through which millions of Catholics have
encountered or accepted Jesus Christ as the Savior who takes
away the sin of the world, our sin, and as Lord . . . There is a
tremendous widespread blossoming of the reading of Scripture and of giving testimony in evangelism.[32]

Martin prefers to talk about what is happening as an "evangelical awakening" in the Catholic Church rather than as a
"charismatic renewal."

I personally feel more comfortable being called a "Catholic
evangelical" than a "Catholic charismatic." The focus in my
life, as it is in most of the renewal movement, is not on the
gifts of the Holy Spirit but on conversion to the person of
Christ and entrance into a life of faithful service to Him.

He recognizes that a struggle over the basic gospel message is
going on right now in the Roman Catholic Church.

Liberal Protestant thought has made serious incursions into
the Roman Catholic church. It is my hope that the charismatic renewal and the evangelical emphasis growing out of it
will be able to contribute to the strengthening of the orthodox
understanding of the Gospel in the Catholic Church. I believe
this struggle for the basic Gospel is an area of common
ground between Protestant and Catholic evangelicals . . . I
look forward to the time when we Catholic evangelicals have
more contact with our Protestant evangelical brothers and
sisters: we desire to serve the same Gospel and the same
Lord.[33]

Protestant Michael Harper rightly looks at this sort of phenomenon with thanksgiving. He even speaks of cases of intercommunion and notes that the world of Catholic officialdom is often sticking rigidly to the rule-book while behind the scenes an "underground ecumenism" is operating where many of those rules are being totally ignored. He quotes Bernard Shaw's play *St. Joan,* where Robert, a law-abiding conservative, turns to Poulengey and says: "What! You are as mad as she [Joan] is." Poulengey answers: "We want a few mad people now. See where the sane ones have landed us!" Harper adds:

> Underground ecumenism may seem to some the product of madness and a dangerous ecclesiastical aberration. But to others it seems a work of the Holy Spirit. The "sane" ecumenists and experts on canon law have got us nowhere very much; perhaps the "insane" will achieve something where others have failed.[34]

Of course, some evangelical critics will argue that Catholic charismatics have not by and large turned from their views on Mary, the saints, the Mass, papal authority, and so on. But that type of doctrinal reformation does not happen overnight, least of all after centuries of conditioning. Some time must be allowed within Catholicism for additional theological thinking on certain issues highlighted by both the Reformation and the charismatic renewal. In the meantime it is less than charitable or honest not to recognize the mighty movements of the Spirit at work in contemporary Catholicism.

Prayer and Worship
Another positive feature of Pentecostal and charismatic witness, the commitment to prayer, impresses me. For example, in our mission to the city of Pietermaritzburg in South Africa in 1975, many people paid varying degrees of lipservice to the importance of prayer. Yet the Pentecostal churches formed a chain of prayer that ran twenty-four hours a day, seven days a week, four weeks a month for six months. Small wonder that we saw such

an amazing response. Pentecostal and charismatic ventures are generally born in hours of prayer. Projects in other sections of the church tend more to be born of talk and organizational expertise.

Then there were the occasional experiences of charismatic worship that came my way. I had been raised on a diet of ancient and modern church music plus the standard fare of evangelical hymnody. I must confess there were times when I wearied of singing theology to other singers, or of singing such lofty exhortations as "Rescue the perishing, Care for the dying." Not that singing about God is to be decried, but what struck me about charismatics was that they sang *to* God. They addressed him in their singing and worship. There was in song a personal sense of fellowship with the Father and the Son through the Spirit. Further, by abolishing excessive anxiety over the clock, time was allowed for people to express their feelings until a sense of communion with God was achieved in the gathering.

Other things were not so positive. To some of these I now turn, not only to underline to charismatics that they still have something to learn, but to remind evangelicals that they still have much to teach.

10
The Obstacle Course

Enthusiasm tramples over prejudice and
opposition, spurns inaction, storms the
citadel of its object and like an avalanche
overwhelms and engulfs all obstacles. It is
nothing more or less than faith in action.
Henry Chester

THE PATH TO GREATER FELLOWSHIP with Pentecostals and charismatics was for me, as I suspect it is for others, not without its
pitfalls. At times I felt I was negotiating an obstacle course.
Some of those obstacles were admittedly tossed into my path
from the wobbly fringes of the movement and not from its more
stable and mature center. That I know. But they were obstacles
nevertheless and my skills at spiritual hurdling were extensively
tested.

One charismatic friend who read the first draft of this chapter
warned me that if I presented all this as typical I would have the
whole charismatic constituency taking up arms against me. He
reassured me that it would, of course, all be done in love, for
which assurance I blessed both him and the gentle and loving
army of waiting warriors with their theological hatchets. Anyway, being a rather devout coward who is far from anxious to be

cudgeled, even in love, let me quickly affirm my recognition that in mushrooming new movements of spiritual life there will always be excesses from those who go off beam, either in weakness or zeal or through old Screwtape's machinations or because of the flesh. All historians of renewal and revival know that.

On the other hand, my experience was my experience. I can't get away from it, and it is this which I am relating. The fact that I initially thought some of these things to be typical only goes to show how easily the exceptions can be thought to prove the rule.

Party Pressure

The first obstacle was neither particularly Pentecostal nor peculiarly charismatic. Found throughout the church, it is perhaps inevitable wherever there are groupings of any sort—social, political, or religious. I am thinking of group pressure.

In my experience it came from two sides, or from two parties, the evangelical and the charismatic. It reminded me of that animal absurdity who appears in children's stories about Dr. Doolittle. The creature has a head at each end of its body. It is called a "Pushmepullyou" and is the contorted consequence of being pulled in two different directions.

On the one hand, I felt a deep loyalty to the evangelical party, as it were, and on the other hand I felt the attraction of the charismatic bandwagon. I did not want to lose acceptance with my evangelical friends, nor did I want to become a charismatic catch to be fêted on the Pentecostal testimony circuit as a scalp won from the other side. Basically I resisted being a feather in anybody's cap. I just wanted to find deeper life in Christ.

Those conflicting pulls highlight two problems in Christendom. The first is that we all tend to find our security in a circle of like-minded people rather than in Christ. We want and need acceptance. We can sympathize with Peter when we learn how on the Gentile issue he compromised the truth in his own search for it by "fearing the circumcision party" (Gal. 2:12).

A second problem is what the party itself does to its members to get them to toe the line, or risk rejection. Commenting on evangelicalism, though his remarks are just as applicable to other parties (e.g., charismatics, Pentecostals, Anglo-Catholics, or ever-so-reformed Reformists), one writer has said:

> Evangelicals fail to achieve the rich diversity that is displayed by independent persons of other convictions; their goal is conformity and they tend therefore to spend their energies on being like others rather than carving their own ideas out of the raw stuff of life. This makes for dullness.[35]

The writer goes on to ask whether evangelicalism (and again I insist on the relevance to all "parties") has not developed into "a closed system" marked by three classic characteristics. The first is a comprehensive way of looking at life which claims to solve all problems and right all wrongs. The second is a refusal to allow itself to be modified by newly observed facts, preferring rather to absorb the impact of those facts by a well-developed casuistry. The third is a tendency to disarm newly initiated persons of their critical faculties once they have stepped inside the system. In this system emotional heat turns disagreement into betrayal and heresy.[36]

All of this results in timidity about spiritual pioneering, in fearfulness about conclusions not prepackaged by the party, and ultimately, unless checked, in that deformity which is the sad consequence of inbreeding. It also, incidentally, leads many religious parties to expel their best people—those who dare to risk a little independent thinking. Anglicans have been quite good at that and among the worthies we have dumped are John Wesley, Methodism's founder, and General William Booth, founder of the Salvation Army. The Catholics did something similar with Martin Luther.

I remember one classic personal experience of this type of pressure. In 1973 I was invited by the Commission on World Mission and Evangelism of the World Council of Churches to Geneva to attend a small dialogue symposium on evangelism. My assignment was to present a paper on evangelism from an evangelical perspective. After this Geneva experience a number of evangelicals in Southern and East Africa decided to write me off. After all, to set foot in Geneva was almost the ultimate evangelical heresy. One prominent evangelical said, "Michael has sold his soul to Geneva." A university Christian group that was thinking of inviting us for a mission to their campus hastily abandoned the idea. The idea that I was invited to Geneva to bring an evangelical witness appeared not to have entered their minds.

Although I have reservations about aspects of current ecumenical theology, on the other hand I could see that kind of pressure only as simplistically judgmental and counterproductive. Likewise, in exploring the work of the Spirit, I felt myself caught in certain party pulls, the one seemingly saying "Don't forsake us—or else" and the other seemingly saying "Please embrace us—or else!" It made the exploration of truth more difficult.

Subculture

Another obstacle on the course was what I might call the Pentecostal subculture. This was the problem of distinguishing form from essence. What was essential to the movement and what were trappings?

The extravagant praying, the boisterous exuberance, the groaning prayers, and the loud noises in the few meetings to which I was exposed became obstacles to my spirit. One high-powered Pentecostal sister once prayed so enthusiastically in our office that the whole street must have heard her. The late Dr. Edgar Brookes, a distinguished historian, scholar, parliamentarian, and then chairman of African Enterprise (South Africa), was coming up the stairs to our office during her prayer. "The Lord couldn't have failed to hear that!" he whispered to me.

Then there was the matter of hands raised in the air. And hugging too. For some years it was a bit much.

Let me illustrate out of someone else's experience. A Methodist pastor in Texas was invited to a renewal weekend. He presumably went because he was seeking personal renewal. The problem to him, however, was the "trappings." Tongue in cheek, he tells his tale:

> We sang a lot during the weekend. Not just plain songs, either, but songs that usually included some motions or actions. We were told to smile broadly, stomp our feet, touch our neighbor and most of all raise our hands. I got to thinking about my own hesitation to elevate my arms. It is not a comfortable position. Nor is it natural. Nor is it common. It is a position that shows vulnerability. Hands up! is... what cops say to robbers, etc. So on a purely subjective level I could see how others who resisted holding their hands up could feel like someone about to be held up or arrested![37]

For my part I used to sense in certain prayer meetings that I was almost being watched to see if I would raise my hands or not, thereby indicating whether I was a bona fide charismatic or not. If you raised your hands you were charismatically there. You had arrived. You were among the initiated. You could be accepted without reserve. After all, it was the public sign, like raising your hand in class when the teacher asks who has done their homework.

My Texan pastor friend also tells his reaction at the camp to all the required hugging. He says: "Those who go in for that sort of expression see it as a sign that the walls are tumbling down. I'm not much of a hugger and am not always thrilled to be a huggee...but those huggers are like steamrollers who plough right through my fence."

Personally I do not now have a hugging hangup. In fact I enjoy it. I have crashed the hug barrier, as it were. But some more sensitive souls, who are still tiptoeing toward a deeper experience of the Holy Spirit, can be both figuratively and literally stopped in their tracks by suddenly being engulfed, midway through divine service, in the arms of the local butcher. I remember once seeing a dear friend of mine, an American black, hugging a white South African politician. I never saw such a struggle between black power and white fear in my life.

Perhaps all this relates to a charismatic tendency at times to measure internal states by external signs, along with an insensitivity to the feelings of quiet, shy, or reserved people. And so, either feeling that they have been delivered from that type of reserve, or forgetting that they were ever marked by it themselves, they periodically batter down the defenses of the seeking or uninitiated.

The Texan pastor put it this way: "We were given fair warning early in the weekend that our dignity would have to go. Maybe you should know that our church is made up mainly of Germans and their descendants, some of whom are upset if you find them in the hospital without a robe on! Dignity is one of their cardinal virtues, especially in church. So the drive to get rid of dignity stalled right away on these Teutonic defenses."[38]

My point is that subcultural baggage, which may or may not include subtle though often unconscious manipulation, is more of a hindrance than a help. It is an obstacle in the course, though foolish is the one who allows it to become insuperable.

Power-Mania
Another obstacle to me was what seemed often to be a spiritual power-mania in charismatic and Pentecostal circles. Not that I would deny the divine promise or the human need of the Spirit's power. Much that I have already said earlier shows that. One amusing though perhaps unusual experience came my way in a meeting of Pentecostal businessmen. In all sorts of ways it was a thoroughly splendid and edifying exercise. However, I once again felt that noise was mistaken for power and volume for victory. The idea that God might have normal hearing appeared not to have entered anyone's mind.

It came to a head for me when one ardent brother, whose rasping and crackling vocal chords suggested he was no stranger to the testimony circuit, yelled out, "We don't need theology" ("Amen" roared the crowd). "We don't need hermeneutics" ("Amen" roared the crowd). "WE-JUST-NEED-THE-P-O-O-O-O-O-W-E-R OF GOD!" (more Amens, hoots of holy laughter, plus sustained clapping as the brother beamed at the multitude). It was the kind of populist rhetoric that was funny to hear but hard to swallow.

I turned to my neighbor, a highly regarded Pentecostal leader from Latin America, and whispered, "I have rarely heard a man in greater need of both theology and hermeneutics!"

Thankfully, he nodded in vigorous assent. And winked!

My relief was great. I could continue to explore the realm of the Spirit without having to embrace that kind of excess! When populist Pentecostals set the Spirit's power over against theology or hermeneutics (the science of interpreting the Bible correctly), they not only create unnecessary complications for people, but they also add substance to the oft-heard accusation that the renewal movement is theologically lightweight and exegetically erratic. I don't think that is by any means generally true, but there is no point in fueling an impression one would presumably want to dispel.

Another unfortunate idea is that weakness and the fullness of the Spirit do not go together. Michael Griffiths has noted that

> the power of the Holy Spirit did not make an apostle into a kind of superstar evangelist. Paul could say he was so utterly, unbearably crushed that he despaired (2 Cor. 1:8) and was "afflicted at every turn—fighting without and fear within. But God...comforts the *downcast*..." (2 Cor. 7:5, 6). God's power is made perfect in weakness (2 Cor. 12:9)...We should be careful when our stereotype of the Spirit-filled leader does not measure up to his being "in weakness and in much fear and trembling" (1 Cor. 2:3), and where his "bodily presence is weak, and his speech of no account" (2 Cor. 10:10). God's power is not intended to make [us] powerful, but rather to display God's transcendent power in the scruffy earthenware of dedicated but frail human vessels.[39]

Paul's point was that one had to proceed in search of the Spirit's power in the realization that it would always be just that, the Spirit's power. Not our own. The treasure is held in an earthen vessel. The Christian who is conscious of weakness often more truly manifests the appeal of Christ than one who projects a self-conscious awareness of great spiritual power.

Doctrine Divides

A related hassle for me was the Pentecostal cliché that "doctrine divides but experience unites." Of course, the slogan is not void of truth, but it is a half-truth and as such almost as perilous as outright falsehood. I was once invited to preach in a Pentecostal church and was informed by one of its laymen that "We keep away from doctrine. It is so divisive." The implication was "And, brother, you'd better too!" Perhaps he meant that they stayed away from talking about baptism, or the millennium, and they didn't want me to push any doctrine of bishops on them. Or maybe he was trying simply to get away from churchiness. But in any event, that sort of thing set off my alarm signals. My evangelical heritage had underlined the importance of truth. The Bible, especially the New Testament, would not have contained so many pages of "teaching" if "doctrine" was of no consequence.

Interestingly, Richard Quebedeaux reports that "there are now even a few Unitarian-Universalist Charismatics."[40] His word *even* obviously expresses surprise that those who are professing a new fullness of the Holy Spirit should continue uncritically in views Unitarian in nature, so manifestly out of line with New Testament teaching. For is not the Holy Spirit the Spirit of truth (John 15:26) and the One who guides into all truth? (John 16:13).

We've Got It

Another hurdle to negotiate is the impression some charismatics convey that they have "got it," that they are a sort of spiritual aristocracy, and everyone else is a second-class citizen. Maybe many groups and individuals are guiltless at this point but it is a common impression and an obstacle.

I remember in one city bumping into a Christian friend. He

was so full of smiles, joys, and overwhelming miracles around
every corner that I quickly felt my inadequacies and insecurities
surfacing. Was he telling me all this to elevate and inspire me or
to show the startling contrast between the supernaturalism
around him and the naturalism around me? One of his points
for rejoicing was put this way: "You know, Mike, I praise God
because in this town he is dividing out the true from the false
Christians."

"Oh!" I said, somewhat startled, not being aware of this
dividing process. "How do you know the true from the false?"

"Well, the true church is made up of those who love Jesus."

"How do you know who loves Jesus?"

"Well, you know—those who *say* they do."

That rationale astonished me. All the Christians in town
would probably claim, once nailed to the wall, that they loved
Jesus, although that vocabulary might not be their natural
choice. My friend's facility at sorting out the true from the false
seemed to be a delusion. In fact, he picked out one pastor in
particular as epitomizing the false, whereas I knew him to be a
man of deep and genuine, even if modestly unorthodox, piety.

No Politics
Another thing that bothered me, especially in the context of
apartheid South Africa, was the difficulty of being accepted by
Pentecostals and charismatics while seeking at the same time to
be true to the socio-political implications of the gospel. A later
chapter will enlarge on this problem, but suffice it for the
moment to indicate that it constituted a real headache for me.

"Michael is political," my Pentecostal friends would say.
"He opposes apartheid and the government." That kind of
remark reveals one of those theological eccentricities so characteristic of many conservative Christians in South Africa—
namely, to label as political those Christians who oppose
apartheid while withholding the label from those who support it.
To oppose the system is to be political; to support or tolerate it is
not. To me the social sins of accepting structural injustice and

racial discrimination are little different in seriousness from personal sins like adultery, dishonesty, or drunkenness. Are we to repent of one category of sin and not the other?

The trouble was compounded for me by the fact that almost all my theologically conservative friends were also political conservatives who tolerated and indeed often supported the South African status quo. They seemed to me to have domesticated God to the support of discriminatory politics. On the other hand, their opinion of me might be that I was seeking to domesticate God to the opposition party and to my own viewpoint. But I am persuaded that God is not headed for the ballot box of any one party. He is on his own side—in favor of holiness, justice, goodness, and compassion wherever those are manifested in private and public life. He is against impurity, injustice, evil, and heartlessness.

Remember that story of the two nineteenth-century sailors, one French and one English, who were discussing their respective national navies. The Frenchman said: "I can't understand how it is that the English navy always seems to win its battles."

"Well," said the English sailor, "before we go into battle we pray."

"But we pray too," insisted the Frenchman.

"Ah, yes, but we pray in English," replied the other.

We dare not turn God into a cosmic Englishman, Afrikaner, or black freedom fighter who is there to promote our private nationalisms. Neither dare we remove him from a compassionate love for the world and from involvement in the whole arena of human life, including the socio-political. If he is concerned about how one person relates to another, isn't he concerned about how one group relates to another? If he is concerned that "not one of the least of these little ones" should be caused to stumble, then surely he is concerned if whole groups or nations of people are caused to stumble through oppressive systems.

Subjectivism

Another obstacle to me was the highly subjective criteria for guidance through visions, prophecies, dreams, or mental pictures. This is sensitive territory and I do not want to be cavalier or skeptical about phenomena that I know can be authentic. But on many occasions in charismatic services or gatherings I have been disturbed by the ease and almost gullibility with which the supposed message behind such phenomena has been received by the faithful as authentic.

My fear relates basically to an undiscerning intrusion of subjectivism untempered by the insights, cautions, and controls both of the Word of God and of the spiritually mature. Apart from anything else, any person with unhealthy ambitions for spiritual authority can easily achieve an improper domination of a group by manipulating them with reports of dreams and "pictures" into a position of spiritual subservience. Every congregation and fellowship has its emotionally dependent people who are too susceptible, ready to be impressed by such "guidance." We must remember that Paul wrote the Colossian letter and John his first epistle in order to counter sincere but deluded claims to divine revelation from certain brethren "who would deceive" (1 John 2:26) or "delude with beguiling speech" (Col. 2:4).

Richard Lovelace, a historian of church renewals, and a sympathizer with charismatic renewal, has made this observation:

It seems difficult to frame a very strong biblical argument for limiting prophetic utterances to the apostolic period. And yet the Church in later eras has repeatedly found that when it goes beyond the canon of Scripture to recognize new revelations, it soon finds itself dealing with severe problems. Outbreaks of fanatical enthusiasm in church history have always been accompanied by a belief in contemporary revelations of the Spirit...Some Reformation groups which began by stressing the contemporary revelation of the Spirit soon ended by treating the Scriptures as an addendum which was more or less unnecessary once a Christian obtained direct access to the mind of God through the Spirit.[41]

The Reformers and Puritans guarded against overly subjective revelations and enthusiasms by stressing the *objectivity* of the written Word within the context of their doctrine of the Holy Spirit. On the other hand they recognized that illumination by the Spirit was necessary for the understanding and application of Scripture.

Edwyn Hoskyns' posthumous commentary on the Gospel of John (16:12-15) says:

> Jesus is the way in which the disciples must be led by the Spirit. He is also the truth to which they must be guided. The author [John] is therefore concerned to impress upon his readers the danger of false conceptions of the work of the Spirit. The inspiration does not detach [human beings] from the truth that is in Jesus and set them free to wander into new realms of truth, apart from the sanctuary of God...The Power of the Spirit does not consist in secret and mystical revelations but in the external preaching of the Gospel which makes them revolt from the world and attaches them to the Church. And His action does not consist in delivering new truths to the disciples but in providing a larger, deeper and more perfect understanding of the teaching which Jesus has given them.[42]

These are important words of caution which many leaders in the charismatic renewal have in fact already sounded themselves.

What I have outlined in this chapter is the obstacle course, or part of it, that faced me as I sought to understand more of what God had shown to Pentecostals and charismatics. Had I been less motivated I might have been paralyzed by the group pressures, stymied by the subculture, offended by the power-mania, frustrated by the apparent indifference to doctrine, squeezed out by the exclusivism, alienated by the apolitical stance, or frightened off by the rampant subjectivism. On the other hand, I was all along encouraged by the vitality and life and reality that I saw in those circles, especially when set alongside the often barren deserts in other sections of Christendom. The renewal seemed to me to be not the ultimate expression of the church, nor the final repository of biblical truth, nor even the purest form of Christian life. But it was the sounding of a gong, a trumpet call, a clarion clang of a bell, calling out to the church at large that the ministry of the Holy Spirit must receive more attention, that new life and power and love are to be found in his release, and that his gifts are there to be appropriated by the twentieth-century church as part of its equipment for service.

So I decided to attend the first South African Renewal Conference on the Holy Spirit—set for the Milner Park Arena in Johannesburg in August 1977.

11

Milner Park
and a
Second Touch

There is a place in the life of the church for
mountaintop experiences.
Caesar Molebatsi of Soweto

GOD HAD TOLD ME TO DEAL WITH an alienated relationship before
going to the renewal conference set for August 1977 at Milner
Park arena in Johannesburg. I knew I had to get right with Jim
and Mary, but I had postponed doing anything about it over the
four months since that sunset walk in the fields. Should I write?
Phone? Do a tape? Undecided, I did nothing. Besides that,
there were so many other distracting pressures. Finally, about a
week before the conference, I decided I would just have to write
to Jim and Mary after it was over. Surely the Lord would make
allowances for how busy I had been.

Just then a phone call came from Kenya saying I should rush
up to Nairobi to meet my colleague, Bishop Festo Kivengere,
leader of our East Africa team, to discuss some emergency matters in connection with our refugee work. It was six and a half
months since Idi Amin had murdered Archbishop Janani

Luwum (who had also been chairman of our African Enterprise work in Uganda). After Janani's death Festo had had to flee into exile; it seemed he was next on Amin's hit list. Then came the deluge of refugees to our Nairobi office. Our East Africa team scarcely paused for breath, especially Festo, who catapulted hither and yon all over the world publicizing Uganda's plight. The continuing flow of refugees from all sections of the society, especially students and professional people, created endless new challenges plus headaches.

It was the Wednesday before the renewal conference was to begin on Monday. No time to write the postponed letter to Jim and Mary. The Lord would understand.

The Uganda problems occupied us day and night for several days. During that time I was contacted by some local Pentecostals who had some overseas friends they wanted me to meet. One was a leader from Canada. He asked what I was doing.

"Well," I said, "I'm involved in a project up here with Bishop Festo Kivengere."

The man looked blank. "Is he an Anglican bishop?"

"Yes, indeed," I replied.

"And is he born again?" was the next question.

"Yes, brother," I said, scarcely concealing my incredulity at such a question about one of the world's leading evangelists, "Festo is born again."

But as I walked away from the conversation I couldn't suppress in my spirit the renewed and horrifying realization of the encapsulated nature of most Christian living. Half the Christian world just does not know how, where, or whether the other half lives. The well-intentioned questions of my new acquaintance were a sad commentary on the state of things.

A Powerful Dream
I went to bed late and tired on Friday night and slept soundly. But about four A.M. I had another dream about Jim and Mary. Once again, in the visual images of this dream I saw myself becoming reconciled to them. I awoke, alert and intensely con-

scious of God's presence and of his injunction. I bounded out of bed, put on the light, sat down at the desk, and finally wrote the letter that would seek to heal a seven-year breach.

About seven A.M. I called Festo in his hotel room and said I'd like to have breakfast with him and share something. Over bacon and eggs I told about the early morning experience and the initiative I had taken. "What if it is rejected or turned down?" I asked, wondering if I could sustain such a rejection.

"Well, brother," said Festo with his inimitable twinkle, "you have entered the Calvary arena. Whatever happens, you have done the right thing in the light of Calvary love. Leave it to the Lord."

Our Ugandan refugee matters were dealt with by Sunday night and on Monday morning I flew back from Nairobi to Johannesburg, wondering what the week would bring forth. I was relieved beyond words that I had finally obeyed the Lord in taking the reconciling initiative about which he had spoken to me: "Do something about that relationship before the renewal conference." After about four months, I had acted, with just two days to go until zero hour. Such are the ways of human procrastination and stubbornness.

Another World

I was met at Jan Smuts airport, driven to Milner Park, and deposited in the speakers' lounge for lunch. I had even been asked to speak. Hope for South Africa was my subject. But this was another world. Familiar evangelical faces were missing. Instead here were the Pentecostal and charismatic faithful. David du Plessis, Bob McAllister of Rio, Cecil Kerr of Northern Ireland, Dan and Al Malachuk of Logos Books, Larry Christenson, Derek Prince, and Francis MacNutt ("Who's he?" I asked of one horrified charismatic, who wore that same look manifested by me with the Canadian brother who had never heard of Festo Kivengere!) I hardly dared say I'd never heard of any of the other big wheels except David du Plessis.

I had in fact also met Derek Prince once at an airport. He had seemed preoccupied, rushed, reserved. "Guess he doesn't like evangelicals," I'd decided defensively, slipping into a negative view. I didn't know that Derek was a shy man. I'd had no time to find out. Judgment was easy; fellowship, harder. I also knew he had certain controversial views. But that does not constitute grounds to break fellowship. Sitting there in the speakers' lounge over coffee, I felt a little nudge from the Spirit. "Go over and greet Derek. You've been distant. Deal with it. Go and greet him." So over I went. It felt good and he was very friendly.

As the conference got underway that night I was struck by the tremendous sincerity, buoyancy, warmth, and devotion that characterized the worship and singing. These people weren't just singing nice theology or exhorting each other in song but were really connecting with their Lord in adoration. As I looked around the auditorium, many indeed seemed "lost in wonder, love, and praise." It was exhilarating.

I recollected the comments made to me about PACLA by Bill Burnett, formerly my chaplain at high school and later Archbishop of Cape Town. PACLA was the Pan African Christian Leadership Assembly, of which I had been program chairman; it had met in Nairobi in December 1976.

"Weak in worship," Archbishop Bill had said, and now I really understood and "felt" what he meant. I also saw that worship takes time. It is not singing three songs in a row and having a quick prayer. It means allowing the majesty and greatness and goodness of God our Father to break in on our inner beings and draw them out in worshipful adoration.

James Packer has expressed "unambiguous approval" of many features of the charismatic renewal when biblically assessed. One of them he notes is

its insistence that each Christian be thoroughly involved in the Church's worship; not necessarily by speaking in the assembly (though that kind of participation, when orderly and well done, must surely be approved) but primarily by opening one's heart to God in worship and seeking to realize for oneself the divine realities about which the church sings, prays and learns from Scripture.[43] It struck me that the church generally, and evangelicals specifically, have very much to learn from charismatics about worship in the Spirit and in truth.

Expectancy
The conference proceeded from Monday night to Thursday. I was struck by the sense of God's presence in almost all the proceedings and by the spirit of expectancy toward God. People saw him as mightily and intimately involved with his people. He was alive, there, active. And he could act now, right now.

That sense of immediacy about God's activity struck me as a positive dimension of charismatic faith, reflecting the New Testament atmosphere and the spirit of the early church. Churchpeople are often like the schoolboy who described faith as "believing in something you know isn't true." These people believed it was true and acted as if they did. The sense of reality was infectious.

Grain of Wheat
On Thursday morning, September 1, I found myself a nice safe seat way back in the bleachers—the sort of seat no one but God would have noticed. I was very reflective about the whole experience. What did it all mean? Here I was in a full-blown renewal conference, sort of a sideline cheerer for the renewal movement. I approved of the game but couldn't quite get into it. Yet I periodically dashed onto the field for a few mischievous moments before running back for the evangelical grandstand, where I felt a bit safer.

Yet I must not sell myself or the grace of God too short. It hadn't all been fear and caution, because through all the preceding years of openness I had also experienced a strange sense of the sovereign purpose, planning, or even strategy of God in allowing that fresh effusion of the Holy Spirit to elude me while it seemed to come so readily and easily to so many around me. I

had accordingly relaxed into a slightly perplexed peace on the
subject, knowing that the Spirit "apportions to each one individually as He wills" (1 Cor. 12:11). Perhaps that important
sense of divine sovereignty for years had also kept me interested
but detached, hungry but content, open but cautious, committed but agnostic, yearning but unmoved.

So there I was. Bob McAllister of Rio was preaching with
extraordinary power on the importance of discerning the body
of Christ. The challenge to see Christ in my brother and my
brother in Christ had struck home afresh and renewed in me
more deeply than ever a commitment to the church worldwide
in all its facets.

The speaker sat down. Then Derek Crumpton, conference
coordinator, moved to the microphone to close the meeting. In a
transitional and apparently throwaway line he said: "Except a
grain of wheat fall into the ground and die, it abides alone. But if
it dies, it brings forth much fruit" (John 12:24). Just a verse of
Scripture well known to me. Later he told me: "I still remember
that moment. I had had that scripture so strongly impressed on
me that I knew it had to be spoken out, even if it appeared out of
context." And so in obedience he spoke it out.

At that moment, totally unexpectedly, I felt as if a surgeon's
knife went through me. Something deep and painful and cruci-
fying and new was happening in me. I couldn't restrain tears.
The grain of wheat that was my life had to die if it was to bring
forth fruit pleasing to God. Somehow I had to get out of the way
more and let God be God. Maybe it was a matter of getting the
self more underground and out of sight like the grain. I knew
God wanted more of me, all of me. But the world, the flesh, and
the devil were still clutching at portions of territory in my life. It
was painful to face. I had the Spirit, but did he have me?

I don't know how long the struggle continued. Half an hour.
Maybe more. During that time, loving brothers and sisters
cared for me and prayed with me. Then the Spirit of peace and
quiet praise began to overtake me. I wondered what it was all
about. At the least I was sure that the attempt to get right with

Jim and Mary had paved the way for this breakthrough.

Of course I knew more work would be needed on that relationship through face-to-face sharing and communication. The healing of deep hurts requires more than a letter, and it doesn't usually happen all at once. But making the start had been crucial. Reconciliation was on its way. Later I would praise God for the warm and generous response from Jim and Mary. We would need to meet, and we did.

In the Milner Park arena that day, however, all I knew was that the Spirit of God was doing something new in me. In the midst of the whole experience I had the distinct sense of the Lord whispering that I should not fear to share this with the greater constituency of evangelicals in South Africa and in the wider world, especially the Lausanne movement for world evangelization. Although I was part of its continuing committee, I was not sure how such an opportunity of sharing would come my way. I would have to wait and see.

Another somewhat disturbing word came through to me about my own plenary address to the conference that night. "Remind them that Soweto is only eight miles away." Soweto is the sprawling and tragic creation of urban apartheid. Situated on the edge of Johannesburg, it stands not only as one of the great human sores of South Africa but as a symbol of black frustration, despair, pain, and struggle. The *South West Township*, SO-WE-TO. Not a prepossessing name, nor a prepossessing place.

And now here was the Spirit of God, right in the middle of one of the most momentous spiritual experiences of my life, bringing to my mind a social reality and a political tragedy of epic proportions, saying that neither I nor the South African church should forget it. It seemed I was to remind evangelicals of Pentecost and remind Pentecostals of politics! My spirit blanched. What an assignment. I quietly protested to my Lord. The sense of the Spirit's response was at once impressed on my soul: "Except a grain of wheat fall into the ground and *die*. . . you must die to your will and the desire to please."

My willingness for such a death was to be tested immediately. The thought of having to jar the conference with that sort of challenge had little appeal to me.

But the Spirit's word was also in line with black expectations for me. For a couple of days blacks had been coming up to me and saying "We are praying for you, Mike, and for your message." I couldn't help reflecting that of the many sins of which we had all been exhorted to repent, no one had yet really hit racism. That night just before I got up to speak, one leading black reached forward from behind me, grasped my upper arm, and whispered, "Courage, Mike, courage!" It was helpful.

Hope for South Africa

The rest of the day following my searing experience in the morning proceeded much like any other. No further dramatic experiences. No overwhelming sense of God's presence. Just quiet work on getting my message finally together.

I spoke with relative freedom and with a clear sense of what had to be said. I indicated in my opening comments my concern that "in the great euphoria of these precious days" we should not allow ourselves to "dangle too far above the complicated and ravished soil of South Africa today." If we did, we would "allow the intoxication of these days to open up an unbridgeable gulf between this glorious conference and the tortured tragedy of a city eight miles away called Soweto."

I went on: "At the outset I have to say this, that, humanly speaking (and those are the key words—humanly speaking), I see no hope. Humanly speaking, the tunnel is stygian dark to the eye. Humanly speaking, I believe that we have through our political lifestyle sown a wind and we must, if human events take the normal course, reap the whirlwind. Every human law of history tells me that this is so. Humanly speaking, if we live in a moral universe, as I believe we do, then the judgments of history must surely overtake us. Humanly speaking, thirty years of official discrimination cannot but produce a political convulsion of shattering proportions. So, humanly speaking, I feel the situa-

tion in our land today is absolutely hopeless. Seeing what I
see and hearing what I hear and knowing what I know from
various people, I cannot say otherwise and still be true to
myself..."

But God...
"And yet, I want to say before this gathering that *I am hope-
ful.* I am full of hope in my heart tonight...because of two
words—*But God.* So Acts 2:23 says, 'This Jesus, delivered
up according to the definite plan and foreknowledge of God,
you crucified and killed by the hands of lawless men. *But God*
raised Him up...' Then there is Acts 10:28. 'You yourselves know how unlawful it is for a Jew to associate with or
to visit anyone of another nation: *but God* has shown me that
I should not call any man common or unclean.' And Acts
10:40: '*but God* raised him [Jesus] on the third day and made
him manifest.' In those two words, I see the tremendous
hope we have for this land because they speak of divine initiative, a divine intervention in history."

I went on to elaborate that there was hope for South Africa because of two particular historical precedents—
because there was hope for Israel in Egyptian bondage, and
because there was hope for Judah in Babylonian captivity.

With reference to the first historical situation I concluded
that "in spite of the perversity of many of our Pharaohs, in
spite of the despair of many of our own people, in spite of the
reluctance of many of our men of God, yet God is going to
work and he is going to bring us through. If not by the loving and constant courtship of the Holy Spirit, then by the
persuasion of seven or even seventy-seven plagues of Egypt,
if need be. But he will bring us through."

And in the second historical situation, what could one do
but find even more encouragement and hope? Here were an
apostate people who, in spite of rebellious deafness to their
prophets' pleas for justice and for purity of worship, had
nevertheless found mercy even while under the historical dy-

namics of divine judgment. Ezra said, "Even now there is
hope...in spite of this" (Ezra 10:2).

Then, having spoken to the gathering of that hope which
comes through the faithful mercy of God, I underlined our
human responsibility as the people of God and the church of
Jesus Christ in this land. "As we look at these situations of history, we see that the prophets called a spade a spade. They didn't
cloak what the problem was or what the sin was. Yet I fear lest in
the church or even in a sensitive gathering like this, we fail to
realize that we have to repent of our national sin: discrimination
on the basis of race. I do not know the political solution but I do
know that unless we repent of this sin and of this system, the
judgments of history will become the judgments of God on us."
I ended with a plea not only for repentance but for reconciliation
between husband and wife, race and race, tribe and tribe,
denomination and denomination, nation and nation, friend and
friend.

Other talks had been greeted with huge amounts of laughter,
clapping, and eruptions of "Hallelujah" and "Praise the
Lord." Mine was received with silence. Derek Crumpton said
later: "Had people applauded it would have indicated they had
not heard you."

The Night That Was

Back in my room that night I had a joyful and peaceful time of
prayer with my roommate, Michael Nuttall, then Bishop of Pretoria and now Bishop of Natal. He was a very old and treasured
friend from Cambridge days. Our time of prayer over, sleep
would not come to me. Instead, the spirit of praise came upon
my soul. All seemed to be release. All seemed to be freedom.
Hour after hour I praised my God in unrestrained and unre-
strainable doxology and song. In words "of men and of angels"
I rejoiced. I felt no fatigue from the full day. All my senses were
vibrantly alive to God. The Holy Spirit was blessing me. Wave
upon wave, it seemed. Flow upon flow. He seemed to be bubbling up from within, surrounding from without, ascending
from below and descending from above. Somewhere in the early

hours of the morning I said to myself, "I don't know the correct biblical name for this, but this is the experience I've heard others talk of." I wasn't quite sure of its exact nature. I would have to think about that later.

In the meantime I kept praising until my bishop friend's alarm clock went off at dawn. Never had I had such a wonderfully sleepless night. Then I told him. We kept praising some more until finally the insistent calls of bacon and eggs were allowed to intrude upon the delights of the soul. It had been a monumental night. I had never had one like it. Nor have I had a comparable one since.

A New Day

The new day was totally luminous with the love and light of God. In some ways the experience was similar to the spiritual euphoria that had overwhelmed me at conversion. It was a "second touch," if you like. My spiritual perceptions seemed strangely sharpened and I felt borne along on the wings of my Lord's love. The desire to praise and worship God was the most striking aspect of what the previous day and night had brought.

But one thought plagued me. What about the past and all that had gone before? What about my life and ministry prior to this moment? Had I missed God's highest will? Had I been operating only on half-throttle—on three cylinders? Had it all been second-rate? Was this experience something I should have received years ago?

At first that was how it seemed to me. My prayers on this matter, however, received un unexpected answer the next day—and from an unexpected quarter. Nonetheless I knew that I would also have to get back to the Scriptures and think it all through from the biblical text itself. Anyway, in the meantime help seemed to come from Elsie Buthelezi, a beautiful Zulu woman who bounced up to me full of the joys of life. Cousin to the Kwa-Zulu prime minister, Chief Gatsha Buthelezi, she has a royal look about her and dresses in striking traditional garb. Her dress was a brilliant cascade of African color and design. Her headgear was an intricate mosaic of beadwork. Her arms and legs tinkled with the gentle sound of Zulu bangles. I had known Elsie since the Durban Congress in 1973, and she greeted me with warmth.

"Oh, Mike, my brother, I have been praying I would see you because the Lord has given me a message for you."

"Really, Elsie?" I responded, a bit startled.

"Oh, *yes,* my brother," she replied with emphasis, pulling me aside by the hand out of the hurly-burly of human traffic moving from the main auditorium to the seminar sessions. "But first let me thank you for the other night. Oh, Mike, it was wonderful. We were all praying for you so much, especially the brothers and sisters from Soweto. We knew you would speak for us. Thank you, my brother, thank you. We are proud of you." I again sensed the privilege of being a white African bound in the love of Jesus Christ to black Africans.

"Now, Mike, I must give you a word. All yesterday the Lord impressed on my heart to tell you that all the past has been just right and in his will. Nothing has been wasted. This has been his plan, and now, and not before now, is his timing of this blessing for you. Nothing is to be regretted. He has been leading you forward in his sovereign and perfect purposes."

It was an astonishing and incredibly important word for me. In fact, if I remember correctly, those questions about the past were whirling round in my mind at the moment Elsie came up to me. Strange and wonderful indeed are the ways of God to us. He was saying that my past was being beautifully interwoven into his plan for my future. We may seek new blessings, but the timing of their receipt is God's, not ours. I found myself experiencing a renewed commitment not only to biblical and evangelical truth, but also to ecumenical relationships, holistic evangelism, and compassionate socio-political concern.

Wind-up
The wind-up to that conference was a precious blur of happy and rewarding encounters, each of which enriched me in some way. First came a momentous Communion Service on the final

Sunday morning. For many people it was too long, but for me it was the greatest experience ever of Holy Communion. My heart was locked in the heavenlies in worship and adoration. The Communion hymn said it all:

> *When I survey the wondrous cross*
> *On which the Prince of glory died,*
> *My richest gain I count but loss,*
> *And pour contempt on all my pride.*
>
> *Were the whole realm of nature mine,*
> *That were an offering far too small.*
> *Love so amazing, so divine,*
> *Demands my soul, my life, my all.*

Then that night came the last evening meeting and in fact the final experience of the conference for me, because I had to fly out early the next morning to Zimbabwe, thereby missing the closing session.

The last evening, however, is memorable in my mind for two things—a prayer and a frolic. First the prayer. In the latter part of the meeting someone gave me a slip of paper to pass on to conference coordinator, Derek Crumpton. It said, "Please pray for Rhodesia."

"Why don't you lead us, Mike," whispered Derek. "After all you're going up there in the next day or so."

"OK," I agreed, stepping up to the microphone. In praying that prayer I recollect a deep sense of being given the faith to believe for the ultimate healing and salvation of what was then Rhodesia. It was a strange experience—the sudden ability to believe God for a place, a seemingly hopeless place at that time. I felt God wanted to heal that land and would do it his way. Rhodesia has, of course, since then become Zimbabwe. My faith in the future of that great land still stands, having held firm since that prayer on Sunday evening, September 4, 1977, in the Milner Park Renewal Conference.

The frolic came a little later, at the end of the meeting.

"What shall we sing?" said Derek Crumpton to the crowd just before wind-up time.

"Let us sing, let us sing a song unto the Lord," I called out, referring to that exuberant, rhythmic, and joyful spiritual song. It was the closing song of the closing evening meeting. The place was ready for an explosion of joy. And it came. The roof was almost lifted as the conferees erupted into song. It was exhilarating. Liberating. Almost intoxicating. Tapping feet and waving arms became more vigorous.

Suddenly Francis MacNutt and Derek Prince burst into a sort of jig on the platform. Now this really *was* something different, I thought. I'm not sure about this. Scarcely had I formulated my reservation when I saw Derek Prince heading across the platform toward me like some sort of highland dancer who has not quite made up his mind whether he is in a Scottish reel, a barn dance, or a bull-fight. His arm, crooked against his side, was extended toward me in invitation. There was nothing to do, short of being a spoil-sport, and the next minute I too was jigging between Prince, MacNutt, Bishop Bruce Evans of Port Elizabeth, and Sipho Bhengu of Soweto.

Down in the "body of the kirk," as it were, my staggered colleagues, John Tooke, Ebenezer Sikakane, Bill Winter, and David Peters, looked on—their eyes popping, their sides convulsed, and their minds boggled. "There's Cassidy dancing for joy on a platform in front of three thousand South Africans—the ultimate de-tribalizing of an inhibited conservative!"

The service over, I left the platform a little self-conscious but full of joy. My heart was still praising God even though I realized that my spiritual freedom in living it up would now have to be followed by living it down!

12

Toddling
in the
Spirit

However far the Christian has gone in the
life of faith, he knows he is still only
a child playing in the shallows and that
there is far more to be discovered
of the riches of the friendship of Christ.
Bishop Stephen Neill

THE DAY THE MILNER PARK CONFERENCE ENDED, I flew up to
Zimbabwe to meet with some of my colleagues. On the plane I
pondered the experience of the previous week and realized that
the test of it all was now about to begin. How would this affect
my personal walk with Christ, my relationships at home, my
ministry, my social concern?

What came to me with new force was St. Paul's injunction to
the Galatians to "walk by [or in] the Spirit" (Gal. 5:16). Having
supposedly entered a deeper experience of the Spirit, I was now
faced with the challenge of a deeper walk. I felt like a toddler. I
saw that somehow I had to penetrate more seriously into what
the apostle highlighted as his major theme in the book of
Romans, "the obedience of faith." That phrase, coming at the
beginning and end of the Roman epistle, makes clear that *obedience* is what the life of faith is all about.

In his opening lines, Paul indicates that both the "grace" he had received and his "apostleship" were granted in order to bring about the *obedience of faith* (Rom. 1:5). In effect he is saying "This is what I am going to talk about in this letter." Then, like any good author, he summarizes in the same terms at the end of the letter what he has been saying in the body of it: that the "gospel and the preaching of Jesus Christ, according to the...command of the eternal God" have one basic purpose which is "to bring about the *obedience of faith*" (Rom. 16:25-26).

Wasn't it this, then, that my new experience was all about—the obedience of faith? Certainly it tied in with another passage which I noticed with new understanding during those days in Zimbabwe. Jesus says in John 14:15: "If you love me, you will keep my commandments. And I will pray the Father, and he will give you another Counselor...even the Spirit of truth..." The fourfold word stood out:

If you love—
You will keep—
I will pray—
He will give—

Here is the second person of the Trinity praying to the first person of the Trinity for the giving of the third person of the Trinity to those who show him their love by keeping and obeying his commandments. The work of the Spirit and the obedience of faith seemed to be very intimately tied together.

In Him

Flying back from Salisbury, I decided to reread Colossians and Ephesians. In those epistles a number of things struck me. First of all, in both, the phrase *In him* stood out with new meaning. We have been blessed "in Christ with every spiritual blessing" (Eph. 1:3). This means that:

1. *In him* we are chosen before the foundation of the world (Eph. 1:4).

2. *In him* we have redemption (Eph. 1:7).
3. *In him* the mystery of his will is made known to us (Eph. 1:9).
4. *In him* is a plan to unite all things (Eph. 1:10).
5. *In him* we have been destined and appointed to live for the praise of his glory (Eph. 1:12).
6. *In him* all who have heard the word of truth and believed in him have been sealed with the promised Holy Spirit (Eph. 1:13).
7. *In him* we sit in heavenly places (Eph. 2:6).
8. *In him* all things were created (Col. 1:16).
9. *In him* all things hold together (Col. 1:17).
10. *In him* all the fullness of God was pleased to dwell (Col. 1:19).
11. *In him* we who were estranged and hostile are now reconciled (Col. 1:21, 22).
12. *In him* are hid all the treasures of wisdom and knowledge (Col 2:3).
13. *In him* we are to be rooted and built up (Col. 2:7).
14. *In him* the whole fullness of deity dwells bodily (Col. 2:9).
15. *In him* we have come to fullness of life (Col. 2:10).

This struck me with tremendous force. I realized that much of the time our spiritual eyes are just not open to discovering and appreciating all that is in him and all that we as believers have in him.

Paul's prayer for the Ephesians hit me like a thunderbolt: "I do not cease to give thanks for you, remembering you in my prayers, that the God of our Lord Jesus Christ, the Father of glory, may give you a spirit of *wisdom* and of *revelation* in the knowledge of him, having the eyes of your hearts enlightened, that you may know" three things:

first—"What is the *hope* to which he has called you,"
second—"what are the *riches of his glorious inheritance* in the saints," and
third—"what is the *immeasurable greatness of his power* in us who believe . . ." (Eph. 1:16-19).

I remember Johannesburg coming into view, the plane banking and descending toward the runway. That's it, I thought. Paul's prayer is being answered in me because in this whole experience I am receiving a new "spirit of wisdom and of revelation." The "eyes of [my] heart" are being enlightened.

Homecoming
When I got home all ready to tell Carol all about it, I was greeted with that look that wives reserve for delinquent husbands: "Whatever have you been up to?"

I sensed she was concerned. Some eager beaver who had gotten back home from the renewal conference before me had phoned Carol. "Oh, praise the Lord, he's worked mightily in Michael. We saw him dancing on the stage in front of the whole conference."

Carol nearly had kittens, as the saying goes. What on earth had happened to her husband? Had he gone off his rocker? Had he made a total fool of himself? How on earth could she get the whole thing in perspective? That advance word complicated for me the process of sharing my experience.

We were scheduled to go away for some days of leave to the coast, which turned out to be a wonderful time of sharing, prayer, and studying together. For hours we searched the Scriptures together, listened to tapes, and sought God's face in new ways.

Listening
I found myself waking very early every morning and wanting to pray and study the Scriptures with fresh intensity. What began to come home to me was the importance of listening—listening for the whisper of the Spirit of God so that I might walk more obediently in the daily details of life. To walk obediently one had to get orders. To get orders one had to listen. Was God interested in the detailed unfolding of each day in the life of his children? I began to believe he was.

First of all, in three consecutive chapters of the book of Acts (chapters 8, 9, 10), I saw three acts of listening along with the astonishing consequences flowing from each.

First there was Philip in Samaria conducting mass rallies, and having a citywide campaign that even Billy Graham would have envied. "Multitudes with one accord gave heed to what was said" (verse 6). Then came the word from God, "Rise and go...to Gaza" (verse 26). So "He rose and went" (verse 27). "And the Spirit said to Philip, "Go up and join this chariot" (verse 29). Philip then witnessed to an Ethiopian government official, won him to Christ—and sent him on his way to *open up a continent.*

Then in Acts 9 there was the word to Ananias. Again it was "Rise and go" (verse 11) and again there was prompt obedience. In fear and trembling Ananias went to pray for the notorious Saul of Tarsus. Ananias prayed for Saul, who was filled with the Holy Spirit—and the *world's greatest missionary and evangelist* was galvanized into mission.

Finally, in Acts 10, it was Peter, a Jew, getting commissioned to go to a Gentile, Cornelius. A tougher job for the Lord this time because Peter, with all his cultural and religious hangups, was a tougher character. But after a few human refusals and a few divine visions, Peter went on his way to Cornelius. Once more it was "Rise and go" (verse 20) as a word from the Spirit. Once again there was obedience. "And Peter went..." (verse 21). Peter won Cornelius to Christ. That time the *whole mission to the Gentile world* was launched.

Three words from God. Three men. Three acts of obedience. Three astounding sets of consequences. A continent was opened. The greatest evangelist ever was empowered. The mission to the Gentiles was launched.

Could the Holy Spirit guide like that in our times? Obviously God had a plan for Philip, Ananias, and Peter. In Acts 13 the Holy Spirit clearly had a will and spoke it out: "Set apart for me Barnabas and Saul for the work to which I have called them" (verse 2). Equally clearly the Holy Spirit had a detailed plan for Barnabas and Paul because, after they had preached in Phrygia and Galatia, they were "forbidden by the Holy Spirit to speak the word in Asia" (Acts 16:6). When they wanted to go into Bithynia, "the Spirit of Jesus did not allow them" (verse 7). Then came the Macedonian call. That was where they were meant to go.

Obviously, both in general and in detail, these men walked in the Spirit in obedience to the whispered word of God to their spirits. I began to long to know more of such a walk. I saw afresh that "to obey is better than sacrifice, and to hearken than the fat of rams" (1 Sam. 15:22).

Three Waves

The morning after we arrived at the coast, I woke particularly early. I felt almost as if I had been shaken awake and found myself with a strong compulsion to get down to the beach. It was about five o'clock and the sun was just lifting over the horizon in a blaze of orange. I began to walk along the deserted beach in a spirit of prayer and rejoicing. When I had gone some distance I spotted a lone surfer out in the waves. I began to watch him with some fascination. A wave came along and he tried with much flurrying and paddling to catch it. He missed it and the wave flowed on leaving him behind in its wake. Then came a second wave. There was more flurrying and paddling and this time the surfer caught the wave, moved beautifully with it for a few yards, then twisted, turned, and tumbled in a great surging mass of sea and board and surf and surfer. A spectacular tumble. I kept watching, fascinated.

The young man retrieved his board, paddled out into the sea again, and waited. A third wave came. This time he moved quickly into its flow, was borne up on its surging power, and began to ride it with perfect balance all the way in to shore. An astonishing spectacle. He just seemed to keep going and going, moving sensitively with the wave's momentum until he was literally landed on the sand.

No sooner had that happened than I suddenly became aware

of the Spirit of God seeming to say to me: "I brought you down here to see this parable. Each wave represents the movement of my Spirit through the world at this time. The three experiences of the surfer represent three categories of people faced with this wave. Some miss the wave altogether and are left behind. A second group gets into the wave but they do not ride it sensitively or with skill and they tumble and fall and they too are left behind. A third category moves into the flow of my Spirit and is borne along as on a wave. They are landed safely on every shore to which I send them and on that final shore of a fulfilled ministry and a completed task. Do not be left behind by the wave of my Spirit. Do not tumble and fall. Ride the wave and know its power."

That experience left me reflective. I kept walking along the beach thinking about what it meant to ride the wave to all the shores, appointments, of God. After a while I turned around and began to retrace my tracks. As I got back to where the surfer was still enjoying himself, I saw another person standing on the beach, also by himself watching the surfer. As I walked toward him our eyes met. Although I had never seen him before, he smiled a warm smile of recognition. "Aren't you Michael Cassidy?" he asked. He introduced himself and we began to chat amicably.

Suddenly I had a strong sense that this was part two of the lesson for the morning. I began to tell my new friend about my insights from the surfer in the waves a few minutes previously. He was a church member and seemed open and hungry for the word I was sharing with him. It seemed the Lord could indeed organize His appointments to be my appointments if I would listen to the whispers of His Spirit and be ready to obey.

Ministry on the Wing
Soon I had to leave for California for a time of overseas ministry. My office had a pretty full schedule worked out for me. The only times that weren't structured were my hours in the plane. I said to the Lord that I would like to put myself at his disposal on the different flights.

We took off from Jan Smuts Airport, Johannesburg, and headed, via Ilha do Sol off the western bulge of Africa, for New York. Also on the plane was my good friend Peter Eliastam, a brilliant Jewish commercial artist who had been led into Christian commitment through one of my colleagues, John Tooke.

Sitting together we had a wonderful time of fellowship. The first thing that happened was that one of the stewards spotted my Bible, came up, and began to tell me that he too was a Christian. He brought another steward until finally we were quite a little cluster. In the early hours of the morning, when we were still two or three hours from New York, Peter suggested that we should have a little service together, which we did, somewhat to the astonishment of an isolated passenger who went by us to the restroom during the night. A little later a Chinese woman suddenly appeared by my seat.

"I heard you talking about Christ," she said, "and I want to hear more. I have great problems." She had been sitting just behind us so for the next hour or so I listened to her story and talked to her. Her marriage was in deep trouble. She said she had been praying for guidance and help and what I shared with her was just what she needed. I knew this was another of God's appointments.

After we got to New York, I headed for my connecting flight to California. "Lord," I prayed, "that was a wonderful time of ministry, praise your Name. Let me be available again." I was ushered to my seat on the next flight and began to settle down. I hadn't been seated more than two or three minutes when the steward said he wanted to move me and the man next to me and put a couple where we were. He then took me all the way up the length of the plane right out the other end of the economy class section and into the first class, where he put me down next to a well-groomed young executive. I had never flown first class, so it was a new experience. If this was what toddling in the Spirit was all about, I was in favor of it.

Although the happening was almost comical, I nevertheless felt that God was in this changing of seats. Before long I was chatting away with this young man and hearing his story. He had been planning on going into a Catholic order, but had begun to have problems with his faith, and had gone into the airline business instead. We had a Christ-centered talk.

"Listen, Peter," I said, "I really believe the Lord has something for me to share with you that is important for your life. In fact, I have been moved from economy class to first class to share it with you!" He seemed impressed and in between the caviar and all that, we covered considerable spiritual ground! I later had a warm Christmas card from him.

Another Divine Appointment

The ministry in California and in St. Louis, Missouri, came and went and then I was on my way back. My excitement about the Lord's work on planes and what he was teaching me knew no bounds. I took my seat in the center section of a relatively empty aircraft bound for Newark, New Jersey. It seemed as if I would have this flight to myself, as there were no other passengers close by. The plane was almost empty, in fact, so I settled down to read. Just before takeoff, a young woman entered the center block of seats and sat down one seat away from me. She was open and friendly and while settling into her seat she shivered and said: "My, but this plane's freezing. There must be something wrong with the air conditioning." I made some polite comeback, she bounced into further conversation, and we were off. Detecting my accent she asked me where I was from and what I did. Then she looked at me quizzically. "Aren't you with African Enterprise? In fact, aren't you Michael Cassidy?"

"Well, Lord, you're on the job again," I chortled inwardly. "This is really fun!"

"Yes," I replied, astonished, "I am Michael Cassidy. How did you know?"

"Now, how about that!" she said. "I come from the First Presbyterian Church of Salinas, which supports your ministry. I know all about your work."

In no time she was telling me about herself. She was in a

difficult situation with her boyfriend. He wanted to marry her, but she wasn't sure. "Anyway," she went on, "early this morning my roommate and I prayed earnestly that the Lord would give me some guidance quickly. I am on my way to meet him now in Newark and I desperately need clarity. I think you may be able to help me. I think this is part of the answer to my prayers."

We talked at length about the principles of guidance and clarification which the Lord can often use with us in the process of choosing a life-partner. Not knowing the details of the relationship I could only talk in generalities but I felt great freedom in articulating to her certain insights that might be relevant. Later in the airport she introduced me to her boyfriend and I waved them both a cheery goodbye. Six months later she sent me a letter saying that our conversation had been important and that God had shown her clearly during the following few weeks that it was not right for her to become engaged to that boyfriend. She had tremendous peace about this and knew in new ways that God had his hand on her life. Then she added an interesting detail. "You know, I quite often fly and whenever I do, I sit in a window seat. I never like sitting anywhere else. But that night as I went to check in for my flight I heard a very clear voice within me saying 'Don't ask for a window seat. Allow the reservation clerk to assign your seat.' The allocation, which put me next to you, was the first time in my life I had flown in the center section of a plane."

Bishop Muzorewa

Leaving the East Coast I headed back via London to Africa. My last stop before heading into Johannesburg was Nairobi. By that time, every flight had taken on an excitement of its own. What would happen now? Having cleared Nairobi customs, all the passengers were herded aboard an airport bus to take us out to the plane. The little man, pressed against me in the bus, looked familiar.

"Aren't you Bishop Abel Muzorewa?" I asked.

"Yes," replied the black bishop, who was one of the main political leaders in what was then Rhodesia. The Rhodesian situation was one that had been of concern to me for some time and I had had contact with many of the political leaders there in the different major political groupings. In the course of things I had met a number of Muzorewa's assistants, but not him. He was an important man and one who needed much prayer. Once again, I had an overpowering sense that God had ordered this encounter. The bishop happily agreed that we should sit together and for the next three hours we discussed the Rhodesian question. I was amazed that he opened his heart to me as freely as he did. Later on, back in Rhodesia, about eight or nine months before he became prime minister of the interim government, we had fellowship once again, and I, along with two friends, was able to pray with him on the very day when he and his party had to make up their minds about whether to cooperate with the whites in seeking a political settlement. Although Muzorewa later lost out to Robert Mugabe, I believe that in the mysterious economy of God, he played an important political role in moving Rhodesia toward majority rule.

In any event, our encounter on the plane and our subsequent prayer together was, I believe, part of the Lord's plan—part of what he was teaching me about conscious surrender to the agenda of the Holy Spirit, both in general and in detail. That overseas trip had provided new lessons in what ministry on the wing and life on the wave was all about.

Failure

Not long after getting home full of the joys of my recent trip, I went away on holiday for our annual leave with the family. As suddenly as I had been fired up a few months previously with new life in the Spirit, so just as suddenly it seemed as if I had run out of steam. I found myself "down." Perhaps I was exhausted, but certainly I was not making it spiritually. I entered a spell of not wanting to pray or even read the Bible. I was irritable with everyone around me and impatient with myself. Where was all this newfound joy and power in the Holy Spirit? Poor Carol! To be seeing her husband no longer riding the crest of the wave, she must have wondered how authentic it all was. It was a depressing few weeks. I knew I was badly failing my Lord in witness to him and to the work of the Spirit. I wasn't walking in the Spirit. I wasn't even toddling. I was just falling all over the place like the surfer on the second wave.

As high as the hill had been, so low now seemed the trough. That really shook me; I had hoped this sort of spiritual fainting-fit would be something of the past.

Rising early one morning, I went out for a walk. High on a sand dune I called on the Lord to show me what was wrong. Fiddling in the dry compressed sand with a stick I started a little slide of sand. It was like a mini-avalanche. Each time I moved any blockage to the sand it seemed to flow more freely down the dune.

I began to think. Had some blockages come in my life in recent weeks? After all, I wasn't consciously appropriating the Spirit's presence. I wasn't "practicing the presence of God." I wasn't keeping myself alert for spiritual opportunity. I wasn't being considerate of Carol and the children. I was being introspective and self-centered. Above all, I had allowed myself through fatigue and weariness to stop my regular devotions.

That was it. There were blocks. Remove those and the flow would start again. Go back down the road and see where I had taken a wrong turn. Reflect on words from the Lord that had been quickened to my heart and see where I was disobeying. That was the key.

I did it. It seemed one had to maintain an almost constant state of appropriation along with up-to-the-minute repentances for one's constant failures in love or care or discipline. Some time later I met an African Christian outside the Nairobi Cathedral. I asked him how he was. "Repenting and praising," he beamed. Yes, that was the key. If you kept repenting and kept removing the blocks of sin, one's heart would continue praising.

It was good for me during that holiday on the coast to be

reminded that failure, dryness, and the work of the Spirit are not mutually exclusive. New experiences of the Spirit are no short-cut to spiritual growth, no guarantee of avoiding spiritual failure. No one spiritual experience lands one safely in any Canaan of spiritual maturity. There remains the constant demand of walking, appropriating, practicing, remembering that God has a will and a way and an agenda for the day. As I acted on all these ideas by faith, it seemed to work for me. When I forgot to live by faith, my floundering recurred. It has been a constant battle ever since. I haven't got it all licked. I am still a beginner, a pilgrim.

A further challenge to walk in the Spirit came from David du Plessis's autobiography:

> I began to be sensitive to the Lord's checking rather than relying only on those times when He said, "Thou shalt do that..." It became my practice to dedicate my mind to the Lord daily, often before I got out of bed in the morning, something like this: "I am yours today, Lord, and whatever comes to my mind, every guidance I get, I'll just follow on. I will do what my hands find to do. I won't stop unless you stop me. Guide me hour by hour, and I don't want to know this morning what I am to do this afternoon. I have an idea of what duties there are, and I am going to do my duty. If there is any point in which I am losing the way or going where you don't want me to go, check me."[44]

David du Plessis learned to trust the "checks" of the Holy Spirit.

> I just proceeded along the course that seemed right. And I learned to recognize the checks. My mind might say one thing, but my heart felt something else. I began to pay attention to those feelings. If I developed a marvelous thought in my mind, but didn't feel comfortable down in my heart, then I knew that I was being checked. I stopped and waited.[45]

So then, although I knew I was still far from living that out, I had caught a vision of what the Spirit wants from us. Perhaps it is summed up in the concept of yielding oneself consciously on a moment-by-moment basis to the indwelling Spirit. Was this what the apostle Paul was after when he said, "Yield yourselves to God as men who have been brought from death to life, and your members to God as instruments of righteousness" (Rom. 6:13)?

I recollect a conversation in 1965 with author John Pollock, then busy on a biography of Billy Graham.

"What is Billy Graham's outstanding quality?" I asked.

"Two qualities go together," he replied. "He is integrity personified, and he has the deepest sense of anyone I know of being an instrument of God." Perhaps that yieldedness to instrumentality explains the fullness of the Spirit that is evident in the life and ministry of Billy Graham.

As far as I was concerned, it was good to work at walking in the Spirit, even if one ended up toddling much of the time.

13

A Filling
or the
Baptism?

The church must lay down its norms
for doctrine and practice, but we should
be as ready as the Weather Forecaster to
admit that however reliable our calculations,
most of the time we cannot command the
wind. And when the Spirit disobeys our
canons we should avoid
the absurd sin of rigidity.
Canon John Taylor

OF COURSE, I COULDN'T DELAY for too long the serious matter of putting on my theological thinking cap and reflecting on what seemed to have taken place in my life, both the new experience at Milner Park and the successes and especially failures in the period after it. I had reflected before on the theology of the Holy Spirit, but this was adding new grist to the mill. What had happened? Was my Milner Park experience a filling of the Spirit, one in a possible series of experiences? Or was it *the* baptism in the Spirit, a once-for-all, nonrepeatable phenomenon?

I realized that neither I nor anyone else should build a theology on an experience. Rather, we build our theologies on the Word of God and fit our experiences into that biblical framework. Without that procedure we can land up in all kinds of confusion.

Humility

Having said that, I want to add the importance of approaching our theological formulations with humility, flexibility, and grace. How foolish to dare to present a final or definitive word on the Holy Spirit. He is God the surpriser, God the unpredictable, God the iconoclast, God the box-breaker, God the desystematizer of systematic theologians.

Much of the current confusion on the person and work of the Holy Spirit lies in just this—that we have tried to systematize One who is extraordinarily unsystematic. We have tried to confine in neat theological categories One who, like the wind, blows where he wishes, unfettered by the theological formulations in which we seek to contain him, or the human predictables by which we hope to anticipate him.

In my library, I have dozens of books by authors not only orthodox, neo-orthodox, and unorthodox, but also Pentecostal, neo-Pentecostal, anti-Pentecostal, all presenting, equally dogmatically, the definitive word on the Spirit's person and work! Every one, I suspect, has some of the truth. No one has it all.

Three Dangers

What I see in most of those books highlights three dangers. Either we lock into talking a lot of theory about the Spirit without letting him disturb our lives in any significant or creative way. Or we simply give up on the subject and say it's all too confusing and should therefore be pushed to the edge of our lives and thinking. Or we hungrily pursue an emotional experience of the Spirit on which we then build a theology regardless of the Bible's teaching, without struggling with the New Testament data.

Dangers one and two (academic theologizing on the one hand and intellectual despairing on the other) leave our lives impoverished. Danger three (theologizing on experience) leaves our theology unbalanced.

In other words, neither the danger of dogmatizing nor the impossibility of finalizing our view of the Spirit's work must make us retreat from an honest attempt to understand the biblical data and apply it to our lives. After all, we don't tolerate such retreats when it comes to the Bible's teaching on the atonement or on conversion or on prayer. Nor can we tolerate such a retreat from the Bible's view of the Holy Spirit. Rather, in formulating our view we are to do so with humility and flexibility, trying to distinguish between those areas where real clarity is possible and those areas where differences of viewpoint will remain and where a measure of agnosticism is necessary.

Procedure
Evangelicals and charismatics tend to have two slightly different approaches to the text of the Bible as they seek to determine their views. Evangelicals tend to build their theology of the Spirit from the distinctly theological sections of the New Testament (e.g., the Gospels and Epistles). Charismatics and Pentecostals build theirs more on the historical sections of the New Testament (e.g., the book of Acts). That is a slight oversimplification but perhaps a serviceable one in highlighting the approaches.

Many evangelicals believe it to be an important principle of interpretation (*hermeneutics* is the technical word) that theology is built on theological rather than on historical sections of the text. History illustrates doctrine rather than constituting it, at least in any primary sense, we say, though there is an obvious interplay. In other words, we start with theology and end with practice, not vice versa. Put differently, we could say we are to move from the general to the specific, from the systematic to the historical, from doctrine, as found in the Gospels but especially in the Epistles, to the historical outworking of it, as found in the book of Acts. Pentecostals and charismatics are less persuaded of this as a rigid principle of interpretation and are therefore less squeamish about drawing their theology from the book of Acts.

Perhaps a little give and take from each side would be useful. We must ask evangelicals who press this so-called hermeneutical principle to avoid doing so rigidly. After all, Paul asserted in 2 Timothy 3:16 that "All scripture is profitable for teaching" (i.e., *all* scripture—not just doctrinal sections). In the Old Testament, historical sections and prophetic sections are intertwined. In the New Testament, history and teaching are certainly profoundly interrelated in the Gospels. So we must be careful not to push this principle too artificially.

On the other hand, charismatics and Pentecostals need to exercise caution in their use of Acts, particularly if their handling of Acts lands them in doctrinal formulations that are hard to square with the systematic doctrinal statements of the Epistles. Nowhere is this more classically seen than in the controversy surrounding the phenomenon of "the baptism in the Holy Spirit." The Epistles do not speak of any two-tier or double-staged process of initiation into the Christian life, but the book of Acts at points seems to suggest this.

Put differently and more personally, if I were to attach a label to my own experience at the Milner Park Conference, what should I call it? Basically two terms are used in the modern situation. One is "the filling of the Spirit" and the other is "the baptism in the Spirit." Which is correct?

Be Filled

First of all, the Bible commands us to "be filled with the Spirit" (Eph. 5:18). This is not a desirable spiritual option but a clear biblical command. If I received the Holy Spirit when I was born again, as I believe I did, and if he indwells me, as I believe he does, then Paul's exhortation must mean something like this: "You have the Spirit, but does he have you? You have taken him into your life, but you must now allow him to fill you—in the sense of releasing yourself so that he can occupy and control every area, every corner, of your being."

It is like the progression in the Second World War from the landings in Normandy on D-Day to the final conquest of Europe heralded on V-E (Victory in Europe) Day. When we are born again it is as if God by his Spirit lands on alien occupied territory. Then he must be allowed to advance from that bridgehead, as it were, to occupy and fill all the territory with his presence and rule. This is the process of sanctification, the advance of the king and of his kingdom or kingship in our lives.

In many ways this must, of necessity, be a lifetime matter, but sometimes God may make an extremely dramatic breakthrough when all at once we allow him by our surrender to capture massive and hitherto unsurrendered tracts of our lives. At such moments we may experience overwhelming joy, release, power, and praise.

All Blessings

Then we must recognize another important truth that is especially brought home in Paul's epistles: in Christ the believer has *already* been blessed with all spiritual blessings. It has already happened, if we are in Christ. Thus the apostle can say in Ephesians 1:3, "Blessed be the God and Father of our Lord Jesus Christ, who *has* blessed us [here, the aorist tense in the Greek conveys the sense of a past happening] with every spiritual blessing in the heavenly places." In other words, if we are in Christ, every spiritual blessing is already potentially ours. It is all reckoned to our account. It is our possession. We "have come to fullness of life in him" (Col. 2:10). But we must appropriate our heritage, our rightful inheritance. Most of us do not do that and as a result we seriously impoverish ourselves.

John Stott has put it this way:

For a healthy Christian life today it is of the utmost importance to follow Paul's example and keep christian praise and christian prayer together. Yet many do not manage to preserve this balance. Some Christians seem to do little but pray for new spiritual blessings, apparently oblivious of the fact that God has already blessed them in Christ with every spiritual blessing. Others lay such emphasis on the undoubted truth that everything is already theirs in Christ, that they become complacent and appear to have no appetite to know or experience their christian privileges more deeply. But these groups must be declared unbalanced. They have created a polarization which Scripture will not tolerate. What Paul does in Ephesians 1, and therefore encourages us to copy, is both to keep praising God that in Christ all spiritual blessings are ours and to keep praying that we may know the fullness of what He has given us. If we keep together praise and prayer, benediction and petition, we are unlikely to lose our spiritual equilibrium.[46]

Stott goes on to stress that in this prayer for the Ephesians, Paul is not praying "that they may receive the second blessing, but rather that they may appreciate to the fullest possible extent the implications of the blessing they have already received."[47] Hence the apostle's prayer that God may give them not only "a spirit of wisdom and of revelation in the knowledge of him," but also a set of enlightened eyes, the eyes of their hearts, to understand the immeasurable greatness of the power already in those who believe, and waiting presumably to be released as it is recognized and understood (see Eph. 1:19).

If there are varying degrees of understanding and of surrender leading to various degrees of spiritual control and spiritual power, then we should not be surprised if Scripture recognizes different levels of Christians. And that is exactly what we find with Paul's threefold categorizing of human beings. He speaks first of "natural" men (those not possessing the Spirit at all), second of "carnal" men (those indwelt by the Spirit but governed by the flesh), and third of "spiritual" men (those both indwelt and controlled by the Spirit in fullness). This is set out in 1 Corinthians 2:14 and 3:1.

Degrees of Surrender
This says to me that our fullness in the Holy Spirit is in proportion to the degree of our surrender. We are as full of the Holy Spirit as our commitment permits. Disobedience can both "quench the Spirit" (1 Thess. 5:19) and "grieve" him (Eph. 4:30). We do this when we fail to allow him to do in us that for which he has been given.

We can also say that a person who is filled with the Spirit is a person in whose life the fruit of the Spirit is evident (Gal. 5:22) and the ministries of the Spirit operative (1 Cor. 12:4-14). The key evidence of fullness is moral rather than overtly miraculous. It is something more evident to observers of one's life and ministry than to the person. No one in Scripture ever claimed to be filled with the Spirit.

Crisis Infilling

I would not want, however, to deny the validity of the "crisis infilling" when, sick of ourselves, our sin, and our anemia, we again cast ourselves on Christ with a cry for the infilling, anointing, and visitation of his Spirit. That is when God in his faithfulness may come upon us or be released in us in power, sometimes with and sometimes without the accompanying gift of tongues, but always with joy and release.

On this, most of us can agree. And wouldn't we all agree with A. W. Tozer when he made the following observation:

> Satan has opposed the doctrine of the Spirit-filled life about as bitterly as any doctrine there is. He has confused it, opposed it, surrounded it with false notions and fears. He has blocked every effort of the Church of Christ to receive from the Father her divine and blood-bought patrimony. The church has tragically neglected this great liberating truth—that there is now for the child of God a full and wonderful and completely satisfying anointing with the Holy Spirit. The Spirit-filled life is not a special, deluxe edition of Christianity. It is part and parcel of the total plan of God for His people.[48]

Unquestionably, multitudes of believers feel that somewhere along the line they have entered some such experience, some in charismatic or Pentecostal settings, and some not. Inevitably there are varying understandings and labels. Some call it a "second blessing." Others call it "crisis sanctification" or "the filling with the Spirit" or "the release of the Spirit" or the "baptism in the Spirit." The term "filled with the Spirit" (Eph. 5:18) or "full of the Spirit" (Acts 6:3) regularly occurs in Scripture and seems best to describe the experience we are talking about. It also seems to be the term the greatest number of people can live with amicably, the preferred term. It can fit either the once-for-all, nonrepeatable experience or the on-going experience of appropriation, rededication, and, as it were, refilling.

Certainly those holding this view should not fight anyone who attaches a different label, for example "baptism in the Spirit," to the same reality. If any of my readers wants to explore the term "baptism in the Spirit" more fully, refer to Appendix B on page 235. There I have sought to set out, in more theological terms and in more detail, my own efforts to come to terms with exactly what the Bible means when it speaks of being baptized in the Holy Spirit.

A Letter

New freedom was certainly what I felt had come my way back in 1977. Terminology was far less important than the sense that I had met my Lord in a new way through his Spirit. About then I got a very helpful letter from a friend.

> Praise God for what has happened. It is he who is speaking to you...but he has much more to say to you in every area of your life and for this reason I would strongly advise you not to describe your experience now but rather to live with it and let the Lord continue to work in you. Don't let it become a thing of the past, till it becomes a fossil and you are left high and dry. You can ride on a "high" for some time, but it might be in his plan that you walk in darkness through the valley with him. This is not what others would have you do or be. But walk in your freedom with him. Accept your own weakness, as he does, so that his strength will flow through you.

> Praise God for friends and for the wisdom and perspectives that come through different members of his body.

14
On the Merry-Go-Rounds

It is not easy to describe my religious
development during these years, for
my heart and mind were a battlefield of
the most diverse influences.
W. A. Visser't Hooft, describing his late teens

THE YEAR 1978, after the Milner Park Renewal Conference, opened with my attendance in mid-January at a Full Gospel Businessmen's Convention in Washington, D.C., followed by a meeting in Bermuda of the Lausanne Committee for World Evangelization, of which I was a member. Then came three missions with Festo Kivengere in Panama, one in Balboa (the Canal Zone), another in Colon at the Atlantic end of the Canal, and another in Panama City. In March, Festo and I and a large African Enterprise team were in Egypt for three missions (Asyut, Cairo, and Alexandria). We were again together for a mission in Australia in May and finally in September in Nairobi, for our second citywide push, the first having been in 1969.

Those international experiences and their demanding ministry requirements created many challenges for personal growth and for seeking to integrate the work of the Spirit in a new way into my life and thinking. They also gave me a bird's-eye view of the state of things between evangelicals and charismatics in different parts of the world. All those developments stood me in good stead for 1979 when we sought to draw the whole South African body of Christ together for the South African Christian Leadership Assembly. But first back to January 1978 when I set off for Washington, D.C., Bermuda, and Panama.

Great Gulfs Fixed

Dan and Al Malachuk of Logos Books had asked me to attend the national convention of the Full Gospel Businessmen's Association. This is a group started a good many years ago by Demos Shakarian, an Armenian refugee who had come to the United States. His rise both as a businessman and as a lay Christian leader had been meteoric. The movement he had started was already worldwide.

Graciously I was introduced to the leadership group and met with them behind the scenes—fine, warm, loving men, one and all. The meetings were spectacular extravaganzas of bubbling life, dramatic testimonies, and exhilarating worship. When I shared my own modest testimony, I was given a rousing and caring reception.

Three things struck me about that experience. First of all, there was immense spiritual energy in the group. Second, it was light on theology. Third, no one I knew from the so-called evangelical scene of the U.S. was there. It seemed there was a great gulf fixed. On either side of the gulf were enormous merry-go-rounds of Christians, and ne'er the twain did meet.

Picking up *Logos Magazine* and *Christianity Today*, two national U.S. religious magazines edited respectively at that time by two personal friends, Dan Malachuk and Harold Lindsell, one might have concluded they were talking about the national Christian scene of two separate countries. There seemed to be no overlap, which struck me as not only sad and unhealthy, but unnecessary.

After saying in my testimony that I was going on to Bermuda

for the Lausanne meetings they prayed for me, with the whole gathering holding out its arms in blessing toward me that I would be empowered in going and that I would be able to share something there that would encourage a greater evangelical openness to the Pentecostal world. There seemed to be a longing for meaningful contact, a yearning for greater fellowship.

In Bermuda for the Lausanne meetings, I was at once struck by the contrast, on the one hand negatively, and on the other positively. Negatively, the spirit of worship seemed to me utterly impoverished by comparison with what I had just experienced in Washington, D.C. Positively, there was a depth of theological perception which, even allowing for the lay status of the Full Gospel group, was almost wholly absent in the Washington experience. The one group seemed to have the theology, the other the vitality. Didn't God want the two together?

In my own Bible study one morning with the Lausanne group I said as much. Curiously enough, the day of my new experience at Milner Park in August 1977, I had the distinct sense of the Spirit saying to me, "Share this with South African evangelicals and with the Lausanne Group." When I retorted in my heart that I could see no way I could suddenly stand up and talk about this to my Lausanne friends, the Lord seemed to say "I will make a way." So I sat back and waited. About two weeks before leaving for Bermuda a letter came from my dear friend Leighton Ford, chairman of the Lausanne Committee. Would I give one of the morning devotional addresses? "This is my way," the Spirit seemed to say. "Share your testimony." So there I was doing it. I spoke on "Obedience and the Holy Spirit" and in the process challenged those two great constituencies of Christendom—the evangelical and the Pentecostal—to come together.

Afterward, a number of the Lausanne members came up to me like secret agents giving a password and whispered: "We agree with that, but we have been scared to come out into the open and say so." Dear me, I thought. What have we done to Christ's church?

Leaving Bermuda, Festo and I flew on to Panama. We were joined for a few days there by two Lausanne colleagues, Orlando Costas of Costa Rica, a sort of ecumenical-evangelical gadfly, and Bruno Frigoli of Bolivia, director of evangelism for the Assemblies of God in Latin America and one-time bodyguard to Mussolini. He was, incidentally, the only one of Mussolini's bodyguards to escape public hanging. That was before he was converted out of gunrunning and diamond smuggling through a Pentecostal missionary in Bolivia. Now he has generated one of the fastest-growing churches in the world through his work in that country.

In our hotel room Bruno asked me: "Are the Pentecostals backing this mission? You know, there are thousands of Pentecostals here in Panama City."

"I don't know. I have my doubts."

"Let me find out," said the volcanic Bruno with a vigorous look of resolution as he left the room.

He was back that evening. "They weren't even asked," he said with a defiant look. "Can you believe it? They could have made all the difference in this mission." Then his countenance fell. "Anyway, it would not have made much difference," he mumbled. "They say they would have stayed out anyway because an Anglican bishop is taking part!" Poor Festo. Pushing the Pentecostals out like that. Too bad they never stopped to hear him preach. Obviously, the gulf was even wider than I had thought.

The next afternoon I listened to Orlando Costas, with his passionate social concerns, locking horns with the passionately evangelistic Bruno. It was great. They were miles apart, although congenially so. Yet each had much to give the other. I resolved to invite them *both* as speakers to the South African Christian Leadership Assembly, which was set for July the following year (1979). Maybe battered old South Africa could contribute to a rapprochement between Latin American evangelicals and Pentecostals.

Guidance and Gifts

When the missions in Panama were over, three options faced me. One was to attend a healing seminar in British Honduras with Francis MacNutt. Another was to look over the Pentecostal ministries of Bob McAllister in Rio en route home. The third was to respond to Doug Coe's invitation to attend the National Prayer Breakfast in Washington, D.C. After praying about it, the strongest compulsion came over me to decline all three and hurry back to South Africa. I didn't know why. But I had to go home.

Half an hour after getting in to Johannesburg, I phoned Carol, who told me that one of our dearest friends had just committed suicide in Cape Town. That was why I had to get back. Although longing to be together again, both Carol and I knew I had to go to the wife and children in Cape Town at once. Once there, I was assured there was no place in all the planet where I was meant to be right then than with that panting, huddled, distraught family. Yes, I thought on my flight home from Cape Town to Durban, the Spirit really does know where we are meant to be. I must keep listening.

Land of the Pyramids

A month or so later Festo and I were in Egypt, the land of the Pyramids. Here I did not have a success experience of listening, but a failure. It was highly instructive and provocative.

It happened like this. One evening during an evangelistic series in Cairo, Festo and I decided to speak on the work of the Holy Spirit. During the course of my own talk I said that God was moving in new ways across the world and I spoke among other things of the charismatic renewal. I also alluded to the way the healing power of God was being manifested and I quoted my eye-witness experiences in a couple of Kathryn Kuhlman services. Then Festo spoke from his perspective. It seemed a good evening.

After the service, one engaging young Egyptian who couldn't

quite believe our interracial mix—a white South African and a black Ugandan—said to me through a wide beaming smile: "Michael, you are the milk of the gospel and Festo is the chocolate!"

But that was where the fun ended. Several of the Egyptian clergy were quite upset. One came out in the open and said, "Michael, if you ever want to preach in Egypt again, don't mention charismatics or Kathryn Kuhlman."

"Why?" I asked in bewilderment.

"Well," he replied, "last year some charismatics came through here and they tried to manipulate everyone to speak in tongues. They created chaos and left behind so many divisions and so much confusion that we don't want any more of that stuff here."

I was dreadfully distressed. Obviously I had touched some very raw nerves. Seemingly I had rushed in, like the proverbial fool, where angels feared to tread.

A couple of days later we were all in the train on the way up to Alexandria where our next series was to open that night. A delightful and scintillating young Egyptian pastor came over and sat with me.

"Brother," he said with loving concern, "we were very anxious about your reference the other night to healing and the other gifts of the Spirit. Don't you feel the gifts were just for the first century? After all, Mark 16:20 says, 'They went forth and preached everywhere, while the Lord worked with them and confirmed the message by the signs that attended it.' Now do you believe that the message was confirmed?"

"Yes, indeed," I replied. "Obviously."

"Then why does it need further confirmation now? It was confirmed then, and that has now happened. The miraculous gifts were just for that time to authenticate the message. This is what the great B. B. Warfield taught and in Egypt we evangelicals go along with that."

"But what would you do if you had actually seen, let's say, the gift of healing in action?"

"I'm not sure," he answered. "I suppose I would have to question its authenticity."

"Or else," I suggested, "you *could* question your interpretation."

He smiled at me with a quizzical look and changed the subject. Just then the train pulled into Alexandria where more wonderful brothers met us and took us to our hotel on the Sea Front. That afternoon, with the waters of the Mediterranean lapping near my window, I reflected on the train conversation of the morning. Were Clement, Origen, Athanasius, and other early church giants of Alexandria, listening in on my thoughts, I wondered.

Gifts

The point at issue was whether all the gifts of the Spirit were still operative or not. My friend on the train had articulated a view known as Dispensationalism, with which I had become familiar in my seminary days in California. This view says that God has dealt with his people in different ways during different dispensations of redemptive history. Commenting on that position in its more extravagant forms, Michael Griffiths, principal of London Bible College, has said:

> There is a serious danger that extreme dispensationalists will adopt an attitude to Scripture little different from that of destructive Biblical criticism, attacking the Bible with a pair of dispensational scissors. Both "Apostles and Prophets" are eliminated from Ephesians 4:11 as "not for this age" while references to prophecy, miracles, healing and tongues must all be cavalierly cut out of 1 Cor. 12-14 as "long since ceased." If the Bible is indeed the "Only infallible rule of faith and practice" (Lausanne Covenant Clause II), then we must be faithful to what we believe about Scripture. According to Scripture, the gifts are given by the Holy Spirit to "edify" the Body of Christ.[49]

Michael Harper adds this in his book:

With the evangelical world thoroughly penetrated now by the charismatic experience, there are fewer and fewer who still subscribe to a dispensationalism that relegates spiritual gifts and miracles to the first century, or to the express views of B. B. Warfield, whose influence on evangelicalism in the first half of the twentieth century was profound, that the "supernatural" gifts were so wholly associated with the apostles that when they had all died the gifts were buried with them. What we see now is a faith in the "supernatural" breaking out from the narrow confines of Biblical fundamentalism, mechanical sacramentalism and traditional dispensationalism. The ghosts of Scofield and Warfield are being well and truly laid.[50]

I agree. Even Karl Barth, who would not be catalogued in most minds as unduly partial toward charismatics, expressed a concern that when there is a lack in the church of these "supremely astonishing activities resting on an endowment with extraordinary capacities . . . there is reason to ask whether in pride or sloth the community as such has perhaps evaded this endowment, thus falsifying its relationship to its Lord."[51]

Those are strong words which, if accurate, suggest that we ignore the gifts of the Holy Spirit at the peril of our personal growth, and the forward movement of the church as a whole. Not that such a conclusion is to exalt any one of the gifts above another, and least of all to make one gift (e. g., tongues) the normative experience of every believer as evidence of the fullness of the Holy Spirit, but only to assert that ignoring the spiritual gifts is not biblical.

C. Peter Wagner puts it this way: "Ignorance of spiritual gifts may be a chief cause of retarded church growth today. It also may be the root of much of the discouragement, insecurity, frustration and guilt that plagues many Christian individuals and curtails their total effectiveness for God."[52]

A catalog of these gifts, as Wagner sees them, is to be found in Appendix C at the back of this volume, space not permitting a full presentation of them here. Appendix D presents a different sort of cataloging. I know for myself that a deeper reflection on the workings of the spiritual gifts generally and on my own specifically has helped me in my life and ministry in these last years. I am in accord with Wagner when he says:

> People who know their gifts have a handle on their "spiritual job description," so to speak. They find their place in the church with more ease...Christian people who know their spiritual gifts tend to develop healthy self-esteem. This does not mean that "They think more highly of themselves than they ought to think." They learn that no matter what their gift is, they are important to God and to the Body... Secondly, not only does knowing about spiritual gifts help individual Christians, but it helps the church as a whole. Ephesians 4 tells us that when spiritual gifts are in operation, the whole Body matures...When the church matures predictably it grows. When the Body is functioning well and "each separate part works as it should, the whole body grows" (Eph. 4:16 TEV). There is clearly a biblical relationship between spiritual gifts and church growth. The third and most important thing that knowing about spiritual gifts does is that it glorifies God. 1 Peter 4:10-11 advises Christians to use their spiritual gifts, then adds the reason why: "That God in all things may be glorified through Jesus Christ to whom be praise and dominion for ever and ever." What could be better than glorifying God?[53]

I believe so strongly in the universality of spiritual gifts. Every Christian has them and every church has them. Many are still buried in the ground like the talent in Matthew 25, but they can be unearthed and used for the glory of God and the growth of the church.[54]

To say that is not, of course, to affirm that the gifts are of the essence of the Spirit-filled life. Paul clearly indicates that they are marked by transience. They will in time pass away, not having the permanence of faith, hope, and love. But to minimize them or deny them is, I believe, to frustrate one's own growth and that of the church. This was my conclusion that afternoon in Alexandria, and I have had no cause to modify my views since then.

Postscript

I must add a postscript to my Egyptian experience, related to the distress I felt after my talk in Cairo when I was reprimanded for referring to the gifts of the Spirit generally and to Kathryn Kuhlman and the healing gift specifically. What was I to make of that? Still in my Alexandrian hotel, I took the matter earnestly to God in prayer.

Then the Lord ministered to me from 1 Corinthians 3, where Paul wrote about going among the Corinthians as "a skilled master builder" (verse 10). Here was the picture of an immensely careful, competent, trained craftsman who lays his foundation and his individual teaching bricks with care and skill. The Spirit seemed to say to me: "Those people who came into Egypt last year and upset everyone by pushing tongues and so on did not come in as skilled master builders. They did not sensitively lay a foundation of understanding. Because they were not wise, they complicated everything. They were not skilled master builders."

"Ah, yes, Lord—the people who came in last year—they were not skilled master builders."

Then, ever so gently came the Spirit's further word to me: "Nor were you." Hard though that was to face, I saw it at once. I had blundered in insensitively without understanding my context properly, without praying through thoroughly on what I should say. I had failed my Lord and the Holy Spirit. I had further complicated the processes of the Spirit in building the Egyptian church.

Down Under

Other experiences of moving between Christian constituencies, jumping Christendom's merry-go-rounds, followed some months later in Australia. When I got there, a local Baptist pastor, who was one of the participating clergy in a mission Festo and I were doing in the suburbs of Sydney, told me he had received an advance letter about me from a conservative evangelical in South Africa. The letter told him not to have me in his church. "Cassidy is too political and too Pentecostal." I roared with laughter. "Goodness gracious," I said, "both my political and my Pentecostal friends in South Africa would have a good laugh over that. The Pentecostals think I'm much too tame and the political crowd views me as way too conservative."

The recipient of that letter told me that in his area the charismatic renewal had often had divisive consequences in churches and some people's so-called experiences of tongues had been in his judgment positively demonic. He played me a tape of an interview he had had with one aspiring charismatic; certainly it suggested something counterfeit. It was a reminder that the powers of darkness can indeed masquerade as angels of light. One couldn't be too careful. All spirits had to be "tested" (1 John 4:1).

But none of that could in my judgment excuse the gaping chasm I saw in Australia between charismatics and evangelicals. I was convinced that the gap was between brothers, not cousins, and certainly not between enemies. How glad I was therefore when I was later invited to return to Australia in May 1981 to speak at the National Evangelical Anglican Congress on "Christ and the Spirit." In so doing I could seek to bridge the chasm between those two groups.

These international experiences in 1978 proved to be preparation for the experience of Christian togetherness (and pain) that lay ahead when leaders from virtually the whole South African church got together in 1979 in Pretoria for SACLA.

15
Forward through Crossfire

I baptize you with water for repentance,
but he who is coming after me is mightier
than I, whose sandals I am not worthy to
carry; he will baptize you with the Holy
Spirit and with fire.
John the Baptist, Matthew 3:11

THE TWO YEARS OF 1977-78 MADE UP an extended period of seeking to go forward in my Christian walk, but finding often that growth came, first, in situations of pain and purging and, second, when I was caught in the crossfire between evangelicals and charismatics. The twin concepts of taking up one's cross and of being baptized not only with the Spirit but with fire became the only spiritual framework through which I could interpret many of the things that happened. The Cross-and-the-fire. Yes, we grow and move forward through crossfire.

Holiness and Fire
Early in my Christian experience I heard the adage that God is more interested in our characters than in our happiness. He knows that the more our characters are conformed to the image of Christ, the happier we will be. I read Hebrews 12:11 in that

light. "For the moment all discipline seems painful rather than pleasant; later it yields the peaceful fruit of righteousness to those who have been trained by it."

I had not, however, clearly linked up the phenomena of the baptism with the Spirit and the "baptism with fire." Yet they were inseparable in John the Baptist's mind. This One who was to come, whose sandals John was unworthy to untie, would perform a twin work on his disciples. He would baptize not only with the Spirit, but with fire. He would come to his disciples with "his winnowing fork in his hand." He would "clear his threshing floor and gather his wheat into the granary" but burn "the chaff with unquenchable fire" (Matt. 3:12).

As those years unfolded, that truth again impressed itself on me. To say "Lord, fill me with your Spirit," is to say "Lord, step up the heat of the fire and burn the chaff in me more freely," because the two baptisms belong together. Put differently, the one baptism involves two elements—the Spirit and fire.

We forget that the Spirit is the Holy Spirit, described that way over ninety times in the Bible. Yet from the beginning there was failure in the church to grasp this. Michael Green has observed that

> the Corinthians, with all their claims to fullness and to having entered on their heavenly reign, were distressingly defective in Christian behavior. Party strife, litigiousness, immorality of a dimension unheard of in paganism, coupled with greed and disorder in the assemblies, marked their lives. No wonder Paul had to castigate them as carnal Christians and yet they were the very people who possessed these gifts of tongues, miracles, faith, healing and the like which convinced them that they were the favored children of Heaven and had already become full. It is still an observable fact that those who speak most about being full of the Holy Spirit are often governed by other spirits such as arrogance, divisiveness and party spirit, disorder, lack of love and criticism. It is hard to see how a [person] can be full of the Spirit if these glaring failures of character persist.[55]

That kind of behavioral deficiency was what Paul was onto when he wrote to the Corinthians. It is just as relevant today. "Brethren, I could not address you as spiritual men, but as men of the flesh, as babes in Christ . . . For while there is jealousy and strife among you, are you not of the flesh, and behaving like ordinary men?" (1 Cor. 3:1-3). Paul's concern was to get the Corinthians to behave not like ordinary people but as extraordinary ones. That could happen only as the flesh or old nature in them was subordinate to the Spirit, brought under his control.

Spirit and Flesh

If I had felt in previous years how much work God still had to do in me, I continued to feel it even more acutely. One is always a beginner. How hard it is to yield to the discipling processes of the Spirit. Jesus said to Peter, "You are Simon. You shall be called Peter [the Rock]." There was a difference between what Peter was, and what he would become. Mercifully, Jesus left him ignorant as to how painful the process would be.

As with Moses in Midian and Paul in Arabia, an "unlearning" process has to go on as each of us is led to learn the ways of God and to unlearn the ways of man. It is the challenge of learning to have a godly attitude in situations of pain, pressure, personal crisis, and interpersonal alienation. It is learning to allow the Spirit and the new nature to predominate rather than the flesh or old nature. The way it happens is the way of the Cross. It is the way of the baptism with fire.

I found that each year seemed to have its own furnace with its particular lessons in the school of the Spirit.

The Pain of Bereavement (1978)

In mid-1978 my father became seriously ill, and we knew he was dying. Death and sadness had come my way in the lives of close friends and extended family, but never with someone in my immediate family. I had always been close to my father, and his influence on me had been enormous. It was he who first pointed me to God in a way I can consciously remember. This illness had come out of the blue and I now faced the prospect of seeing him slowly slip into the clutches of the Last Enemy. I knew these would be weeks when the Spirit's wisdom, strength, and guidance would be specially needed.

Several weeks before Dad fell ill I had had an argument with him about South African politics (not the first, I might say). These were curious exchanges because much of what I knew about racial justice and fair play between peoples I had learned from him, yet here he was taking a reactionary stand against more progressive politics in South Africa. His reaction was the result of wounds and disillusionment experienced during the independence process in Lesotho where Dad had served pretty thanklessly for over thirty years, but I in my obtuseness had failed to show any understanding.

I recollect his phoning me the same evening of our argument. I had the powerful sense of the Holy Spirit whispering, "Apologize to him for all those stupid political discussions that got nowhere." But my pride was too great. I didn't apologize. A few days later he was in the hospital with the medical death sentence over him. I continued to feel I should apologize for my insensitivity and heated attitudes in those discussions, but events swept us along and the opportunity seemed to slip away. Remorse and regret gripped me.

Then early one morning I woke with a sense of the Spirit's word: "Say to him today what is in your heart." By this time the end was very close. After breakfast my sister Olave Snelling, who had come out from the U.K. to be with us and who knew nothing of my feelings about the political discussions, came to me in my study and said, "In my devotional time this morning the Spirit said to me that we should say everything to Dad today that is on our hearts and that we may need to say." It was confirmation.

That afternoon I whispered my words of apology in Dad's ear, thanked him for all he had meant as a father, and asked his forgiveness for where I had failed him as a son. He shook his head vigorously, as if to say "No, you haven't failed," smiled a smile of understanding and reassurance, and gripped my hand as if to say "Thank you." But what blessed me over and above

Dad's reaction was the Spirit's gentle dealing with both of us in this detail, his gracious leading and enabling so that the decks could be cleared of this one bit of clutter.

Also in those days of anxiety and sadness I saw other evidence of the Spirit's work. One nurse tending Dad, Athene, was a Christian. Week after week I observed her give extra care to all her patients, and especially to Dad. One day I spoke to her about this. "Well," she said, "I believe the Lord Jesus would express his care through me to all these people, especially the dying ones. You know, it's the little things that mean much to them. For example, few nurses will bother to help these old folk in the terminal ward to clean their teeth. I make it my business to help them to do their teeth. They feel better for it as they turn in. Other nurses say I'm silly to expend energy on things like that, but I feel the Spirit has led me to this."

Now, I thought to myself, how about that for an evidence of the fullness of the Spirit? Not a lot of extravagant talk about tongues and so on, but helping dying people to clean their teeth. Later that night I wrote in my diary: "Thank you, Lord, for pressing on my heart that the ultimate mark of your Spirit's work is the Spirit of care. Baptize me into that Spirit and anoint me to care for people as never before."

I was learning new things in the midst of anguish and sadness. A little poem of Robert Browning Hamilton's came back to me.

> *I walked a mile with Pleasure;*
> *She chatted all the way;*
> *But left me none the wiser*
> *For all she had to say.*
>
> *I walked a mile with Sorrow,*
> *And ne'er a word said she;*
> *But, oh! the many things I learned*
> *When Sorrow walked with me.*

I was due in those weeks to go up to Rhodesia (now Zimbabwe) to speak at a huge interchurch conference called NACLA (National Christian Leadership Assembly). It was an overflow of PACLA, the 1976 Pan African Christian Leadership Assembly referred to earlier. Six hundred leaders from over fifty denominations were to be present.

The question was—how long would Dad linger? Could I slip away early the next day, speak at the conference, and get back to be with Dad? Should I cancel out? Should I have my message delayed in the conference, or what?

Assured of the Spirit's ability to speak in such situations, I went into the garden, sat on the children's swing, pored over my Bible, and asked the Spirit of God to guide me as to whether I should board the plane early the next morning or not.

Somehow I was constrained toward Psalm 90. I came on verses 9-10: "For all our days pass away under thy wrath, our years come to an end like a sigh. The years of our life are three-score and ten, or even by reason of strength fourscore; yet their span is but toil and trouble; they are soon gone, and we fly away." The words *soon gone* literally leaped at me from the page, as if radiating with the Spirit's quickened life. Dad would very soon be gone. That was the Spirit's word.

I went up to my study, phoned Rhodesia, and said I would not be on the plane the next day, but I believed I would be up there before the end of the conference. And that is how it ultimately worked out. I then took out my journal and noted: "Lord, I feel you are showing your mind. It seems I should stay and walk a day at a time on Rhodesia. Perhaps I am meant to speak a word at the end. In any event I am on standby to do your bidding."

Early next morning I was called from a prayer meeting at our church to go to the hospital. A long, searing, but precious morning followed. As a family we were knit closer than ever before. At one point Dad whispered, "I am sorry I am taking so long." It was characteristic of his selfless nature to be worrying even then over our pain. He died at 1:11 p.m. Had I not heard the Spirit's word the day before, I would have been landing at Salisbury airport at that very time.

How precious the sense of Jesus' presence was throughout that experience and after it. I remembered Paul's words, "For the law of the Spirit of life in Christ Jesus has set me free from the law of sin and death" (Rom. 8:2). Yes, the Spirit is the one who embodies the law of life in Christ Jesus; he frees us from those dreadful clutches of sin and death. I now knew this in a new way.

I remembered the words of Elizabeth Barrett Browning:

When some beloved voice that was to you
Both sound and sweetness, faileth suddenly,
And silence, against which you dare not cry,
Aches round you like a strong disease and new—
What hope? What help? What music will undo
That silence to your sense? Not friendship's sigh,
Not reason's subtle count. . .
Not songs of poets, nor of nightingales . . .
Nay, none of these,
Speak Thou, availing Christ!—and fill this pause.

It had been a Calvary time. Yet how gloriously real had been the Holy Spirit's ministry to us all.

A Year of Pressure (1979)

Another growth point came in the immense pressures some of us faced especially in 1979 as we sought to mount the South African Christian Leadership Assembly. The idea was to assemble leaders from the whole South African Church "in order to discover together what it means to be faithful and effective witnesses to Jesus Christ as Lord in South Africa today."

In order to get the thing to happen, those of us in leadership had to walk an extraordinarily traumatic gauntlet of misunderstanding, criticism, opposition, and obstructionism, on top of a crushing workload. Many times we felt at the end of our tether as, caught between different flanks or wings of the church, we took the flak from both sides. Anonymous documents, slander, political suspicion, character assassination, police investigations, Christian pamphleteering, and a thousand deadly darts constantly made life difficult and occasionally almost unbearable. I finally opened a file in my filing cabinet under M for "Mudslingers." It makes fascinating though unedifying reading, and constitutes a sad commentary on the Christian church. But in all these pressures the gentle, guiding, controlling work of the Holy Spirit brought relief and ability to cope.

Even so I couldn't help from time to time putting the question to myself, "If I have sought the release of the Spirit in new ways, how come all this trauma?" Then I would turn again to the fire that John the Baptist had stressed, and it all made sense. God was allowing these things in order to purge. It was an age-old principle. I hadn't grasped before so clearly the top priority Jesus placed on "clearing his threshing floor" (Matt. 3:12). It came to a head for me just before SACLA opened. I was in the office of one cabinet minister in whose mind much suspicion against SACLA and against me had been sown.

"If SACLA blows up and gets out of hand, the government will move in to close it down and we'll hold you accountable."

"It won't blow up, Mr. Minister," I said quietly, "because God is in it."

By that time, however, after so many months of these difficulties, my soul was pretty tattered. The whole thing had been almost too much; it had taken its toll on our morale. I felt stricken. Last straws can do that. I needed to hear a word of assurance from the Lord.

I drove over to the Pretoria Show Grounds and went to the large assembly hall to check out the public address and sound reinforcement system. Sitting way back in the empty bleachers I called to our African Enterprise media team to let me hear the system work. They put on a tape. Suddenly the whole auditorium exploded into magnificent stereophonic sound. The words of "Great Is Thy Faithfulness" along with a thousand strings filled the air. Then suddenly it was not just a hymn, a glorious cavalcade of sound, but a word from the Spirit of God. It just seemed as if Jesus by his Spirit, had entered, bringing me the affirmations of that magnificent hymn: "Great is Thy faithfulness, O God my Father, There is no shadow of turning with Thee." My tears began to flow and I was bathed in the warm and gracious assurance of the Spirit of God that all would be well. SACLA would not disintegrate in racial explosion. God's faithfulness would once again be demonstrated. I learned once more not only how the Spirit ministers to us just when we need it most, but how he can use anything to bring his sustenance to us. My point is that these were very tough experiences, which previously I had not seen as so integral to a fresh work of the Spirit in me. Yet all these happenings were slowly being revealed as necessary for God's work in the world and for his work in me.

SACLA

Then came the SACLA Assembly itself, as 6,000 South African Christian leaders came together in probably the most significant ecumenical assembly ever to happen in South Africa. Again for me it was both ecstasy and agony, both Spirit and fire.

As I prepared for my own address on the Holy Spirit I was led into the most unusual pre-address experience I have ever had. I was simply overcome for nearly three hours with grief for South Africa. A great weeping seized my soul for nearly an entire morning as I sought God's face and final guidance for my message. Never had anything like that happened to me. Not surprisingly, much of my text ended up in a new form. I was powerfully drawn to elucidate Isaiah 58:6–9:

> *Is not this the fast that I choose:*
> *to loose the bonds of wickedness,*
> *to undo the thongs of the yoke,*
> *to let the oppressed go free,*
> *and to break every yoke?*
> *Is it not to share your bread with the hungry,*
> *and bring the homeless poor into your house;*
> *when you see the naked, to cover him,*
> *and not to hide yourself from your own flesh?*
> *Then shall your light break forth like the dawn,*
> *and your healing shall spring up speedily;*
> *your righteousness shall go before you,*
> *the glory of God shall be your rear guard.*
> *Then you shall call, and the Lord will answer;*
> *you shall cry, and he will say, Here I am.*

Unless the Grain Die

This leads back to that verse so powerfully applied to my heart in the Milner Park experience, John 12:24. "Unless a grain of wheat falls into the earth and dies, it remains alone: but if it dies, it bears much fruit."

That kind of dying is hard. Some months before SACLA, returning from one of my trips related to the conference, I had been gearing up to prepare my paper on the work of the Holy Spirit. That Spirit convicted me that there was another brother in a neighboring country who had something against me, and I needed to try to reconcile with him before the conference.

"But, Lord, he has hurt me; I haven't hurt him," I protested. "Why should I go?"

"What does my Word say?" seemed to be the response of the Spirit of God. Then I thought of Matthew 5:23–24. "If you are offering your gift at the altar [i.e., if you are busy with your religious exercises], and there [i.e., at the place of religious service] remember that your brother has something against you, leave your gift there before the altar and go; first be reconciled to your brother, and then come and offer your gift."

"But, Lord, that's far away. It will mean a plane trip."

"Go, first be reconciled, then preach at SACLA."

"But, Lord, it will be expensive. Who will pay?"

"You've got some savings, haven't you?" the Spirit seemed to say.

Rather presumptuous of God to touch my savings, I thought. Anyway, the next day I was on my way. A strange, beautiful, but difficult journey in spirit leading to a partial healing of the relationship; later it became complete. But so much *dying* had to happen in the process.

In the closing meeting of SACLA I described that experience and challenged all to reconciliation. A young English woman who had just arrived in South Africa to do Christian work felt convicted. She had left her family in England totally alienated when she went abroad for Christian service. A few days later she humbled her proud heart, went to the bank, drew out all her savings, and set off for England. Her astonished family, whom she had left only weeks previously, all thoroughly alienated from the gospel as much as from her, now stood on spiritual tiptoe as she came back to seek forgiveness and reconciliation. Suddenly her gospel had credibility.

That process took place in many others while they were at SACLA. Each evening we broke the 6,000-member assembly into small groups where pietists faced activists, white heard from black, evangelical was confronted by nonevangelical, and charismatics and noncharismatics prayed and sometimes agonized with each other. Often there were tears. At times there was anger. Generally there was pain. And nearly always there was the cross, repentance, and growth. SACLA was a baptism with fire for many of us. That is why I knew so truly that it was a work of the Holy Spirit.

Calvary Love

In due time I had the opportunity to discuss this whole aspect of spiritual growth with Festo Kivengere. He underlined to me a truth at the heart of his own ministry in the East African Revival. Pentecost flowed from Calvary. The Holy Spirit is the Spirit of Jesus and Jesus is the Christ of Calvary. Unless, therefore, our teaching on the Holy Spirit is allied to the Cross and its self-sacrificing imperatives, we can miss the fact that the Spirit is primarily concerned to conform us to the image of Christ. His fruit, especially love, is to be produced in the life of the believer. The person who is full of the Holy Spirit is the one who loves and who is like Christ. That is the ultimate test.

We have to reason and preach from Calvary. We have to sustain the view from the Cross, not just as our place of conversion and salvation but as our means of growth. As self is crucified, the Spirit is released more and more in fullness. That has been the key in the East African Revival.

In Festo's book, *When God Moves,* the first paragraph is as follows:

The word *revival* has seven letters: three on one side, R-E-V; and three on the other side, V-A-L. In the center is the letter I.

How do we get to revival? By crossing out the I. Try writing the word carefully with a capital I in the center. Then put a line through the I and it becomes a cross. . .

Self-centeredness is the greatest enemy of spiritual life. You are going to be involved in inward battle and conflict as long as the center of your personality is occupied by that little god. It's too little to be your god. It can't occupy the throne. The throne is for him who died in love for you—I mean God in Jesus Christ. When self is on the throne, it is conspicuously out of place. It is too weak to meet your needs, too small to satisfy your hunger, too dry to quench your thirst. Revival begins by putting a line through the I which is at the center and turning it into a cross.[56]

Personal Crisis

In spite of starting to learn something more of this principle in 1979, I was scarcely prepared for the greater depths in which I was to face it during a deep personal crisis in 1980.

After SACLA I was worn out in more ways than one. In fact, the pressures of 1978 and 1979 were simply the culmination of a decade of pressure. I was more then ready for a sabbatical break, which had been granted me sometime previously by the African Enterprise board. With Carol and our three children I set off in January 1981 for three months in the U.S., two in ministry and one in rest, followed by three months of reading and study at Cambridge and Oxford.

They were not easy months. In the first place I had become deeply concerned about aspects of our ministry in African Enterprise. My concern related to whether we always took care to discern the will of the Spirit before we plunged into miscellaneous ministry opportunities or social care projects. The load, both financial and personal, was becoming crushing for many in the work, yet Jesus had said, "My yoke is easy, and my burden is light" (Matt. 11:30). What is one to say when the yoke is anything but easy and the burden anything but light?

Moreover, I was becoming increasingly suspicious of frenzied ministries that seemed not only to destroy one's spiritual peace but to threaten one's health. I remembered again the Lord's word through Jeremiah: "I did not send the prophets, yet they ran; I did not speak to them, yet they prophesied" (Jer. 23:21). Here was a picture of frenzied, fruitless, and wasted ministry which had nothing to do with the will of God. Then the Lord added his commentary: "But if they had stood in my council, then they would have proclaimed my words to my people, and they would have turned them from their evil way, and from the evil of their doings" (Jer. 23:22).

In a sense the issue was whether we in African Enterprise would really seek the agenda of God, or whether we would just do our own thing in our own energy. Could self-will be eliminated in the scheduling of an entire organization? It was no light matter. It clearly applied to the whole purpose of God for one's earthly walk. Imagine getting to heaven, facing the Lord Jesus, and hearing him say: "Well done, my son. You did pretty well. The only problem is that you worked the rose garden of your choosing and not the cabbage patch of mine. You poured out great and sincere energy, but on the wrong thing."

The thought plagued me day and night. For months I woke at four a.m. or earlier. Were we functioning the right way? Was I personally doing the right thing? Had the time come for a change in my life? Was evangelism still my work? Should I enter the political process? Get back to teaching? Should I stay in South Africa? Should I go to Zimbabwe or East Africa? Should I leave African Enterprise and let others run with it as they saw fit?

Beyond that I saw the dangers of hitting the "bigtime." African Enterprise was now a large organization, spanning a number of countries across the world. Our budget was expanding and the whole machine had to be kept on the road. Money was an endless anxiety, though I knew I should be more relaxed and trusting in the Lord over this than I was.

There was also the now obvious danger of the ego trip. I wanted to succeed, be well thought of, widely called on, written up in periodicals, and all that. Suddenly it sickened me. The spirit of the manger and the carpenter's bench could vanish so easily from a work. The whole point of what Jesus was about could be subtly, slowly, and lethally lost.

What suddenly began to worry me as much about myself as about our ministry as a whole was that it seemed at certain points to be operating more in the flesh and in the ways of the world than in the Spirit and in the ways of God. Not that we were being consciously disobedient. We were just functioning as "ordinary men" and doing many things in human ways, in human energy and in human wisdom—i.e., at certain points we were not being spiritual. We were not full of the Spirit.

Those were hard thoughts to entertain of myself, or of the organization I belonged to. They are equally hard for any individual or group or congregation, especially if habits of "doing it my way" have become established. Breaking out of old ways hurts. It is difficult. It involves constant crucifixion, which God uses to try and bring us more fully under his control—so that where the Master is, there is the servant also. Regrettably, we his servants are often scampering across the Christian landscape on our own self-inflating errands, which of course we want the Master to bless mightily. He is somewhere else on his agenda, no doubt wondering when his high-powered and ever so important servants will get where he is.

In Hiding

About this time I was due to leave Oxford, where I was studying under Bishop Stephen Neill, and go to Thailand for several weeks for the International Congress on World Evangelization. I had a paper to give and a study group to lead. One morning the Spirit mightily convicted me in prayer that I was not to go. I was to stay where I was. "Hide yourself," God's word to Elijah in 1 Kings 17:3, gripped me firmly. Perhaps, had I known what the next three weeks were to bring forth, I would have opted for the long journey east, like Jonah heading for Tarshish. But Oxford was my divinely appointed Nineveh for those days.

The mechanics of how it all happened are of less consequence than the spiritual process itself. But in effect in those following weeks all my Isaacs were systematically taken up my Mount

Moriah and forced to the altar of sacrifice. My desire to be a good evangelist, my continuing involvement in African Enterprise, my ministry of evangelism, my presence in South Africa, our beautiful home near Pietermaritzburg, all were taken by the Spirit of God—not theoretically but existentially and truly. It was all gone or almost gone. I was left camping on Mount Moriah, with the knife poised over my Isaacs, not knowing whether or not there would be a ram caught in the thicket.

My Isaacs—all things that in themselves were good—were in danger of becoming idols. They were getting in the way of God. That was especially true of my relationship to African Enterprise, which I saw, as Abraham had with Isaac, as the means by which I would bless the world. God went for that one hardest, and finally I let go. It was gone. I felt light, as if a massive weight had been lifted.

On Monday morning, May 26, 1980, after a weekend in London, I walked on the Wimbledon Common with Carol. We talked about what our future held, now that the Lord had seemingly taken us out of African Enterprise. My journal says: "It was a time of searing crisis when I basically faced up to leaving A.E. and all that would mean. It was not an easy time. I experienced all the emotions of bereavement."

Servanthood

Two days later my journal records: "The word of Philippians 2 came home to me. Jesus made himself of no reputation and *became obedient*—unto death—even death on a cross. He also emptied himself of all to which he was entitled. The challenge to me was obvious in terms of laying down everything on which in a sense my reputation rests, yet which is now a potential if not actual impediment to my own obedience."

Next day a new insight came which my journal again captures: "I think I have cultivated a fairly healthy, or perhaps unhealthy, though certainly not uncommon, desire to succeed, and to be someone! That I saw too must go and if A.E. is an unconscious vehicle to that relatively unconscious desire, then the altar of sacrifice must have yet another offering upon it!"

The end of a long week finally came. I went to church on Sunday. The message was on Nehemiah the leader, the rebuilder, the mourner, the lamenter for Israel. It was momentous for me. The Holy Spirit was in it. The word was to rebuild. The word was to keep courage. "Should such a man as I flee?" asked Nehemiah (6:11). The word was to persevere. "So the wall was finished" (6:15).

Drake's prayer came to mind: "Lord, when thou givest to thy servants to endeavor any great matter, grant us also to know that it is not the beginning but the continuing of the same until it be thoroughly finished which yieldeth the true glory; through Him, who for the finishing of Thy work, laid down His life, our Redeemer Jesus Christ."

I was out of the woods: re-commissioned, re-called, renewed. African Enterprise was handed back to me, though I now held it in freedom. It did not hold me, nor could it ever again in the same way as before. South Africa came back to me. We could return to our precious home, Namirembe. Above all, I could continue evangelizing, which was my love, but more as God's servant than as one of A.E.'s preachers.

It had been a time of going forward through crossfire.

Calvary Road

But, lest anyone imagine I was now soaring on some new height of sparkling spirituality, I must add that the Calvary process kept going on. We are never finally on top. We never arrive. Not until Glory!

I was setting off on leave that Christmas, in 1980. The car was packed and the family waiting. As I left my study the words *Calvary Road* popped into my mind. That made me anxious, because I remembered it as the title of a powerful little book by Roy Hession. I remembered picking it up twenty years ago as a seminary student and finding it too hot to handle.

The prompting to take the book on leave scared me a bit, but I did. I duly read it and was greatly challenged by it. Commenting on this Cross experience, Hession writes:

Dying to self is not a thing we do once and for all. There may be an initial dying when God first shows these things, but ever after, it will be a constant dying, for only so can the Lord Jesus be revealed constantly through us. All day long the choice will be before us in a thousand ways.[57]

Returning some weeks later with all this Calvary theology, and somewhat apprehensive as to why I was being led further into this truth, I was confronted almost immediately with the situation of a friend who had exercised my patience at several points. In fact, perhaps unconsciously, he had hurt me. I was mad at him. Wanting to face him with his supposed affronts to my person, I set off to set him straight. The words *mote* and *beam* sizzled into my spiritual consciousness from Hession's book.

"Lord, you mean, my mote and his beam."

"No, my son, I mean your beam and his mote. You leave him to me to deal with and in the meantime ask his forgiveness for your attitude."

Oh, my! That meant a kingsize helping of humble pie. But if my brother has a mote, or a speck, and I have a beam, what is that beam, I wondered. Hession had the answer:

Now we all know what Jesus meant by the mote in the other person's eye. It is some fault which we fancy we can discern in him; it may be an act he has done against us, or some attitude he adopts toward us. But what did the Lord Jesus mean by the beam in our eye? I suggest that the beam in our eye is simply our unloving reaction to the other man's mote. Without doubt there is a wrong in the other person. But our reaction to that wrong is a wrong too! The mote in him has provoked in us resentment, or coldness, or criticism, or bitterness, or evil speaking, or illwill—all of them variants of the basic ill, unlove. And that, said the Lord Jesus, is far, far worse than the tiny wrong (sometimes quite unconscious) that provoked it. A beam means a rafter. And the Lord Jesus means by this comparison to tell us that our unloving reaction to the other's wrong is what a great rafter is to a little splinter![58] But let us not think that a beam is of necessity some violent reaction on our part. The first beginning of resentment is a beam, as is also the first flicker of an unkind thought, or the first suggestion of unloving criticism. Where that is so, it only distorts our vision and we shall never see our brother as he really is, beloved of God. If we speak to our brother with that in our hearts, it will only provoke him to adopt the same attitude to us, for it is a law of human relationships that "with what measure ye mete, it shall be measured to you again."[59]

Does that mean that my brother is without fault and I who would judge am the only one who is guilty? Not at all, says the author of *Calvary Road*.

But as we take these simple steps of repentance, then we see clearly to cast the mote out of the other's eye, for the beam in our eye has gone. In that moment God will pour light in on us as to the other's need, that neither he nor we ever had before. We may see then that the mote we were so conscious of before, is virtually nonexistent—it was but the projection of something that was in us. On the other hand, we may have revealed to us hidden underlying things, of which he himself was hardly conscious. Then as God leads us, we must lovingly and humbly challenge him, so that he may see them too, and bring them to the Fountain and find deliverance. He will be more likely than ever to let us do it—indeed if he is a humble man, he will be grateful to us, for he will know now that there is no selfish motive in our heart, but only love and concern for him.[60]

With all these thoughts rushing through my mind, I met my friend and confessed my fault. It was hard. It was a Calvary road for my pride, but it was good. He confessed that he had indeed failed me. We went forward in light—growing.

Cross Central

To sum up, over these years in many ways the Spirit of God has seemed to be pointing to the dangers, in my own renewal personally and in the church's renewal generally, of triumphalism and fleshly responses with all their self-satisfaction and self-assertiveness. God has seemed to be underlining that the true mark of the Spirit's working is self-sacrifice, humility, servanthood, and finally forgiving love as the hallmark of the Spirit's presence. The cross must remain central. It is a tough challenge, but an unavoidable one. For this was and is the way of love.

16

The
Jesus Way
in the World

Too many evangelical Christians
are irresponsible escapists: Fellowship
with one another in the church
is much more congenial than service
in the world's hostile environment.
John Stott

SHORTLY AFTER THE FIRST RENEWAL CONFERENCE in August 1977, a young black consciousness leader, Stephen Biko, died by torture in a South African jail. He had been arrested without charge, detained without trial, and now was dead without explanation. He was not the first young black to die like that. He was part of an epidemic. Against a backdrop of silence from most conservative South African Christians, the world and the rest of the South African church lifted their voices yet again in grief and protest.

Detainee Deaths
I expressed my profound concern in a newspaper column titled "Detainee Deaths" (*The Natal Witness*, September 17, 1977). It included the following:

Perhaps the most shattering aspect of this is that having become accustomed to the neo-pagan practice of detentions without trial, we are now in danger of becoming accustomed to the deaths without adequate explanation of people detained without trial. That justice in any country must be done goes without saying. It should also go without saying, especially in a professedly Christian country, that it must also be seen to be done. Even heathen and pre-Christian civilizations, such as the Roman and the Greek, followed this principle.

Our country, because of its Christian profession, thus has a very special obligation to its citizens and to the world to exercise its judicial processes in a manner compatible with its spiritual heritage. In other words, we also need to have established in open court why the Steve Bikos of this world should be in prison in the first place.

None of this is to deny that the State has judicial, statutory and security responsibilities. This is a clear New Testament principle. But the State is meant to be "God's servant for [our] good" (Rom. 13:4). Carrying the awesome responsibility of a divine servant, the State has the accompanying duty to pattern its principles of justice on those of its Master. Otherwise it will be held more fearfully guilty than any citizens on whom its own condemnation has fallen.

Therefore we need to recognize afresh that the New Testament is a book of means as well as ends. The end does not justify the means. Nothing therefore which is morally wrong can ever be politically right. Expediency is not justice.

The challenge then to our authorities is clear. It is a challenge left to us not only from Christian principle but even from the pagan Roman Empire where people knew they could say: "If [they] have a complaint against any one, the courts are open, and there are proconsuls; let them bring charges" (Acts 19:38).

Is it too much to ask for this—not in pagan Rome but in Christian South Africa? Is it too much to request an independent inquiry into these detainee deaths so that a restive public may have its troubled mind set at rest? If so, then we all must truly Cry for the Beloved Country.

Reaction

Not long after that article appeared, a white local parishioner, very high on spiritual renewal, approached one of my colleagues.

"I thought Michael got sorted out at Milner Park and now here he writes in his column about Steve Biko."

"Did you read what he said?" asked my colleague.

"No," said the irate parishioner, "I just saw he was writing on Steve Biko and that was enough for me. I'm not going to support African Enterprise any more."

We in African Enterprise were no strangers to that sort of response, because whenever we have addressed any social issue in this avowedly Christian country (a breathtaking 87 percent of South Africans profess to be Christians), we have met with a similar response from white Christians in varying degrees of intensity, though never yet from any black Christian. Even when I told this Biko story at the second South African Renewal Conference in January 1980 I was faced with a barrage of criticism from whites and put the Conference Executive Committee into crisis. I had asked if a new desire to know the fullness of the Holy Spirit made one more—or less—interested in a man dying by torture in one of our prisons.

I was told by one sincere person that even to mention Biko, let alone to quote Martin Luther King with approval, as I had done, was inappropriate in a South African religious gathering. Apart from anything else it created a psychological guilt complex and made reconciliation more difficult. That is a sincerely held viewpoint among many white Christians in my country. Of course the fact that we may suffer from the psychological ravages of authentic corporate guilt, rather than simply from a guilt complex, and that reconciliation is impossible until we have faced the true extent of our socio-political crimes, does not seem

to have impressed itself too deeply on many of us in this complicated end of the world.

"South Africa hasn't just got a guilt complex," I commented
to a friend, apropos of that reaction. "South Africa is *guilty!*"

Was I right or wrong as a Christian to lend my voice in challenge to the brutal pattern of political happenings of which
Biko's death was only one aspect? Put differently, should Christians take part in any form of socio-political action? Should they
indulge in actions of social concern? Should they ever challenge
the state?

It is a complicated issue, but for me it becomes less confusing
if one asks the question, What are the obligations of love in such
a situation? On the other hand it becomes more confusing when
you ask in addition, What are the obligations of love to the
authorities also in such a situation?

I remember my anger, almost bitterness, at the time of Biko's
death when our then Minister of Justice, Mr. Jimmy Kruger,
came on television with excuses and hollow explanations for the
black leader's death, when he had already said publicly, "Steve
Biko's death leaves me cold."

Midstream in my anger, I realized I also had to ask, What
does it mean to love Jimmy Kruger? How do I voice my Christian protest in a manner that does not betray the gospel whose
priorities I am trying to protect?

Tough questions. Trying to find the Spirit's way had been a
fairly lengthy process, though basically there were only two steps
in it. The first step involved being brought to an understanding
of the implications simply of being a human being. It related
really to the doctrine of creation and seeing all human beings as
valuable. The second step involved being brought to an understanding of the implications of Jesus' own way in the world. It
related to the doctrine of Christ and seeing all people as recipients of his compassionate concern. Step one happened over my
childhood years and was really the result of powerful influences
in my upbringing. Step two took place through my later high
school and student years.

Step One: Being Human

I grew up in the little British Protectorate of Basutoland (as it then was called—now Lesotho). My earliest recollections of my father were of a man who treated all people fairly. He had both blacks and whites under him in his capacity as senior engineer in the territory. To him people were people, regardless of their color.

I don't think his view was based on anything very self-consciously Christian. It was just a corollary of being a human being. It was basically related to the way God had created us. To treat people differently on the basis of race was in a sense to deny something of one's own humanity, not to mention theirs.

Another very important influence on me through childhood was Patrick Duncan, son of Sir Patrick Duncan who had been Governor General of South Africa under Smuts. Pat lived next door to us and he was an easy candidate for a child's hero worship. He had a sparkling personality, was constantly full of hilarious fun, and could mimic anyone. More than that, he shared my childhood passion for horses, showed me how to raid a beehive, taught me about birds and butterflies, and scared my mother silly as he introduced me to the giant size bow and arrow. He was the most stimulating and interesting person I ever knew. But above all he had passionate political commitments to justice and a fair shake for all. He abominated *apartheid* and all its ways, but he equally abominated anything to do with violence. Mahatma Gandhi and his philosophy of *Satyagraha* (passive resistance or soul force) constituted his guiding star.

I became a childhood convert. Discrimination was wrong. Justice was right. Apartheid would doom South Africa. I was glad and proud when Pat joined Peter Brown and Alan Paton in founding the South African Liberal Party. Tragically, over the following twenty years a desperate and disillusioned Pat gradually turned to violence, and we parted political company. He was banned in South Africa and fled the country.

Years later I talked to him about Christ but I never knew if I got through. Once in New York he said to my sister, "In

Michael's message lies the answer." Perhaps he came full circle. In any event, the commitments of his early years, based like my father's on the common humanity of the human race under God, had made their mark on me.

Then there was my prep school in Johannesburg. My headmaster, another of my heroes, smoked a pipe shaped like the head of Dr. Malan. "It seems to please both sides," he once commented wryly between puffs! (Malan had become prime minister in the 1948 election when the Afrikaner Nationalists came to power by defeating Smuts and the United Party.) What I again remember was the headmaster's basic conviction that discrimination was wrong. The 1948 Nationalist victory filled him with gloom, though as a twelve-year-old, more full of soccer, cricket, and Latin principal parts than political savvy, I couldn't quite understand why. I gathered it had something to do with how the new government viewed blacks. Pat Duncan gave me the same line on the election. I concluded 1948 was a bad year.

On the other hand I was not allowed to become crudely anti-Afrikaner. My maternal grandfather and grandmother saw to that. Although grandfather had come out with the Royal Canadian Cavalry to fight in the Boer War in 1899 and Granny had come as a British nurse, they had both developed strongly sympathetic views of the Boer cause after the war. Granny who had nursed both British and Boer soldiers and won from Lord Kitchener the Royal Red Cross in the process, the highest women's decoration for bravery, always taught me that there were wonderful qualities in the Afrikaner. She was right. Naturally therefore both she and Grandfather longed for a new South Africa in which all races would live happily. They held out the hand of fellowship and reconciliation, especially to Afrikaners.

It was the way of healing for South Africa, the godly way, Grandfather said. It was also simply the right and human thing to do.

Step Two: Being Christian
During high school those commitments took greater shape

around a specifically Christian framework. At Michaelhouse I learned that one was concerned for the world because Jesus was concerned for the world. That developing framework set me up for a mighty step forward—reading Alan Paton's *Cry the Beloved Country.* When he came to our school in 1952 I was moved by his words and warnings and especially the lament in the last words of his book that, when the white man turns to loving, the black man will have turned to hating. He was a good prophet.

Then came my conversion at Cambridge in 1955, which crystalized my convictions that Jesus was the answer for South Africa, his Way the only Way.

Trevor Huddleston came to the university shortly after the publication of *Naught for Your Comfort,* which I avidly read. He was followed by Alexander Steward from South Africa House who had just put out a book titled *You Are Wrong Father Huddleston.* After Steward had given his lecture, during which my brave roommate Alasdair Macaulay tried his first hand at heckling, the famous South African historian Eric Walker was asked to speak a word of thanks to the speaker. What stuck in my mind were Walker's words to the effect that the only thing Mr. Steward had missed was "Jesus—and he was interested in blokes." It was a shattering condemnation of the politics of apartness because in its terseness it went to the heart of the matter. People mattered. They shouldn't be treated differently.

I became quite militant and with other friends wrote vigorous letters of protest about South African policies to *The Times.* We even picketed South Africa House, carrying a cross and wearing black armbands. The South African High Commissioner was overheard by one of my friends saying to an official, "I can understand the picket, but why the Cross?" A good question.

I then reacted somewhat to that militancy, and embraced the view that all that was needed was for people to be converted. Then society would come right. Imagine my horror as a very young Christian when I began to find converted people not just tolerating but actively working to maintain the South African status quo.

On the other hand one couldn't get away from the fact that

Jesus was "interested in blokes." Although some Christians got it wrong, his way had to be right. I heard that again in an interview several years later with Nobel Prize winner Chief Albert Luthuli, then head of the African National Congress and later banned by the South African authorities. His movement at that time was deeply pacifist and he said, "It's only the Way of the Master that will work in South Africa." He went on to add that the ANC would go radical and violent if its aspirations and pleas for a fair deal went unheard. He too was a good prophet.

Luthuli's word about the Jesus Way struck me powerfully, though I had to wait until 1969 to grasp its depth. Then it became a profound and settled conviction.

The Jesus Way

In 1969 our team was gearing up for a citywide mission to Nairobi when we learned that veteran missionary statesman E. Stanley Jones could join us. How much we learned from him! It was he who first gave us a clear picture of the cosmic Christ and of his Way as *the* Way in all things, moral, political, marital, personal. If the universe is his, then doing things his way is to do them the way that works.

Stanley Jones referred us to his wonderful little devotional volume, *The Way*, where this principle is lucidly spelled out in 365 daily readings. The heart of his teaching was this:

If the Christian way is a way among ways, you can take it or leave it, and nothing much happens. It doesn't really matter. But if it is true—if it is *the* Way—then nothing else matters. This is the one thing in life with which we must come to terms, or ruin life itself. If the Way is imposed upon life, then it is A Way, but if it is a revelation of life, of life itself, then it is THE Way. If it is written in the Scriptures only, then it is A Way. If it is written in the nature of reality and the Scriptures, then it is THE Way.[61]

That principle is so helpful in thinking about this socio-political issue. What we are getting back to is the Bible's teaching on creation. There we discern the moral nature of the universe with its implications for our lives in society. People like my father, grandfather, Pat Duncan, and Albert Luthuli were onto that principle, though not couching it in theological categories.

The Moral Nature of the Universe

Slowly things began to come into clearer focus. Suddenly Colossians 1:16 made sense politically, as well as theologically. Here Jesus is presented as the agent and goal in creation. "All things were made through him and for him," the apostle says. The socio-political implications of that fact for Christians become obvious. Because the universe has Jesus' stamp on it we must tell society, both governments and the governed, that for life to work, whether private, marital, social, or political, the game must be played in Jesus' way.

Later on I tried to spell this out in a letter to a member of the South African cabinet. First of all, bearing in mind the politics of love, I felt constrained to come to him not in judgment, but in love. I wrote: "I come to you as a brother, not to complicate, but to try and help. The challenge is to think through more deeply *as a Christian* the *ethical* and *moral* factors involved in the policies of our country. Let me elaborate, first on the principle—and then on some precedents." I then went on to try and spell out the principle which is the focus of our attention in this chapter.

The letter put it this way: "You see, I believe that *apartheid* or separate development, or whatever we now call it, is doomed and it threatens to doom all of us with it, not because it is meeting with opposition which will make it fail, but because I believe it violates a fundamental ethical principle in treating people differently on the basis of race.

"Now that may sound to you like old hat, but let me go further and share with you as Christian to Christian.

"The Bible teaches us that Jesus is the agent in creation. 'Without him was not anything made that was made' (John 1:3). 'All things were created through him and for him' (Col. 1:16). This has dramatic and fundamental implications for us."

I saw the implications as fivefold and spelled them out as follows:

1. It means that the universe is his and his stamp is on it at every level.
2. It means that his laws—scientific, social, personal, psychological, and moral—are operative throughout.
3. It means that if we want life and the universe to cooperate with us we must play the game his way. If we do, life and the universe cooperate with us. Things work.
4. It means that if we do not go the Jesus way at every level of life—whether personal, marital, or political—then life and the universe do not cooperate with us. We lose their backing and instead of producing that which is integrative we produce that which is disintegrative. Thus a teenager violating the laws of sex is not breaking the laws but illustrating them when he or she becomes fragmented. Likewise a politician who violates Jesus' corporate and social laws (e.g., 'Do unto others as you would have them do to you'—or 'Love your neighbor as yourself') will find not that they are breaking laws but that the laws are breaking them and the society around them. Nor will anyone persuade me that apartheid laws are not violating those two principles at every turn. Not one white South African, least of all any member of the Cabinet, would want to be on the *receiving* end of apartheid legislation.
5. It means that a thing is not wrong simply because the Bible says so (as if it were something arbitrary), but rather the Bible says a thing is wrong because it doesn't work. It is not in accord with the moral fabric of the universe. In other words, biblical morality (whether personal, social, or political) is not an *imposed* morality but rather an *exposed* morality. The Bible simply *exposes* the morality that is there and says 'If you want life to work, then do it this way.' It is like finding the direction of grain on a piece of wood so that one may plane it correctly. The plane works when it follows the grain that is there. Likewise if by faulty policy we go against the moral grain of the universe, the political plane just will not work.

This is very close to Plato's definition of the good as that which best relates function to purpose. Thus a good knife is one that cuts well because its functions according to its purpose. A good man is a man who functions as God purposed him to function. A good government is one that functions according to the divine intent. From a biblical perspective this means functioning "as God's servant" for the "good" of *all* its peoples (Rom. 13:4).

This is why I have often said in South Africa that the fundamental issue facing us is whether we live in a moral universe or not. If we do not, then we can discriminate (whether in microcosm or in macrocosm) and get away with it. But if we do live in a moral universe, and if we discriminate, then we can't and won't get away with it. And the judgments of life, of history, and of the universe will become the judgments of God—because he has made one sort of universe and not another—a universe in which we reap what we sow.

After sharing several biblical and historical precedents I concluded my hopefully not too presumptuous homily to my political friend with these words: "I realize that all of this is almost certainly familiar ethical territory to you, but you are a Christian brother and therefore these things are worth underlining to one another. Exactly how all this is to be worked out within the realities of the South African situation is for those of you who are Christian politicians and statesmen to decide. But of this I am sure—anything that breaks with Christian principle will not work. It will only produce the kind of mounting fury that is now threatening to engulf our whole society—if not right now, then within a few years. It is self-deceiving to see all this as the work of a few agitators. It is not. It is a reflex in the machine, as it were, to what happens when the rules are broken. It is the cogs in a watch grinding because of sand that should not be there.

"Put differently, it is life and the universe in *re-action*. This is not to discount agitating, exploitive, or even Marxist elements. But Marxists are never foolish enough to *exploit* anything except *just* causes. The devil always has a sound eye for the genuine grievance! We can head him off only by cleaving to what is right—no matter how much the darkness may call us to the dictates of expediency.

"So my challenge is to encourage subordination of policy to principle, bearing in mind it is better in the eyes of both time and eternity to lose in the short term with what must ultimately win rather than win in the short term with what will ultimately lose." There my letter concluded.

I had discharged my soul to a key political figure and felt glad and relieved to have done so. I was of course trying to project into the future as to the dread consequences in my own land of violating the moral fabric of the universe. No Christian who has grasped the principles of the moral nature of the universe can stand aside and let governments and societies (or even so-called "liberation" movements) try to do their own thing without reference to Jesus and his guidebook. It would be as criminal as letting a ten-year-old drive a car without learning the principles of driving, and without reference to traffic law.

Human Dignity and Value

Another principle that relates to the moral nature of the universe is the principle of human dignity and value. It too is an extension of the doctrine of creation. E. M. Howse is a recent chronicler of the influences of the English Clapham Sect, the group of people who got together around William Wilberforce (1759-1833) to support him in the abolition of slavery. Howse observes that this sect "sprang out of a new doctrine of responsibility toward the underprivileged, a doctrine which received its chief impulse from the evangelical emphasis on the *value of the human soul* and hence of the individual."[62]

That biblical concern was renewed by the Wesleyan revival. In fact, says Howse, the evangelical revival "created a moral sentiment that permanently changed England's attitude to distant and defenseless peoples, and to her own brutal and degraded masses at home. Within a lifetime, like a group of mountain springs, there appeared in England a series of religious and humanitarian movements which altered the whole course of English history, influenced most of Europe and affected the life of three other continents."[63]

All this sprang from a renewed appreciation of the value of the human soul. It is the rediscovery of the doctrine of creation. In making us in his image, God has endowed each of us with immense value and sacrosanct dignity. Anything that undermines that, whether political or social or personal, is to be opposed in the name of Christ.

No Dichotomy

What was becoming increasingly clear to me was the fact that one cannot divide life or people into secular or sacred compartments. Nor can one decide to care for the needs of one group, say one's own, and not those of another. To be a friend of Jesus Christ means also to be a friend of the human race. While a common redemption identifies us with other Christians, a common creation identifies us with all people everywhere. The God of grace is also the God of nature. In the New Testament I could see no Greek dichotomy between the material and the spiritual.

My doctrines of the Fall and redemption told me that all people need saving, challenging me as an evangelist. My doctrine of creation told me that all people are worth saving, challenging me as a human being. Every individual, although a sinner needing salvation, is also immensely valuable because he or she is made in the image of God. That gives each person equality, dignity, and value in the eyes of God. Anything that denies that equality or threatens that dignity or minimizes that value is to be challenged in the name of the God of both Old and New Testaments.

There was also the fact that we are in community. That fact thrusts in on us constantly in South Africa. We are not a soul without a body or a body without a soul. Nor are we a body-soul without a community. No one survives or grows in a vacuum. We develop within a complicated interweaving of relationships that influences us for good or ill. Society's immense power to shape and mold individuals, and how it does so, depends on the nature of that society. A society can either stunt or warp its people, or it can stimulate and inspire their fullest growth into freedom, wholeness, and happiness.

George Carey in *I Believe in Man* makes this observation:

> If we wish [human beings] to develop into responsible, mature citizens, society as a whole must demonstrate values it wishes to see reflected in its citizens. It follows, that in a corrupt system of society, with injustice, inequality and a mockery of moral standards, the odds are against a [person] becoming a truly harmonious self.[64]

John Stott adds a corollary about the church, which has allowed a corrupt system of society to develop:

> When any community deteriorates, the blame should be attached where it belongs: not to the community which is going bad, but to the church which is failing in its responsibility as salt to stop it going bad. And the salt will be effective only if it permeates society, only if Christians learn again the wide diversity of divine callings, and if many penetrate deeply into secular society to serve Christ there.[65]

One performs such service not out of a desire to be politically provocative but because alongside the Great Commission to evangelize the whole world stands the Great Commandment to love the whole world, as a fundamental adjunct of loving God with all our being. Regrettably, some sincere Christians act as if the Great Commission supersedes the Great Commandment. However, while New Testament love certainly obligates us to share with our neighbors the greatest good news, the story of salvation and forgiveness in Christ, it does not stop there. It goes on into any areas of activity or initiative that are demanded by plain, straightforward compassion.

South African Situation
In our South African situation that sort of challenge to compassion keeps coming before us. Take, for example, the ongoing

removals of black squatters on the edge of some of our major cities. At the moment of writing, many people of color in the Western Cape are being moved by our authorities from squatter situations back to the Transkei (a supposedly independent South African homeland) where, in the judgment of our authorities, "they belong." Government officials moved in on one of the squatter camps near Cape Town early one winter morning. The pathetic little shacks, some made only of plastic, were knocked down, and the people put onto buses and sent 600 miles back to Transkei. A number of mothers were separated from their babies and the consequent situation of trauma passed description, according to many who saw it.

Let a local newspaper tell the tale. (And while one reads it one can ask, "Is it being improperly political to judge such actions?")

About 1,000 squatters deported from Nyanga arrived in Umtata yesterday on the first leg of a journey back to nowhere—and took the Transkei Government completely by surprise. The refugees—mostly women and children—had been loaded into a single train at Kei Bridge where they had been brought in 14 buses from Cape Town. They arrived at the Umtata railway station in driving rain. At least 600 streamed down the main street of Umtata to the Catholic and Anglican churches to seek shelter...

An Umtata social worker said: "The deportation happened so quickly for them that many just grabbed what they could and ran. One woman, whose baby is in a Cape Town hospital, was caught by the police. Before she knew it, she was on a Transkei-bound bus and found herself in the Catholic centre in Umtata yesterday. Two babies of about six months also came along with two women this morning—but nobody knows whose children they are."

According to the refugees at the centre, most of them want to return to Cape Town. "We don't want to remain in Transkei. There's no housing for us, there are no jobs and there is no future," one woman said.[66]

Another article in that same paper filled out a poignant detail:

Of the many possessions the squatters left behind when they
were deported to Transkei, one was most poignant. The bundle, lying in the sun, was small enough to contain a pair of
castoff shoes. But the bundle stirred and a seven-week-old
baby began displaying hunger pangs. His mother was not
there to feed him. She was one of more than 1,000 squatters
arrested and put on railway buses bound for the Transkei.
Her friends identified him as Alfred Baatjie... He is now
warmly clad and being fed and cradled by the squatters who
have now taken refuge outside the nearby Holy Cross
Church.[67]

The newspaper also noted that

Johannesburg's Chief Rabbi, Mr. B. M. Casper, making a
rare entry into a national issue during his Sabbath sermon last
night at the Great Synagogue in Wolmarans Street, Joubert
Park, attacked the deportations and called on the Government to let justice and compassion prevail. "The forcible
removal of homeless squatters from their pitiful, miserable
shacks, in the midst of winter, must surely touch even the
most heartless of men. Every humanitarian instinct cries out
against it," he said.

The rabbi is right. It is not even Christian instinct that cries out,
it is humanitarian instinct. Are conservative Christians to stand
back and say, "We don't believe in being political. You must
obey the government and submit"? Doesn't the law of love call
for both involvement and caring?

One could multiply incidents and situations like this ad infini-
tum out of South Africa. Not that our land alone is guilty. My
travels in many parts of Africa, plus experiences in Australia,
Latin America, England, and the U.S. are enough to assure me
otherwise. But I illustrate from my own context because that is
the one for which I am uniquely accountable and in whose guilt I
am irrevocably caught up.

As far as I can see, I cannot love my Lord or my neighbor

without somewhere along the line entering the political arena. That is why, when Stephen Biko died, it was clear to me that my responsibility was to speak out.

Hot Water
To speak out is to land in hot water. It is "not appropriate," conservative Christians constantly affirm. One Christian leader, who recently wrote to me, said, "The only effective means of eradicating the evils of social mal-conditions and racism is the blood of Jesus Christ." For a long time, as I already said, I had believed just that—get people converted and all will be fine thereafter with their racial attitudes and social concerns. But the evidence to the contrary is overwhelming.

Something Wrong
It seemed increasingly to me that those who were advising the stance that Christians keep their hands out of such unspiritual things as politics, economics, and the problems of society, were often concerned not so much for souls and spirituality as they were for their own freedom to do as they pleased in social, economic, and political matters. Is Christ the Lord over private matters such as food, drink, sex, and entertainment, but not over public matters like racism, voting, education, and justice? Are we to call for repentance from adultery and drunkenness but not from racial prejudice, discriminatory practices, and participation in unjust structures?

With hindsight everyone recognizes that the Victorian factory system, with children working twelve to sixteen hours a day, was evil. Yet child-labor, like slavery, was legal. Legal or not, those practices destroyed people by the millions. Were those Christians right who abstained from challenging those things because they didn't believe in getting "involved in politics"? What about Idi Amin's Uganda? Should Ugandan Christians have remained silent because "involvement in politics" is *out* for the evangelical or Pentecostal Christian? After all, the powers that be are ordained by God!

It seemed to me that Ron Sider was right in his view that

neglect of the biblical teaching on structural injustice and insti-
tutionalized evil ranks as one of the deadliest omissions in theologically conservative sections of the church today. Sider notes
several interesting Old Testament Scriptures, e.g., Amos 2:6-7:
"For three transgressions of Israel, and for four, I will not revoke
the punishment; because they sell the righteous for silver, and
the needy for a pair of shoes—they that trample the head of the
poor into the dust of the earth, and turn aside the way of the
afflicted; a man and his father go in to the same maiden, so that
my holy name is profaned." Here, "In one breath," observes
Sider, "God condemns both sexual misconduct and legalized
oppression of the poor. Sexual sins and economic injustice are
equally displeasing to God."[68]

To me as a South African Christian the structural question
became a particular challenge. South African structures were
not only frustrating true social progress but also full human happiness and dignity. Shouldn't they be challenged? Especially
when one saw a generation of young blacks slowly turning away
from the Christian gospel because it seemed to have no relevance to the issues and pains they were facing.

Soweto

In 1970 African Enterprise conducted a major mission in
Soweto. Young blacks were losing patience with the Christian
church and becoming suspicious of the Bible. "Why do the
authorities give us the Bible free but make us pay for our school-
books?" they demanded as we visited high schools. "It must be
the book of the status quo, something to keep us quiet." The
place was clearly simmering.

"Soweto is going to blow," I told the mayor of Johannesburg.
We told white Christians too. "Surely it can't be that bad," they
said. "Things will work themselves out."

Six years later, as the whole world knows, Soweto did blow.
Hundreds died as the army and police quelled the rioting. Even-
tually the rioting stopped. But the alienation of thousands of
teenagers from the gospel did not and has not stopped. The

result of Christian silence and lack of adequate political reform has pushed multitudes of young blacks toward the Marxist option at the expense of the Christian one.

Playing into Marxist Hands

When Christians stand aloof from socio-political issues we play right into the hands of the Marxists. We verify their hypothesis that church members actually want to escape from the world and want their churches to escape with them.

Wasn't that the case with Karl Marx himself? The young Marx saw himself as "an alienated man," and he was. He and his family suffered from discriminatory anti-Jewish laws in his Prussian homeland. As he grew up in his mid-nineteenth-century world he saw human suffering, exploitation, and class oppression all around him: the rich getting richer, the poor getting poorer. He saw, for example, awful poverty among the Mosel wine-growers. They typified the plight of the underpaid worker and the consequences of trade agreements that protect vested self-interest among those with power and privilege. He saw gags on the press so that the voice of the poor could not be heard. He saw pitiful living conditions for the masses of Europe. He saw humanity and dignity constantly destroyed or undermined as people were economically and politically manipulated. He found a kindred spirit in Friedrich Engels, who had been gathering material for a new book to be titled *The Condition of the Working Classes in England in 1844*.

Not only did Marx see this pitiful unhappiness, "suffering humanity" as he called it, but he saw a disengaged, aloof church sitting in the grandstands—detached, preoccupied with itself, concerned "not to be involved in politics." The Prussian state church had become a pathetic caricature of what true Christianity was all about. Not only was it unconcerned about those outside its ranks, but in his judgment it led those it captured to a passive "quietist" attitude to social ills. Religion, he therefore concluded, was "the opiate of the people."[69]

Girardi, a Catholic contributor to the Christian-Marxist dialogue, affirms that historical events support that view: "Whenever the working class expressed its aspirations and demands, the church stood with the opposition, against the workers. The workers grew up, therefore, considering the church as their class enemy."[70] In other words, it is claimed, religion diverts attention from the needs of real people in sometimes desperate situations.

No wonder the British working class turned away from the gospel in the mid-nineteenth century and has never really gotten back to it. The trouble was that personal ethics and social ethics simply never got together. In spite of crowded churches, the social injustices of the time went unchallenged. The church, which had tremendous influence, failed to use it for the healing and transformation of the society around it. Then came disillusionment among the working classes which has continued to this day. They had seen religion that had no challenge to the conscience of the nation. The lessons for our present time are self-evident.

Back to the Law of Love

Back to the basic question as to the right way through this issue for Christians. The answer surely is that it has to be the way of love. As far as biblical principles are concerned, we can not get away from the primacy of the law of love. Perhaps the most political chapter in the Bible is 1 Corinthians 13. Here is the ultimate call to care. Here is the expanded version of Jesus' words, "Whatever you wish that men would do to you, do so to them" (Matt. 7:12). Put differently, "Love your neighbor as yourself" (Matt. 22:39).

Jesus has identified with us incarnationally in our lostness, sin, and need and has said to his church, "As the Father has sent me, even so I send you" (John 20:21). In his love, compassion, and care, he has not only given us a message, but a model: incarnational evangelism and Christian social concern. There are only two options vis a vis the world—either to turn our backs on it in rejection or to face it in compassion, to escape from it or to get involved in it. We can ignore its brokenness or seek to heal its brokenness. The former represents a failure of love, the latter an expression of it.

The law of love also answers the question as to how the Christian opposes injustice in a way that is different from, let's say, how the opposition political party would do it. Love again is a sure guide. Love requires that we hate sin but love the sinner. It requires that we abominate injustice but seek to help the perpetrators of it to see another way. Love demands that we rebuke discriminators but relate to them as precious humans for whom Christ also died. In the South African setup many of us in the English churches have simply denounced Afrikaners and the Afrikaans government without seriously facing the demands of love to care for them, relate to them, pray for them, and seek to be of service to them.

To come back to that squatter business, some South African government apologists would even make a Christian case that they are trying to terminate the hazards of overcrowding the edges of big cities with the unemployed and the poverty-stricken. Removing them prevents mass slums from developing, they would argue. Of course it is simplest to dismiss all such talk as shallow rationalization for the implementation of a basically un-Christian political ideology. But love also requires us to recognize the massive complexities that lawmakers do in fact face in coping with the average modern country, though no excuse can ever be made for brutal methodologies in carrying out even the noblest political schemes.

Love and the Lawmaker

Having said that, however, how do lawmakers build love into political policies and structures? The first point to establish is that the love of Christ will also be the love of right. The late Edgar Brookes put it this way:

> Right consists of a deep respect for personality, combined with a free love of truth. This is that justice by which every so-called 'law' is to be tested.[71] All power is dangerous unless

it is controlled by right. The power of the State, inevitable and
not immoral, can become a raging peril, unless right, and not
mere law, limits its exercise. Right or righteousness or justice—use whichever term you prefer—is the fact which can
make power a blessing...And what love really means in
political life is in the recognition of the other man as a person
to be cared for, to be seen in his infinite possibilities as a
human being.[72]

A refinement of that observation was eloquently made by
Reinhold Niebuhr in his book *An Interpretation of Christian Ethics*.
Recognizing the complexity of human and political situations,
and the difficulty of operating the love ethic in ideal categories,
Niebuhr notes that the problem of politics is how to bring all the
complex mix of human vested interests into some kind of order
so that people are somehow subtly constrained to work toward
one another's mutual benefit. He observes that in collective
human behavior, the selfish passions of people are so strong that
the only way to get any social harmony is to neutralize these
self-centered forces not only by introducing different balances of
power, along with various legal restraints, but also by finding
ways and means of harnessing even the selfish devices of man for
positive social ends that can benefit all!

All those possibilities, we must admit, represent something
less than the ideal of love. Yet the law of love has surely got to be
involved in all approximations of justice. Niebuhr emphasizes
that perhaps the best way forward for Christians is to define
their political ideals in terms of *freedom and equality*. Our highest
good, therefore, will consist in *freedom* to develop the essential
potentialities of our natures without hindrance. This is what
lawmakers who embrace the Christian ideal must recognize.

But since people live in social contexts where other human
beings are also competing with them for the opportunity of a
fuller life, the other highest good is *equality*. Otherwise we have
no means of deciding between conflicting human interests
except that which equates the worth of all the different compet-

ing individuals. Of course we will never achieve perfect equality in our societies, but Christians at least should never rest in an acceptance of inequalities.

On the other hand, both the governing and the governed need to recognize that the principles of equality and of justice are in fact only approximations of the law of love in the kind of imperfect world we have. That insight should slow us down a bit in terms of facile and crude judgments on everything our political leaders do. As the saying goes, it is easier to shoot a lark than sing its song. Perhaps that is why Paul so strongly urged Christians to pray for political leaders (1 Tim. 2:1-2). The fact is that their task is almost impossible.

I have found it a challenge and a blessing to seek to pray regularly and sometimes daily for six or seven South African political leaders, including the prime minister—men who span the total spectrum from status-quo to revolutionary zealot. My prayer is that each may find "the mind of Christ." If all seven converged on that "mind," we'd have a solution for South Africa.

Romans 13 and Obedience

What if the law of love leads us to challenge, criticize, or even disobey the state? How can we reconcile that with Paul's words in Romans 13, to be subject to the powers that be, seeing "the powers that be are ordained of God" (Rom. 13:1 KJV).

At the Pan African Christian Leadership Assembly in Nairobi in 1976 we had a fascinating panel on this subject of church and state relationships. Participants were Gottfried Osei-Mensah of Ghana, Philemon Quaye also of Ghana (one of his country's ambassadors), David Bosch of South Africa, and Itofo Bokeleale of Zaire.

Panel participants recognized the problem in defining the degree to which the church should give uncritical support and obedience to the state, especially when there was a serious discrepancy between the state's activity and the church's understanding of the biblical requirements for the state. Coming to

Romans 13, the panel did not understand this passage as requiring uncritical obedience to the powers that be. It was noted that when Paul wrote that chapter he knew of biblical examples of civil disobedience: Moses challenging the legitimate authority of Pharaoh, Samuel rebuking King Saul, Daniel defying Nebuchadnezzar. So we must not make Romans 13 too absolute, construing it to mean that any form of protest against a legitimate government is out of the question for a Christian.

Two Limits
Romans 13 does not simply speak of the legitimate power of the state, but of the proper limits to the power of the state. Those limits are two in number. The first limiting factor is that the state's authority is under God. The state is to be "God's servant" (verse 4). In other words the state has its true legitimacy only as it works according to what God expects it to do as his serving instrument functioning under him. So Romans 13 has to be set alongside Revelation 13 which describes a state that has become inhuman and unjust. The church must be able to distinguish in which category a given government falls.

The second limit on the state's authority is also found in verse 4. The state is to be "God's servant for *your good*." It exists for the good, not the harm, of those in it and under it. The state is not just God's servant. It is the people's. It not only serves God, it serves human beings. Here is the basis and criterion for protest. When the state ceases to serve God and its people, it deserves the criticism if not the condemnation of Christians. The same conscience that obeys the government may in some cases disobey it.

The panel also saw special significance in 1 Timothy 2:1-2, where the supreme responsibility of the church toward the state is seen as intercession. Prayer is in some ways, as David Bosch stressed, the most radical form of the church's involvement in government.

The government as such cannot pray for itself. It is dependent on the prayers of the church. Indeed, even in times of state persecution, the church will pray for the state and be its conscience. The church will pray even for the unjust state. The church will defend the state against the state and this will be its most radical means of saving and repairing the state.[73]

The Jesus way in the world commits us to the politics of love. What a challenge to allow the Spirit's fruit of love to send us out in care for the world, in prayer for political leaders, in work for better societies, and in demonstration to both powerless and powerful that Jesus is the Way, the Truth, and the Life.

17

Witness
to the
World

You shall receive power when the
Holy Spirit has come upon you; and you
shall be my witnesses...
Jesus, Acts 1:8

BACK IN 1955 WHEN ROBERT FOOTNER LED ME into personal discovery of Jesus Christ as Savior and Lord, I couldn't for the life
of me have told you what the word *evangelism* meant. The concept of *witness* likewise was totally foreign to me.

On the other hand I reflect during a six-month spell of prep-
school teaching, after leaving school and before going to Cambridge, that I did want to influence all those eager little boys
"toward Christianity." That, like motherhood and helping little
old ladies, I deemed a good thing. But neither with those boys or
with friends could I ever say more than "Wouldn't you like to
come to church with me?" In one particular fit of daring I read a
section of *The Greatest Thing in the World* to the senior dormitory of
the school before putting their lights out. I regarded it as an act
of enormous boldness. Then along with teaching my Latin and
French classes I got landed with *Scripture* for most of the school

because no one else wanted to do it. I have no recollection of what I taught them—except that I had modestly benevolent Christian feelings toward my young victims and hoped they would all end up respectable Anglican communicants.

Then came October 1955 and the wonder of conversion to Christ. The Holy Spirit entered my heart as I received Christ and from that very day I began to witness to him. After the Sunday evening service of the Cambridge Inter-Collegiate Christian Union (CICCU), my commitment having taken place that morning, I jumped on my bicycle and roared round to the digs of an old school friend and told him about this incredible person, the Lord Jesus, whom I had come to know that very day. He was staggered because he had known me at Michaelhouse only as sort of churchy. This was something different. I now was before him as a witness to Jesus Christ and what he had done in my life that very day. He looked shaken.

In a short time half my college knew me as a pretty fiery fellow religiously, "a Hot Prot," one friend labeled me. I simply could not keep quiet about what I had found. In retrospect, my irrepressible acts of witness were often ill-advised, insensitive, and tactless. I even appeared to terrify the chaplain. On the other hand, the discovery of new life, love, meaning, purpose, peace, new everything was hardly something to suppress. Wisdom and discretion in sharing about it would have to come later, though I've since learned that a person can be tactful and cautious unto death, inhibited from any kind of witness. Alas when that happens.

What all that early enthusiasm taught me is that the presence of the Holy Spirit along with one's desire and ability to witness were integrally related. That is true in the individual life as well as in the corporate life of the church. When the Spirit is most truly at work, there you will find new burdens and commitments to witness to the person and work of Jesus. After all, that is the Spirit's ministry, whether people call themselves charismatics, Pentecostals, ecumenicals, Reformed, or whatever. To be a Christian at all is to be a Holy Spirit person and therefore to be a witness to Jesus. "He [the Spirit] will bear witness to me," Jesus said (John 15:26) and "He will glorify me, for he will take what is mine and declare it to you" (John 16:14).

The Holy Spirit is the Spirit of mission. The acid test therefore of supposedly renewed individuals and of renewal as a whole is whether it produces new impulses of evangelism and missionary outreach to a lost world. The Spirit was given not so that we might have lovely spiritual experiences and beautiful fellowship in the church, but so that we might be equipped to be witnesses to Jesus in Jerusalem, Judea, Samaria, and to the uttermost parts of the earth.

The Spirit of Mission

Not surprisingly, the work of the Spirit therefore in the book of Acts is a missionary work. It is the story of people being mightily activated to evangelism. The book of Acts reveals the Holy Spirit as the great commander-in-chief of the missionary enterprise as it spread more and more widely throughout the Mediterranean world.

The Spirit came upon those first believers at Pentecost and galvanized Peter into a dynamic Pentecostal address that won three thousand to Christ (Acts 2). "Filled with the Holy Spirit" (Acts 4:8), Peter was able to make his defense before the Sanhedrin after he had healed the lame man at the "Gate Beautiful." The Holy Spirit inspired the apostolic group to speak "the word with boldness" (Acts 4:31). The Holy Spirit guided Philip in his word to the Ethiopian eunuch (Acts 8:29), who in turn would go and penetrate the missionary frontiers of Africa for the cause of Christ. It was the Holy Spirit who "comforted" the church "throughout all Judea, Galilee and Samaria" so that it had peace, was built up, and was multiplied (Acts 9:31).

How spectacular was the Spirit's word to Peter, "Rise and go" (Acts 10:20), sending him to evangelize Cornelius and his family, thereby opening up the whole Christian mission to the gentile world.

Then almost as dramatically, the Holy Spirit interrupted a

beautiful time of worship, fasting, and fellowship in the Antioch church and said, "Set apart for me Barnabas and Saul for the work to which I have called them" (Acts 13:2). Maybe they had planned to settle down there for awhile. But no. *"Being sent out by the Holy Spirit,* they went down to Seleucia and from there sailed to Cyprus" (Acts 13:4). Thereafter we see the Holy Spirit directing missionary expansion, forbidding them to speak in Asia (Acts 16:7), not allowing them to go into Bithynia (Acts 16:7), but directing them by vision to Macedonia (Acts 16:10).

And so the apostles and others criss-crossed their world sharing the Good News of Jesus. Always it was the Holy Spirit initiating and inspiring. More than that, he was always elevating Jesus. Nowhere do we see a stress on the Holy Spirit per se, with Jesus being squeezed out, as if allegiance to him somehow revealed a lower-level walk of Christian experience.

Once those early Christians were on their way, nothing could stop them. They were, as one might say, an overwhelming minority. Not the opposition of Jewish religious orthodoxy, nor Roman political might, nor Greek intellectual sophistication, nor Mediterranean moral decadence could hold them back. When attacked, persecuted, and scattered, they just "went about preaching the Word" (Acts 8:4).

"Something like a forest fire had started . . . and it centered on Jesus. Those commissioned had begun in Jerusalem as instructed and, as instructed, they had not stopped there."[74] Certainly the early church, in the power of the Holy Spirit, faced the missionary task of their world with incredible dedication, faithfulness, courage, and effectiveness. What about us?

Testimony

My vision of witness to the world first became real when Billy Graham came to Cambridge not long after my conversion. I saw evangelism in action for the first time—though not without opposition and reservation from both within the church and out of it. Apart from the spirited correspondence in *The Times* when British Christians poured out their views regarding an evangelist being let loose in the supposedly rarified intellectual atmosphere of Cambridge, there was also vigorous opposition in Cambridge itself. Students threatening to kidnap the evangelist were deliciously foiled; Billy Graham was smuggled into Cambridge by some ingenious back door.

In his first Bible study to the CICCU, fireworks were lobbed into the Union Debating Chamber, and I recollect the startled British jumping as the vicious little explosives detonated at their feet. It's amazing what a good firecracker can do for the prayer life! That was when I first began to see that evangelism and witness often produce opposition. No wonder the early church had to pray for boldness through the Holy Spirit.

I also saw the spiritual hunger of the human heart because, in spite of all the resistance and turmoil elicited by Graham's presence, the majority of the university turned out in force to hear the gospel preached. Hundreds responded to the claims and call of our Lord Jesus. In spite of lots of academic learning, the hearts of students were yearning for reality, peace, and purpose.

Contemporary Challenge

The world's spiritual need has escalated spectacularly with the population explosion. Christian statisticians tell us now that somewhere in the region of three billion people have yet to hear the message of Christ. Most of those have not even heard the name of Christ, let alone had an intelligible presentation of the gospel made to them to which they could respond positively or negatively. A friend of mine in the Orient asked a young student if he had heard of Jesus Christ and his reply was "Is that a new kind of soap?"

Certainly the task before us is daunting. It has been said that if we were to bring 50,000 people a day from among this number of unreached into a stadium so that Billy Graham could preach to them, and to a different crowd each day, it would still take more than 165 years to let all those billions hear the gospel clearly just one time. In the meantime, billions more would be born. That is the challenge facing the church of Christ at this time. The task is made more daunting by the fact that so many Christians have lost their vision for evangelism, especially for world missions. In 1975 a group of British Christian leaders were surveyed about world missions. Of them 23 percent thought missions were optional, 21 percent saw it as a duty, though a nuisance, and 16 percent no longer thought it concerned the western church. An extraordinary state of affairs. Surely if the renewing work of the Holy Spirit around the world has a unique contribution to bring for our time, it should be in inspiring God's people the world over with the evangelistic and missionary enterprise.

Speaking at the Lausanne International Congress on World Evangelization in 1974, Billy Graham said:

> Many sincere Christians around the world are concerned for evangelism. They are delighted at evangelizing in their own communities and even in their own countries. But they do not see God's big picture of "world need" and the "global responsibility" that he has put on the church in his world. The Christians in Nigeria are not just to evangelize Nigeria, nor the Christians in Peru just the people in Peru. God's heartbeat is for the world.

David Bryant, an American missionary thinker, has challenged the church to step out of our pea-sized Christianity to stand in the immense gap between God's worldwide purpose and the fulfillment of it. He believes that a new breed of "World Christians" should step into the gap.

> World Christians are day to day disciples for whom Christ's global cause has become the integrating, overriding priority for all that He is for them. As disciples should, they actively investigate all that their Master's Great Commission means. Then they act on what they learn . . . World Christians are Christians whose life directions have been solidly transformed by a world vision.

> Some World Christians are missionaries who stand in the gap by physically crossing major human barriers (cultural,

political, etc.) to bring the gospel to those who can hear no other way. But every Christian is meant to be a World Christian, whether you physically go or stay at home to provide the sacrificial love, prayers, training, money, and quality of corporate life that backs the witness of those that go.[75]

Why Bother?

Does it matter? Will it make any difference, either now or after people die? After all, aren't people managing pretty well? Isn't their religion a private personal matter with which we have no right to interfere? "Pie in the sky when we die by and by" seems to have almost no appeal to "live-it-up-now" twentieth-century men and women. Divine condemnation or eternal separation from God is a concept that is counted antidiluvian by most moderns—until they stare death in the face.

The question "Why bother?" is an important one. The issue first came deeply before my mind in Madison Square Garden in New York during Billy Graham's crusade there in 1957. The fact that I was there at all, I believe, was part of the Lord's own special plan for my life.

In early '57 I heard of some very cheap student charter flights from London to New York. Those were the days! I booked, and although the plane had three false starts trying to get away from London because of the precarious state of its mechanical innards, we finally made it. Gracious relatives in New York took me in, and I had my first exhilarating taste of the New World.

By then I was beginning to think of theological training. Not being a candidate for the ordained Anglican ministry, I could not secure a scholarship to an English theological college. That led me to think of the U.S. But who could advise me about seminaries? I knew no Christians in the States at all. But there was that distant hero, Billy Graham. I heard he had a crusade on in New York. I would write to him. My letter, along with thousands of others filling multiple bags of mail, went into the Crusade office. I naively believed he might get it. That was not to be. God had other plans.

Among the teams of people helping to sort mail was an American Japanese student from Fuller Seminary named Harry Kawahara. The mail bag with my letter landed on his desk. He opened my letter, read it, and phoned me. I was mad with excitement when I was called to the phone for a call from the Crusade office. "Billy Graham is phoning me," I exulted. My disappointment that it was a mere seminary student from who knows where was scarcely concealed, I suspect, in my flat response to the voice on the other end.

"You want to know about seminaries?" asked Harry.

"Indeed," I replied.

"Well, why not come down to the Garden? Come to a Crusade meeting and we can talk about it."

I went, probably one of the most momentous things I ever did. My whole future destiny turned on that phone call and that visit to Madison Square Garden. There I received my call to evangelism and also set my face toward Fuller Seminary and all it meant for my later life, ministry, and the founding of African Enterprise with Dr. Charles Fuller's help.

While listening many evenings to the preaching of the gospel in Madison Square Garden I began to come to terms with three basic reasons why I ought personally to bother about world evangelization: They were:

—because Christ commands us to bother. He urges us to take the gospel to all the world.

—because men and women without Christ are lost.

—because the deep and desperate needs of human beings can be fully met only through the transforming, reconciling, and saving power of Jesus Christ.

Christ's Command

To come to Christ is to come to his Great Commission to go out into all the world and take the gospel to every creature. I couldn't get around the Great Commission without getting around Jesus altogether. Reaching out into all the world in his name became a matter of obedience. "As thou didst send me into the world, so I have sent them into the world" (John 17:18). "As the Father has sent me, even so I send you" (John 20:21).

Jesus made his mission the model of ours. Not only was his mission costly, compassionate, and humble, but it went out in penetration of the world. He moved into the nitty-gritty needs of the men and women around him.

Lostness?

The meetings in Madison Square Garden (which went on for some three months) also underscored people's lostness and longing to find their way home. Individual stories and testimonies night after night revealed that they felt like sheep without a shepherd. When they heard clear preaching of the gospel, they responded. Now, after twenty years of ministry, I am still convinced that there is nothing in time or eternity men and women need more than salvation in Christ. Otherwise they are lost both in time and in eternity.

I knew that this conviction would put me at odds with theological liberalism, which opts for a rather loose interpretation of the Bible, and which taught, in Reinhold Niebuhr's pithy phrase, that a god without wrath brought men without sin into a kingdom without judgment and to a Christ without a cross. That stance, popular in the latter part of the last century and in the early part of this century, has lingered on in much contemporary Christian thinking. Most believers in eras before our own accepted that people without Christ were lost. But early twentieth-century liberalism had collapsed that "saved-lost" division of humanity. People were seen as part of a general brotherhood of man under the benign and general fatherhood of God.

At seminary I read about the famous ecumenical conference in Jerusalem in 1928. Almost for the first time in such a gathering, I learned, there was no clear-cut biblical proclamation, but rather a religious syncretism basically saying that all religions were part of the way of God. Commenting on this, Bishop Stephen Neill once remarked that "this was the moment at which liberal theology exercised its most fatal influence on missionary thinking, the lowest valley out of which the missionary movement has ever since been trying to make its way."

Not long after that a book called *Rethinking Missions* by W. B. Hocking was published (1932). Hocking, a Harvard philosophy professor and prominent layman, stressed his view that the time had come to set the educational and other philanthropic aspects of mission work free from the work of conscious and direct evangelism. He saw the missionary as working to find the most harmonious coexistence with non-Christian religions so that each could stimulate the other in growth toward the ultimate goal of unity in the completest religious truth.[76]

A response came in a volume called *The Christian Message in a Non-Christian World* by Hendrik Kraemer (1938). The author warned of the dangers of this sort of thinking because it "blurs and relativizes the question of truth . . . It constitutes a perennial threat to the distinct character of the truth of the Christian message."[77] In other words, if we are placing Jesus among the general pantheon of religious leaders and prophets, saying there is nothing distinctive about him, we are in fact challenging his deity and the exclusiveness of his claims. We are denying his assertion that humankind is "lost" and that at the heart of his coming into the world was his intention to "seek and to save the lost" (Luke 19:10). If the lost will turn to him and repent they will not perish (Luke 13:3) but will have "eternal life" (John 3:16). There is no other way of salvation (John 14:6; Acts 4:12).

In 1973 I was thrown out of Uganda, my crime being that my passport announced me as a missionary. "Missionaries are no longer welcome," I was told. Men from Amin's security squad tracked me down and I was ordered to report to a particular official at the Foreign Affairs Department. While this man was out of the room collecting a form to declare me "undesirable," John Wilson, one of my African colleagues from Uganda, said to me: "This fellow's name is very interesting. It means 'Without him [i.e., Jesus] I will not get there [i.e., to heaven].' "

When the official returned to the room I commented on his interesting name. "I'm told it means 'Without him I will not get there.' Do you believe that?"

"Oh, no!" he snorted. "My parents believed that, but not I."

"Well, I believe it," I said, "and I hope you come to believe it too, because that is what the Bible says."

I believe that still. Without Jesus we will not get there. In both time and eternity we are lost without him. That is the Bad News. But, praise God, there is Good News. "God sent the Son into the world, *not* to condemn the world, but that the world might be saved through him" (John 3:17). Forgiveness and eternal salvation through Christ. That is worth heralding to the ends of the earth.

Human Needs

As compelling as any other reason for getting out to the world is the immense extent of human need on all sides. This need is felt and experienced in so many ways.

One of these is emptiness. Many psychiatrists believe that this is the chief neurosis and central problem of modern man. Pascal wrote about "the God-shaped vacuum in the human heart." It is not even that people do not know what they want, they often don't even have any clear idea of what they feel. A little girl once said to her father, "I want something, Daddy, but I don't know what." Many twentieth-century people are like that. They can identify with what T. S. Eliot wrote back in 1925:

We are the hollow men
We are the stuffed men
Leaning together
Headpiece filled with straw.

Loneliness, Boredom, and Anxiety

The problem of lostness is experienced also as loneliness. How many lonely people I have encountered. Many people, even when surrounded by swarms of other people, still feel totally isolated. Many people really fear finding themselves alone and so they don't find themselves at all.

The problem of lostness is also experienced as chronic boredom, a sense of futility, and that peculiar psychological pain and turmoil that we call anxiety. Yet Jesus said repeatedly, "Do not be anxious" (Matt. 6:25, 34; 24:6, etc.). St. Paul wrote, "Have no anxiety about anything" (Phil. 4:6). That is impossible apart from Christ.

Possessing a prescription for peace of mind and freedom from anxiety, how can the church refrain from taking its gospel to a lonely, bored, and anxiety-stricken world?

Alienation and Escape

Perhaps the greatest crusher of our times is alienation. Blacks are alienated from whites, husbands from wives, children from parents, business colleagues from one another, old from young. People are chronically at odds with each other. The average modern marriage lasts only seven or eight years, often less, and as a result even the institution of marriage is coming into question. It seems to be an unworkable relationship.

Multitudes of people take the escapist routes of illicit sex, extravagant drink, or enslaving drugs. All are cul-de-sacs. But in Jesus is a way out. Dare we keep such news to ourselves?

People sense that there must be some answers, whether they articulate that sense or not. In his *Story of Philosophy* Will Durant said:

> So much of our lives is meaningless—a self-cancelling vacillation and futility. But we strive with the chaos about us and within: and we want to believe all the while that there is something vital and significant in us, could we but decipher our souls. We want to understand. We want to seize the value and perspective of passing things and so pull ourselves up out of the maelstrom of daily circumstances.[78]

New Initiatives of Evangelism

In light of the overwhelming needs of modern times, dare Christians who have the ultimate answer in Jesus Christ remain silent? Dare we be part of a church that never looks beyond its own doors? Dare we embrace a Christian fellowship that is introverted and self-preoccupied with charismatic kicks at the expense of the pressing spiritual and physical needs outside? Believers who do those things fail their Lord, their church, their society, their world, their neighbors, and themselves.

With the tremendous spiritual energy that has been released into the church by the renewing activity of the Holy Spirit in modern times, we will quench that Spirit and hinder his working unless we look from the church to the world with massive new initiatives of evangelism, missionary enterprise, socio-political concern, and Christian witness. But how are we to do it?

How?

First, we must explore further the work of the Holy Spirit. As he is released more in us, he will make us not only shine more brightly with the character of Jesus Christ but burn more fully with a zeal to let his caring love be felt across the globe.

Nor will we bog down in the problems of vocabulary, semantics, and terminology but will press on to appropriate the Spirit's power to energize us for the task. Three billion people are waiting to hear the gospel, multitudes are oppressed, millions are hungry, countless relationships are daily shattered, and if we are only busy singing and clapping in our little religious ghettos then we can be quite sure that those untold millions will remain untold. They will never know the compassionate, practical care of our Lord.

Second, we will need to repent of what I call SIWs, a military term referring to Self-Inflicted Wounds. Nothing is more tragic than when the church participates in all sorts of acts by which it tears itself down. I don't believe that in African Enterprise we have ever had any of our projects immobilized by Marxists, pagans, free lovers, atheists, or Muslims. The only people who have ever torn down any Christian initiatives in which I have personally been involved have been other Christians. That is inexcusable; it will incur the judgment of God.

My plea therefore is that Christians should cooperate in holistic, incarnational witness to the world. Particularly is this true of those who share a high view of the Bible and an identical understanding of the deity of our Lord Jesus Christ, who believe in the importance of the Spirit's work—even if their vocabularies and terminologies are different.

However, this is not to be construed as a call for evangelical-charismatic-Pentecostal solidarity at the expense of total solidarity in the total church. All sections of the church need each other. No one has twenty-twenty vision on the truth of God. It takes the full-orbed whole church of Christ to reflect the full-orbed truth of the gospel of Christ. We don't have to agree in every detail. But we can make dramatic progress at this moment of history if we see other Christians not only as brothers and sisters, but also as our teachers, and if they will see us in the same light.

The new wine is there. But the old wineskins of rigidity, inflexible denominationalism, hide-bound traditionalism, and Christian factionalism often block its flow. The new wine being created by the work of the Spirit in the old wineskins must be released. And God will provide his own fresh wineskins. But first the old wineskins must burst. Only then will a thirsty world be able to drink.

I believe that God the Father, God the Son, and God the Holy Spirit are waiting for this. The world is waiting too. Let us therefore arise and go.

18
So What's the Difference?

Does the road wind uphill all the way?
Yes, to the very end.
Will the day's journey take
the whole long day?
From morn to night, my friend.
Christina Rossetti

FOR ME THE ROAD CONTINUES TO WIND UPHILL. A deeper appropriation of the Spirit's work has not provided any shortcut to spiritual maturity. A number of my old anxieties, insecurities, and irrational fears are still with me, though less pronounced. Nor am I now the model husband or father or colleague.

That may disappoint some who have followed me through these pages hoping for some dramatic word that I had now found the way to live a peerless Christian life. But to indicate that would be to depart from the facts. If anything, a deeper insight into the Spirit's ways has brought me to a deeper sense of just how far I have to go, just how drastically my old nature still needs dealing with. On the other hand, my yearning to do better for the Lord and to strive upward for his purpose is undoubtedly greater. In spite of both failures and lapses I press on with genuinely renewed determination.

To be frank, I have been disappointed that the change in me has been as modest as it has been. Am I more incorrigible than others, even for the Holy Spirit of God? I don't know. But the battle for holiness of character, charity of heart, and consistency of life goes on. I should have known that, because this is Scripture's word from cover to cover.

"For the Lord disciplines him whom he loves, and chastises every son whom he receives...For the moment all discipline seems painful rather than pleasant; later it yields the peaceful fruit of righteousness to those who have been trained by it" (Heb. 12:6,11).

"Count it all joy, my brethren, *when* [not if!] you meet various trials, for you know that the testing of your faith produces steadfastness. And let steadfastness have its full effect, that you may be perfect and complete, lacking in nothing" (James 1:2–4).

"Beloved, do not be surprised at the fiery ordeal which comes upon you to prove you, as though something strange were happening to you" (1 Pet. 4:12).

Those Scriptures indicate that God is going to be working on our characters all our days. The Spirit's work is an integral aspect of the process, but it offers no magical shortcuts.

Positive Changes

The renewing work of the Spirit has truly changed both my attitude to and my experience of Christian worship. That has been lasting and real and ever deepening. In my pre-Milner Park days I enjoyed Christian singing, but the yearning of my heart to worship the living God—really connect with God in praise—was not there in the same way. I could never quite come to terms with the psalmists' endless fixation on praising God, not only with all voices, but with the most unconservative range of musical instruments, trumpet, lute, harp, timbrel, strings, pipe, even "with loud clashing cymbals" (Ps. 150:3–5). And *dance*.

Now my desire to praise God with freedom of expression and with every musical means at our disposal is real and deep. Worship, which meant little before, means a great deal now. I have been freed up from many previous inhibitions. I can even, on rare occasions where it is not ruled out as shockingly inappropriate, dance a little jig before the Lord and not feel that lightning will strike! That has been exhilarating.

Ministry

Another plus lies in my deeper ability to trust the sovereignty of the Holy Spirit in bringing results from evangelistic preaching. "No one can say 'Jesus is Lord' except by the Holy Spirit" (1 Cor. 12:3). It is his prerogative to bring results. A grasp of that fact prevents inflation when one sees results and deflation when one does not. We can therefore relax into his purposes and plans as we preach the gospel.

In my ministry I no longer fear praying for the healing of people at the end of an evangelistic meeting or whenever called on to do so. Previously I felt paralyzed in this area. I knew of excesses on the Christian lunatic fringe and I feared seeming to fail if nothing happened. I am now willing, particularly in the concept of shared ministry with others in the body of Christ, to pray for those who need healing. And how wonderful it has been to see numbers of people authentically healed in such times of prayer. Not usually anything wildly dramatic, as some can report, but generally a quiet but real work of healing grace, perhaps that night or the next day or over a period of time.

I hope to develop in this dimension as my confidence and understanding deepen. But the point is that I am more open to the miraculous intervention of God in this way than I was before.

Guidance

Earlier teaching and conditioning introduced me to orthodox principles of guidance through God's Word, through the counsel of friends, through the peace of God ruling in one's heart, through the inner whisper of the Spirit, and through the circumstantial opening and closing of doors.

Now, by opening up to the wider possibilities of the Spirit, I have come to see that his guidance can come through *"vision,"* as when Paul received the Macedonian call in Acts 16:9, through *angelic testimony,* as when Paul got the word in Acts 27:23 that none on the ship to Rome would be lost as a result of the storm, or through *prophetic utterance*, as when Agabus was used to alert the Antioch church to imminent famine and the need to send relief to Judea (Acts 11:28–29).

There is also the extraordinary significance in the Scriptures given to dreams. Not that one dare ascribe every dream to the Spirit of God—because the Scriptures clearly warn against "lying dreams" (Jer. 23:32). But from Genesis 20:3, where God "came to Abimelech in a dream," on into the New Testament where "an angel of the Lord appeared to Joseph in a dream" (Matt. 1:20), divine use of the subconscious dream life to communicate God's mind has been a reality. Why should it stop? Since 1977 I have had several meaningful experiences of being guided during my sleep. Maybe that's the only time the Lord can get me when I'm not answering back. Also, it was a series of dreams about my alienated friends Jim and Mary that finally led me to be reconciled to them just before the 1977 conference.

Interestingly, Richard Foster in his little classic, *Celebration of Discipline,* points out that "for fifteen centuries Christians over-whelmingly considered dreams as a natural way in which the spiritual world broke into our lives."[79] He then quotes Morton Kelsey's assertion that "every major Father of the early Church, from Justin Martyr to Irenaeus, from Clement and Tertullian to Origen and Cyprian, believed that dreams were a means of revelation." Foster bemoans the fact that "with the rationalism of the Renaissance came a certain skepticism about dreams." But if in the Scriptures God used dreams to speak to his people, why should he not do so now?

Is it not in fact just a matter of opening up to all the scriptural options and evidence of a supernatural God? This is something the Spirit seems to do. He reworks our presuppositional world, as it were, thus preventing us from screening out by some naturalistic presupposition those miraculous workings of God that are evident in both Old and New Testaments.

Reading All Scripture

That brings us to another bonus, the Spirit's way of getting us to read the whole Bible without prejudice. In the last years I have found myself facing the Spirit-inspired Scriptures with a greater degree of openness to everything they say. Not that I am referring to any doubt as to Scripture's inspiration and authority, nor am I wanting to deny interpretational or hermeneutical problems that do, I know, exist. But I also know that like Martin Luther who judged the epistle of James "a right strawy epistle" because it didn't seem to speak of justification by faith, so we all tend to filter Scripture through our own limited experience. We ride high on certain passages, on our strong points, on what our theological background has decreed as normative. We ignore or subconsciously discard what is outside our experience, our tradition, or the theologically acceptable practice of our denomination, circle, or group.

Social activists thus often ignore the Scriptures on new birth, salvation, human lostness, and evangelism. Many evangelicals overlook prophecy, tongues, dreams, visions, or healing. Charismatics and Pentecostals will in many instances ignore Jesus' injunctions about clothing the naked, feeding the hungry, visiting the prisoner, or taking in the stranger. And so on. We all tend to live in spiritually selective categories based on our selective reading of Scripture. Although I still do this to some degree, I do it much less than before. I have become more open to all Scripture. That has been exciting.

Working with God

Another area where a deepening grasp of the Spirit's work has been helpful lies in my developing aversion to working *for* God on my own agenda as distinct from working *with* God on his. No longer do I want to dash with quite the same impetuosity into my own plans and then drag God in to bless them. What a joy now to relax into the Spirit's agenda and seek to cooperate with the Father's plans rather than my own.

In this connection the beautiful picture in Isaiah 40:30-31 comes to mean so much. There the prophet notes that "even youths shall faint and be weary, and young men shall fall exhausted; but they who wait for the Lord shall renew their strength, they shall mount up with wings like eagles, they shall run and not be weary, they shall walk and not faint." The eagle is a bird of distinctive flight habits. One of these is to wait for the thermals or updrafts of air by which it can mount to incredible altitudes. The eagle doesn't waste its energy by attempting such feats on its own strength. It mounts on the power of the thermal. And it waits for that power.

We are to wait on the thermals or updrafts of what God is doing and where He is going by his Spirit. Then we simply get in on his agenda. In the Spirit we mount up with wings like eagles. We run and are not weary. We walk and do not faint. We are no longer working for God, but with him.

Yes, that's the ideal, and it's a thrilling one to aim for. So the question for the evangelist who contemplates where to go now or what to do next is simply "Where are God's thermals?"

Family Life

This principle of walking in the Spirit's agenda also has relevance for family life. As the inspirer of *agape* love, the Holy Spirit is very much the Spirit of the family. For example, if the Spirit is the one in whose agenda an individual is to walk, then he will know just what absences one's family can sustain as a result of an itinerant ministry or a lifestyle of absenteeism. I have to believe, and do, that the Holy Spirit is deeply concerned for my wife Carol and for my children, Catherine, Debbie, and Martin—for us as a family. So he will not lead me into anything that is emotionally or relationally destructive for them. How important, then, only to be away in travel when he says so.

The other day Marty, age seven, put his little arms around me as I was leaving for an eight-day absence on a citywide mission.

"Daddy," he said, "you think a week is a short time. I think it is a long time." All I could do was hug him tight. And reflect. Yet in that instance I knew so clearly that the Lord was guiding me into that mission. The signs and sense of rightness were very clear. I was walking at that moment in the Spirit's agenda for both my ministry and my family. So I could know that all would be well with Marty and the others. The Spirit would see to that.

Then there is this precious thing of *agape* love, God's love—God's "in spite of" love. It loves in spite of weaknesses in the beloved. It is the love that keeps on loving even when it sees faults. If the fruit of the Spirit is love, then the Spirit is the fundamental prerequisite in the lives of husband and wife. Carol and I have found that our love and commitment to each other are constantly renewed through our common Lord.

Like any couple we have our ups and downs, our dry patches, but the Spirit constantly restores us. More than that, he convicts of sin and of those "little foxes that spoil the vineyards" (Song of Sol. 2:15). What wrecks marriages is SIN—sometimes big Goliaths of sin, other times little foxes of sin. How marvelous to have in the Spirit an inbuilt convictor of sin, whose job is to alert us to either Goliaths or little foxes. He tells us when we are drifting from the Lord's way and hurting or imperiling a relationship. As he shows us what we are doing wrong in our marriage, we are able to confess this to God, or to our partner, or to both. Carol and I have learned this. The way of forgiveness, apology, and reconciliation is the way of marital safety.

Then there is the matter of priorities. I've sometimes said to Carol, "Sweetheart, you are my Number Two." She is my Number Two relationship, next to Jesus himself. She must not be Number One, where Jesus belongs, nor Number Three or Four, after my work or organization or any other human relationship. The Spirit's work is to keep her my Number Two. The fact is, I never made the kind of vows to evangelism or African Enterprise or to any other human being that I made to her. It is the Spirit's task, I believe, as the giver of love, to keep it that way. The Holy Spirit is the guardian of family life.

Building the Body

It will not surprise anyone who has followed me through these pages that my own quest to know more of the Spirit's working should have resulted in an ever deepening commitment to the building up of the body of Christ. In one sense that is what this book has been about, but I must re-declare it as a parting shot.

We need one another. Therefore the lines of estrangement within the body of Christ must be dissolved by a balancing understanding of the Spirit's way in assigning to each of us different gifts and insights. There seems to me no reason why we cannot find a Christian lifestyle of integrating spirituality that can move between different poles of Christian insight without insecurity, threat, or fear. Committed to that, we can all develop into the ideal once verbalized as *ecclesia reformata semper reformanda*—a reformed church always reforming. Ghetto-style living prevents this.

Nor will such reformation happen through facile judgments of supposedly renewed believers that all denominations or groups or individuals who do not think or act or respond as they do are "dead or dying" and therefore are to be forsaken for pastures new, as if those new pastures will forever avoid the same problems. If we are giving up on each other, or if we separate from each other on those grounds, we betray that patience of God which has not yet given up on us. Imagine if the Corinthian church had been abandoned by St. Paul or given up as a lost cause by the Lord himself. And what of all those defective churches in the book of Revelation that received the Spirit's letters of admonition? What if all the "true blue" renewed believers had left those fellowships for some promised land of ecclesiastical purity and perfected spiritual power!

One can of course sympathize with people who despair of "stick-in-the-mud" congregations or of denominations that won't move into the new day of greater life in the Spirit. The hiving off into separatist fellowships or isolated house churches of those who have thus lost hope is up to a point understandable.

Nevertheless I remain personally persuaded that while this may bring short-term gains it is more likely, if church history is anything to go by, to bring long-term losses to the body of Christ as a whole.

Richard Lovelace, the New England historian of spiritual renewal, brings his judgment:

> Revival and division are ultimately antithetical. . . the hope of renewal is ultimately bound up with church unity. . . dividing the church in the interest of renewing it is no more feasible than severing the parts of a body to improve its health. Even if the severed parts survive, they suffer loss and they will never function properly until they are re-united in fellowship. Leaders who secede from imperfect denominations and denominations which eject imperfect leadership simply lose the values of the group they reject while they ensure the unrestrained growth of its defects in a body of future converts.[80]

In one sense one could say that the separatist mentality is a form of pride. It says, "We're better than you or spiritually purer than you." Writing about the eighteenth-century revival in New England, Jonathan Edwards noted that "the spiritually proud person is apt to find fault with other saints, that they are low in grace; and to be much in observance of how cold and dead they are."[81] Richard Lovelace comments:

> Under the guise of prophetic righteousness, pride can move awakened believers to censorious attacks on other Christians, a lack of meekness in rebuking those who really need it and a hair-trigger readiness to separate from those less holy or less orthodox. It can do things to Christians which make their religion grate painfully on the sensibilities of fellow-Christians.[82]

Once again the inimitable Jonathan Edwards got it in a nutshell when he spoke from the renewal experiences of nearly two centuries ago.

Spiritual pride commonly occasions a certain stiffness and inflexibility in persons, in their own judgment and their own way: whereas the eminently humble person, though he be inflexible in his duty, and in those things wherein God's honour is concerned... yet in other things he is of a pliable disposition... ready to pay deference to others' opinions. He loves to comply with their inclinations and has a heart that is tender and flexible, like a little child.[83]

And though he [the humble person] will not be a companion with one that is visibly Christ's enemy... yet he does not love the appearance of an open separation from visible Christians... and will as much as possible shun all appearances of a superiority, or distinguishing himself as better than others.[84]

In these last years that spirit has become more and more beautiful to me. In other words, my own ongoing pilgrimage in the Spirit is committing me more deeply in mercy to the whole church of Christ. I know that it is the mercy of both God and others that I must count on for myself and for my own progress in the body.

Working on the Wrap-Up

To conclude, if I were to try and put in a nutshell what these last years have done for me I would say they have pressed me more and more to work on the wrap-up of the gospel. That this is both worthwhile and possible has been underlined in a thousand ways both in Africa and overseas. For example, this conviction was confirmed during the two Spring Harvest conferences in North Wales where I was privileged to minister in April 1982.

What encouraged me there was to find my own quest reflected in thousands of people, many of them quite young, who were also working on a wrap-up of the gospel embracing zealous evangelism, sane and gentle renewal, profound social concern, deep marital commitments, and solid biblical theology. Thus they were as concerned to see the "Siberian Seven" freed (seven Russian Christians who sought asylum in the U.S. Embassy in Moscow but whom the authorities would not allow to emigrate) and to see a peaceful way through the Falklands crisis which was then looming, as they were for the proposed evangelistic visits to Britain of Billy Graham and Luis Palau. On top of that they were allowing the Holy Spirit to be released in renewing power, in breathtaking worship, and in motivation of believers to deepened intercession and fasting. I thought that was great. The fact is that when the mix truly comes together it is almost intoxicating in its exhilaration, power, and appeal.

To embrace this wrap-up is to embrace the whole word of God, within the fellowship of the whole church of Christ, and to exercise the whole range of the Spirit's gifts in love and humility as he enables.

Not that this comprehensive, inclusive, holistic concern excludes or ignores the reality of specialized callings. We know "there are varieties of gifts, but the same Spirit; and there are varieties of service, but the same Lord; and there are varieties of workings, but it is the same God who inspires them all in every one" (1 Cor. 12:4–6). We need those who major in evangelism, social care, political protest, healing, renewal, pastoring, teaching, helping, administration. But the point is to make real room for one another and to take on one's heart the full range of the Spirit's concerns, even if one is not called oneself to give major or equal expression to each of those concerns.

For me the best statement of faith in the Holy Spirit is still Clause 4 of the Lausanne Covenant, because it so clearly sets the full range of the Spirit's work in the context of the mission of the church in the world. Mission and evangelism and reaching the world for Jesus Christ are still what it's basically all about. Surely all of us who love our Lord Jesus Christ can unite around the Covenant's affirmation of faith and purpose:

We believe in the power of the Holy Spirit. The Father sent His Spirit to bear witness to His Son; without His witness ours is futile. Conviction of sin, faith in Christ, new birth and

Christian growth are all His work. Further, the Holy Spirit is a missionary Spirit; thus evangelism should arise spontaneously from a Spirit-filled church. A church that is not a missionary church is contradicting itself and quenching the Spirit. Worldwide evangelization will become a realistic possibility only when the Spirit renews the Church in truth and wisdom, faith, holiness, love and power. We therefore call upon all Christians to pray for such a visitation of the sovereign Spirit of God that all His fruit may appear in all His people and that all His gifts may enrich the Body of Christ. Only then will the whole Church become a fit instrument in His hands, that the whole earth may hear His voice.

Appendix A

Prophecy in the
New Testament

The word *prophecy* is used basically in three ways in the New Testament.

First, it refers to the *announcement of a revelation from God.* The word is used that way in Acts 19:6, where the Holy Spirit "came on" some Ephesian disciples who then "spoke with tongues and prophesied" (cf. Acts 21:9). In his sermon on the day of Pentecost, Peter affirmed that Joel's prophecy was being fulfilled in that moment, because God had said, "On my menservants and my maidservants in those days I will pour out my Spirit; and they shall prophesy" (Acts 2:18). Paul said that "he who prophesies speaks to men for their upbuilding and encouragement and consolation"; that is, Paul said, "he who prophesies edifies the church" (1 Cor. 14:3–4). In the same passage Paul said explicitly that "prophecy is not for unbelievers but for believers" (1 Cor. 14:22). Thus in its primary meaning prophecy seems to be distinguished from evangelistic preaching and proclamation directed at non-Christians. On the other hand, prophecy on occasion resulted in the conversion of unbelievers (1 Cor. 14:24–25).

A second New Testament usage is *revelation of something for which the evidence is hidden*. For example, the chief priests and their henchmen taunted Jesus, saying "Prophesy to us, you Christ! Who is it that struck you?" (Matt. 26:68). The blow probably came from behind him, so Jesus was challenged to declare what had happened by the supernatural means of prophecy.

A third usage is *foretelling the future*. Thus "All the prophets and the law prophesied until John" (Matt. 11:13); "Well did Isaiah prophesy of you" (Matt. 15:7); and "The prophets who prophesied of the grace that was to be yours searched and inquired about this salvation" (1 Pet. 1:10).

Drawing together these threads, we can say that prophecy is a process whereby a believer, under the inspiration or special anointing of the Holy Spirit, declares or confirms the mind and will of God relating to the past, present, or future, in such a way as to edify Christians and on occasion to convince and convict outsiders. Hence the word of prophecy need not come directly from God in the first person singular, as in "I, the Lord, say to you. . ." I suspect that such direct prophetic words should be the exception rather than the rule. Yet if prophecy is declaring the word and will of God, it is no wonder that in 1 Corinthians 14 Paul began (14:1) and ended (14:39) by saying "earnestly desire to prophesy." Indeed, he said that gift or ability was to be sought "especially" (14:1).

A Gift
Although in the Old Testament prophecy was for a few select giants like Moses, Ezekiel, Jeremiah, or Daniel, in the New Testament it is for all believers. Every Christian is potentially a prophet, as a consequence of the pouring out of the Spirit on all flesh: "and they shall prophesy" (Acts 2:18). Paul told the Corinthians, "I want you all to speak in tongues, but even more

to prophesy" (1 Cor. 14:5). He said they should "earnestly desire to prophesy" (1 Cor. 14:39). Paul seemed to regard prophecy as the most important gift of utterance and perhaps of all gifts.

Ministry of the Prophet

Although Paul recognized that all Christians may prophesy and perhaps should prophesy, he did not expect the ministry of the prophet to be an activity in which all are primarily or totally engaged. Thus he asked "Are all prophets?" (1 Cor. 12:29), clearly expecting a negative answer. In Ephesians 4:11 Paul spoke of only "some" as being prophets. Clearly the New Testament church set apart a special group of people known as prophets. The church at Antioch had in its number both "prophets and teachers" (Acts 13:1).

Agabus, one of the few prophets actually named in the New Testament, had notable gifts of prediction: he prophesied first that there would be a great famine (Acts 11:28) and later that Paul would be "bound" in Jerusalem and handed over to the Gentiles (Acts 21:10–14). Generally, though, the term *prophecy* seems to combine the triple ingredients of proclamation, prediction, and setting forth the divine mind or will on a subject. According to his biographer, Bob Slosser, the Episcopal minister Terry Fullam defined a prophet as "one who speaks, or delivers, the word of the Lord":

Fullam explained that the New Testament teaches all Christians may prophesy as the Holy Spirit wills, depending upon the need of the moment. But, he said, not all Christians are called to be prophets; not all are called to that ministry. It has a special function. In that special sense, viewing it as an office, several passages of Scripture shed light. In Exodus 4, there is the dialogue after God tells Moses He will equip him for leading the people of Israel out of Egypt. Moses cowers, says he's not eloquent and so on. The Lord becomes exasperated and says, in effect, "Okay, Moses, I'll use your brother Aaron."

In verse 16, God adds that Aaron "shall speak for you to the people; and he shall be a *mouth* for you, and you shall be to him as God." Further on, in verse one of chapter seven, God says of the Moses-Aaron relationship, "Aaron your brother shall be your prophet." So we see the Scripture likening Moses to God and likening Aaron to a prophet or a mouth. A prophet was like a mouth. Thus a prophet of God is a mouth or mouthpiece for God.[85]

Purpose

The purpose of the gift of prophecy is the upbuilding, encouragement, and consolation of the church (1 Cor. 14:3) although, as we have seen, it may on occasion be used for the conversion of unbelievers (1 Cor. 14:24–25).

Regulation

Two regulations control prophecy: "Let two or three prophets speak, and let the others weigh what is said" (1 Cor. 14:29). If more than two or three were to speak during a worship service, confusion would result. The weighing or discerning of what is said is to be carried out by the other believers present in the light of their knowledge of God and his truth. One could say that two tests are to be applied—the first of which is the experience of other prophets present. Paul said, "the spirits of prophets are subject to prophets" (1 Cor. 14:32). The second test is the overall test of apostolic truth. "If anyone thinks he is a prophet, or spiritual," the apostle wrote, "he should acknowledge that what I am writing to you is a command of the Lord. If any one does not recognize this, he is not recognized" (1 Cor. 14:37–38).

In other words, prophets are not sources of new truth to the church, but expounders or elaborators of truth already given. The early church was warned to be on guard against false prophets and teachers who would come "speaking perverse things, to draw away disciples after them" (Acts 20:28–30). Prophecy seems to be the cooperative working together of the Holy Spirit with the human spirit to declare the present mind of

God in a given situation or to reveal the future intention of God, while at the same time the Spirit witnesses among other discerning believers who weigh the utterance in the light of Scripture.

What God wants for his children is for us to know and do his will. Prophecy is intended to play a key role in that process. In the words of Terry Fullam: "It is more important for people to hear the word of God than anything else. It is not mere human advice. And it is not always introduced by some stentorian proclamation of 'thus said the Lord' or 'the word of the Lord came unto me today.' It is merely speaking the words of the Lord into a situation, quietly and humbly."[86]

Summary
Prophecy is the exercise of that gift and ministry of the Holy Spirit that takes place when a believer declares the mind, will, or righteousness of God to the church or the world. The utterance is based on knowledge received by understanding the written Word and abiding in the living Word, sometimes by supernatural discernment, hearing, or direct revelation of the Spirit received by faith. The twofold test of prophetic authenticity is, first, whether it is consistent with the revealed Word of God and the apostolic deposit, and, second, whether it receives positive affirmation from the body of Christ especially from other prophets.

Appendix B

The Baptism in
the Holy Spirit

A brief discussion of what is meant by the baptism in the Holy Spirit is presented here, beginning with a resume of what is clear about the person and work of the Holy Spirit and moving to those points that are less clear.

The Holy Spirit

1. What Is Clear

(i) The Holy Spirit is a person
He is not an "it," not an impersonal influence. Jesus used the masculine pronoun *he* when referring to the Holy Spirit (e.g., John 14:26; 15:26; 16:8,13,14). Moreover, Scripture assigns personal attributes to him in speaking of his *mind*, as when he "teaches all things" (John 14:26); his *emotion*, as when he

"grieves" (Eph. 4:30); and his *will,* as when he "forbids" (Acts 16:6–7).

(ii) The Holy Spirit is God

He is co-equal with the Father and the Son and proceeds from both Father and Son, as affirmed in the Nicene Creed. Article V of the Anglican church's Thirty-Nine Articles speaks of him as "of one substance, majesty, and glory with the Father and the Son." Jesus sent his servants out to make disciples and baptize them in the one name "of the Father and of the Son and of the Holy Spirit" (Matt. 28:19). The apostle Paul commended people to "the grace of our Lord Jesus Christ and the love of God and the fellowship of the Holy Spirit" (2 Cor. 13:14).

It should be noted that the doctrine of the Trinity (a word not used in Scripture) arose not from metaphysical speculation but from scriptural evidence and early church experience. In their pre-Christian experience the early followers of Jesus had known God *above* them, as they walked the hills of Galilee and surveyed the star-filled skies at night. Then they had known God *with* them as Jesus shared three breathtaking years of their lives. Finally they knew God *in* them as the Holy Spirit entered their hearts after Pentecost. Having experienced God as Trinity, they could thereafter speak of him in no other way.

(iii) The Holy Spirit is the Spirit of Jesus

Throughout the New Testament, and certainly from Acts to Revelation, the Holy Spirit is seen as the Spirit of Jesus. Jesus said, "I tell you the truth: it is to your advantage that I go away, for if I do not go away, the Counselor will not come to you; but if I go, I will send him to you" (John 16:7). As the Father had sent Jesus into the world, so Jesus would send the Spirit. The Father would share in that sending but the Spirit would be sent in the name of Jesus. Thus John reported Jesus' words: "But the Counselor, the Holy Spirit, whom the Father will send in my name, He will teach you all things" (John 14:26).

In other words, the Holy Spirit was able to universalize the presence of Jesus. The disciples had perhaps sensed the Spirit *with* them during the earthly ministry of Jesus, but after the Resurrection they could know him *in* them. To his disciples Jesus said of the Spirit of truth, "you know him, for he dwells with you, and will be in you" (John 14:17). The Spirit makes it possible for the presence of Jesus to be in the hearts of his disciples everywhere. He cannot be localized as Jesus had to be in his earthly ministry.

The implication is that the Spirit is not there to glorify himself but to glorify Christ. "He will be a witness to me," Jesus said. (John 15:26). The Spirit is like a person operating a movie projector. He is there not to give us an experience and knowledge of himself, but of Christ. That fact gives a certain objectivity and identity to the Spirit's work, especially in an age hankering for subjective experience of any spirit of any kind. To seek after mere spiritual experiences makes for dangerous sentimentality and emotionalism. Christians seek the knowledge and experience of the Spirit of Jesus which will build us into a greater likeness of him. Indeed, any "spiritual" experience that does not result in greater likeness to Christ is to be considered suspect, because the Spirit whom we should be seeking or releasing is the Spirit of *Jesus*. There is therefore only one evidence that we have received the Holy Spirit of the Bible. That evidence is our gradually becoming like Jesus (Gal. 5:22–23) and desiring to bring people to Jesus (Acts 1:8).

The doctrine of Christ (called "christology") is a doctrine about God because God is the Father of our Lord Jesus Christ. The doctrine of the Holy Spirit (called "pneumatology" from the Greek *pneuma*, spirit) is a doctrine about Jesus because the Spirit is the Spirit of Jesus. As Michael Green has said of the Spirit, "You cannot get Him except through Jesus or get to Jesus except through Him."[87]

Thus if we ask how far God will go with us, christology answers, "All the way." If we ask how much Jesus wants to fill us and possess us, pneumatology answers, "completely."

A statement of Christian theology could therefore appropriately follow the outline of the biblical benediction:

Volume 1:   The grace of our Lord Jesus Christ
Volume 2:   And the love of God
Volume 3:   And the fellowship of the Holy Spirit
Volume 4:   Be with you always.

(iv) The Holy Spirit has a threefold ministry

The next item of clarity, as I see it, is that the Holy Spirit has a threefold ministry in the lives of those who become followers of Jesus—as they *seek, believe,* and *follow.* Thus the Holy Spirit works in us:

  a. before conversion—when he illumines the minds of seekers (1 Cor. 12:3) and convicts them of their sin and need of a Savior (John 16:8);

  b. at conversion—when he regenerates (John 3:5-6) and then indwells the lives of believers (Rom. 8:9-10; 1 Cor. 3:16; 2 Cor. 1:22), and finally seals them as purchased possessions (Eph. 1:13);

  c. after conversion—when he sanctifies disciples (1 Thess. 4:7-8; 1 Cor. 6:19-20), guides them (John 16:13), helps them to pray (Rom. 8:26-27), strengthens them (Eph. 3:16), brings forth his fruit (Gal. 5:22-23), and equips them for service through his gifts (1 Cor. 12:4-11).

2. What Is Less Clear

All the above seems to me pretty clear and straightforward. However, several things are not so clear. First is the matter of being "filled with the Holy Spirit." How does that relate to being "baptized in the Holy Spirit"? How do both terms or experiences relate to being "regenerated" or "born again"?

Specifically we must ask whether being filled with the Holy Spirit is the same as or different from the baptism in the Spirit. Are different terms being used to describe the same experience? Moreover, when does the baptism in the Spirit happen? Does it happen once or many times? In other words, what is the exact nature and timing of the baptism in the Holy Spirit? And where does the gift of tongues fit in?

The Nature and Timing of the Baptism in the Holy Spirit

1. The Term Defined

The terms *baptism* and *baptize* come from a Greek word (*baptizo*) which in secular Greek literature meant to plunge, sink, drown, drench, or overwhelm. A person could be drowned or sunk (literally "baptized") by wine or "overwhelmed" by sleep.

In the Old Testament the normal meaning of the word is to overwhelm or immerse. So when John the Baptist, who in one sense links Old and New Testaments, said of Jesus that he would baptize with the Holy Spirit (John 1:33) he meant that Jesus is the one who can immerse us in the Holy Spirit or overwhelm us by the Spirit. The one image carries the idea of being pushed into or under the water and the other of having buckets of water poured over us. And those who profess the baptism in the Spirit according to the charismatic understanding are probably divided pretty evenly as to which of the two metaphors they find most useful to describe their experience. Some say they were baptized in or into the Spirit and others that they felt the Spirit come upon them. Both ideas are brought together in Acts 1, with Acts 1:5 speaking of an imminent baptism in (Greek *en*) the Holy Spirit and Acts 1:8 promising power to witness when the Holy Spirit had "come upon" the disciples.

The phrase "baptized in the Spirit" is not very common in Scripture. It occurs four times in the Gospels (Matt. 3:11; Mark 1:8; Luke 3:16; John 1:33), in John the Baptist's prophecy that just as he had baptized (or immersed or overwhelmed) people with water, so Jesus would baptize, immerse, or overwhelm them in the Spirit. The phrase occurs only once in the Epistles: 1 Corinthians 12:13 tells of all being baptized by one Spirit into the one Body—all are made to drink of one Spirit. Finally, the phrase occurs twice in Acts; first, in Acts 1:5 speaking of the day of Pentecost, and second, in Acts 11:6 where Peter defended his Gentile activities to the critical "circumcision party" (Acts 11:2) by telling them how he saw the Holy Spirit fall on them "just as on us at the beginning." That, he said, reminded him of the Lord's pre-Pentecost word that "John baptized with water but you shall be baptized with the Holy Spirit" (1:6).

2. Light from the Cornelius Story

In the story of Cornelius (Acts 10), several concepts relating to the Holy Spirit are drawn together for us in one package. While Peter was speaking to Cornelius's household, "the Holy Spirit *fell on* [Idea One] all who heard the word" (Acts 10:44). Luke, the author of Acts, reported that the believers who had accompanied Peter were amazed because "the gift of the Holy Spirit had been *poured out* [Idea Two] even on the Gentiles" (Acts 10:45). The evidence Luke cited was that "they heard them *speaking in tongues* [Idea Three] and extolling God" (Acts 10:46). Peter then asked how water baptism could be denied to "these people who have *received* [Idea Four] the Holy Spirit" (Acts 10:47).

Back in Jerusalem, Peter reported how the "Holy Spirit fell on them just as on us at the beginning" (Acts 11:15) and how that had reminded him of Jesus saying that "John baptized with water, but you shall be *baptized with the Holy Spirit*" (Idea Five; Acts 11:16). In the next breath Peter said, "If then God *gave* [Idea Six] the same gift to them as he gave to us when we believed in the Lord Jesus Christ [Note: at the start of their Christian experience], who was I that I could withstand God?" (Acts 11:17).

Then the assembled group of "apostles" and "brethren" (Acts 11:1) who heard the story jumped immediately to the irrevocable conclusion on the basis of the evidence that "to the Gentiles also God has granted *repentance unto life*" (Idea Seven; Acts 11:18). When the whole happening was reported at the

Jerusalem Council (Acts 15), Peter summarized the events as God "giving them the Holy Spirit just as He did to us" (Acts 15:8).

The seven ideas brought together in the story are: (1) the Spirit *falling*; (2) the Spirit being *poured out*; (3) the recipients *speaking in tongues*; (4) the Spirit being *received*; (5) the people being *baptized* with the Spirit; (6) the Spirit being *given*; and (7) the people *repenting*. Five of the terms used (falling, being poured out, being received, being baptized, and being given) seem to refer to the same happening, suggesting that they are interchangeable. These events were followed by immediate water baptism (Acts 10:47–48).

If that early situation of New Testament evangelism were itemized slightly differently, we would observe:

(i) Illumination:
There was the spirit working to prepare Cornelius and his household (Acts 10:22,31).

(ii) Evangelism:
There was proclamation from a Spirit-directed preacher (10:20,34).

(iii) Repentance:
There was the reflex of conversion (15:3), repentance (11:18), and presumably faith, without which God does not pour out his Spirit.

(iv) New Birth:
There must have been the divine response of justification and regeneration, since no true Christian life can begin without those blessings.

(v) Baptism in the Spirit:
There was a falling of the Holy Spirit (10:44) on all who heard, identified by Peter (11:16) as similar to or identical with what

happened to the first group on the day of Pentecost.

(vi) Signs:
There was dramatic evidence of the "poured out" Spirit (10:45) in the form of tongues and praise to God (10:46).

(vii) Incorporation:
There was almost immediate public baptism (10:45) in water (10:47) for those who had "received the Holy Spirit."

(viii) Consolidation:
There was followup as Peter and the believers with him remained "for some days" (10:48).

Some argue that the first preaching to the Gentiles was inevitably unique and special, but I wonder if that argument has not been pushed too far. Maybe there is more of a norm here than we find easy to admit. Certainly neither Peter nor Cornelius (nor God) had to contend with hearers having been told by some minister that they had received the Spirit at the font in infant baptism and were accordingly regenerate; by a bishop at high school that they were getting the Spirit at confirmation; by an evangelist at the town hall that they had missed the Spirit at the font and at confirmation, but would find him either at conversion or in lesson five of the followup series; or by some Pentecostal preacher that they'd missed the Spirit at the font, confirmation, town hall, and followup series, but could receive him—plus tongues no less—at the altar-rail of the Tabernacle at Fifth and Lily Streets, where "revival will be taking place at 7:30 p.m. each night next week." Cornelius, the listener, was spared all that. So was Peter, the preacher.

Some of our problems in this matter are a legacy of the theological tangle that is our context in the semi-Christianized western world. For Peter and Cornelius the slate was clean, so the proclamation, human response, divine initiative, and public incorporation could all take place at once in a situation devoid of theological or ecclesiastical clutter. Perhaps we need to bring all these happenings together again, so that spiritual experiences that belong together are no longer separated.

3. *The Timing of the Baptism in the Spirit*

When the baptism in the Holy Spirit happens, and how, is a major point at issue between Pentecostals and non-Pentecostals and between charismatics and noncharismatics. There are three prominent views.

(i) *View One*
The first view is that regeneration and baptism in the Spirit are synchronized, taking place at the same time when an individual is converted to Christ and indwelt by the Spirit. Broadly speaking, this view is based on 1 Corinthians 12:11-13: "For by one Spirit we were all baptized into one body . . . and all were made to drink of one Spirit." In other words, at conversion all believers are baptized in the Spirit and what charismatics call being baptized in the Spirit belongs strictly to what it means to be a Christian at all.

In this view, one possible gift is that of tongues, given in the sovereignty of the Spirit (1 Cor. 12:11) but not a normative expectation or requirement for every believer. Also, the fullness of the Spirit comes through moral and spiritual surrender to his leading. It is something that happens as we keep coming to drink of the Spirit. The fullness is to be continuously appropriated.

In this view, according to John Stott in his booklet, *The Baptism and Fullness of the Holy Spirit*, "water baptism is the initiatory Christian rite, because Spirit baptism is the initiatory Christian experience."[88] Stott adds: "The Baptism in the Spirit is not a second or subsequent experience, enjoyed by some Christians, but the initial experience enjoyed by all."[89]

(ii) *View Two*
The second view sees a two-stage initiation. The first stage is regeneration, when we are born again and indwelt by the Spirit. The second stage is the

baptism in the Spirit, when we are anointed (filled, flooded, immersed) in the Spirit and empowered for service. The second stage is evidenced by manifestation of gifts of the Spirit, most notably tongues. Some insist on the evidence of tongues as normative. Others prefer to say of those baptized in the Spirit that not all *do* speak in tongues, but all *may.*

This position is based primarily on four passages of Scripture. *The first is the experience at Pentecost (Acts 2).* It is assumed in this view that the disciples received the Spirit after Jesus' resurrection, when he breathed on them and said, "Receive the Holy Spirit" (John 20:22); they were then baptized in the Spirit in a second experience on the day of Pentecost itself.

The second passage is Acts 8, about certain Samaritans who "believed Philip as he preached good news about the kingdom of God and the name of Jesus Christ" (Acts 8:12). They "received the word of God" (8:14) and were baptized (8:13,16) in the name of the Lord Jesus, but without receiving the Holy Spirit (8:15) or having him fall on them (8:16). At least it had "not yet fallen," the implication being that this event would happen before long. Finally the Samaritans did receive the Holy Spirit (8:15–17), but only after being specially prayed for by Peter and John, who had been sent down from Jerusalem by the apostolic band. Note that "baptism in the Holy Spirit" is not referred to as such in this passage, only "receiving" of the Spirit.

The third passage used to sustain view two is Acts 9, with what would seem to be a three-day gap between Saul's conversion on the Damascus road (Acts 9:1–9) and his filling with the Spirit (9:17). Again, note that the term used is "filling" with the Spirit, not baptism with the Spirit.

The fourth passage is Acts 19, which tells of "some disciples" at Ephesus (Acts 19:1), "about twelve in all" (19:7), who had been followers of John the Baptist. They declared that they had neither heard of the Holy Spirit nor "received" him when they "believed" (19:2). They had believed only "in the one who was to come" after John the Baptist (19:4). When they heard about "Jesus," they were baptized in his name, after which Paul laid hands on them, "the Holy Spirit came on them; and they spoke with tongues and prophesied" (19:5-6). Again, no reference is made to baptism in the Spirit but only to the phenomenon of "receiving the Holy Spirit" (19:2) and having the Holy Spirit "come on" one (19:6). Note also the reference to tongues in this Ephesian experience; this is the second instance (the other being Pentecost). There is no indication of tongues in either the Samaritan situation (Acts 8:14-17) or in Saul's Damascus infilling (Acts 9:17-19).

(iii) View Three
The third view accepts the experience of the baptism in the Spirit but rejects the terminology. Thus David Watson has written: "The term, baptism, is undoubtedly linked with Christian initiation, and in that sense, at least, every Christian is already baptized in the Spirit." Watson comes out strongly for the alternative phrase of being "filled with the Holy Spirit."[90]

Cardinal Suenens of Belgium in his book, *A New Pentecost*, rejects the terminology of "baptism in the Spirit" but encourages pursuit of the experience.[91] Michael Green also accepts, approves, and promotes the experience of charismatics, but encourages them "to call the rose by some other name," giving them assurance that "it will smell just as sweet."[92]

Many of those holding this third view would not want to break fellowship over terminology, but they recognize the exegetical problems and caution about pastoral problems if the terminology issue leads to arrogance in those who are supposedly "stage two" Christians, or depression in those who feel locked into "stage one." The idea of first- and second-class Christians is considered inaccurate, especially on this basis. Imagine putting people like Billy Graham, Mother Teresa or John Wesley in an inferior class because they have neither claimed a baptism in the Spirit nor spoken in tongues!

(iv) Pros and Cons
Let us summarize the three views. The first says regeneration

and baptism in the Spirit are synchronized and simultaneous. The second says there are two stages in Christian initiation, the first being regeneration and the second the baptism in the Spirit to equip for life and service. The third accepts the charismatic experience but rejects the label "baptism in the Spirit," choosing to speak rather of a filling with the Spirit as a desired experience and goal following the reception and baptism in the Spirit at conversion. We shall now look at arguments for and against each view in turn.

a. The view that regeneration and baptism in the Spirit synchronize. The idea of synchronization of the two experiences has the backing of some twenty centuries of Christian thinking. To the best of my knowledge, a two-stage initiation in these exact categories was not a part of the church's teaching until the rise of twentieth-century Pentecostalism.

This view is also sustained by a considerable weight of exegetical data. Four presentations of the biblical data in varying degrees of detail are John Stott's *The Baptism and Fullness of the Spirit,* Michael Green's *I Believe in the Holy Spirit* (noting especially chapter 8), James Dunn's elaborate treatise, *The Baptism in the Holy Spirit,* and Billy Graham's more popular study, *The Holy Spirit* (noting especially chapter 5). All of these books make a good case for retaining the term "baptism in the Spirit" as an initiatory spiritual happening. Perhaps only Michael Green's does full justice to the astonishing evidence of the twentieth-century charismatic renewal, however, which has received its major impetus from the sustained preaching of the baptism in the Spirit as a second experience.

My friend Derek Crumpton sees 1 Corinthians 12:13 ("For by one Spirit we were all baptized into one Body . . . and all were made to drink of one Spirit") as referring not to the baptism in the Spirit, as traditional evangelicalism has it, but to a baptism into the body of Christ by the Spirit. He sees that as something different:

There is a baptism by the Spirit into the body of Christ and a drink of the Spirit. The Spirit is the agent, we are the subjects of the baptism, the element is the body of Christ and he gives us to "drink" of Himself. He becomes thereby the "indwelling" Spirit, the Spirit of Christ of whose fullness we have all received. So I would see the Baptism into the Body of Christ. Then the Baptism in the Spirit has *Jesus* as the agent, we are still the subjects and the Spirit is the element in which we are baptized.[93]

Such an argument presses us either to reexamine our traditional exegesis, or, if we remain sure of it, to reexamine exactly *what* it is that the renewal movement is preaching that has brought such life and blessing across the world. Crumpton continues:

Evangelicals may argue about the terminology. But the evidence is that where this teaching is given, the resultant response is undeniable. . . I have also observed that wherever this emphasis (i.e., on Baptism in the Spirit as a second clear experience) is lacking, the renewing move of the Spirit loses impact, momentum, and meaning. . . For myself I would be very happy to testify anywhere to my being baptized in the Spirit by Jesus. I would be very reluctant to claim, even with my dearest brother, that I am filled with the Spirit. That is my daily longing. The evidence, I fear, indicates that there is so much more to gain.[94]

Alternatively, while retaining the traditional evangelical view of baptism in the Spirit as initiatory and belonging with the gift of the Spirit at conversion, one could conclude more generally that what God is honoring is not so much the concept of a second spiritual experience as it is a renewed emphasis on the work of the Spirit as a whole. Maybe the Holy Spirit has indeed been the stepchild of theology and a neglected person of the Trinity in much church life. Perhaps the Pentecostals and charismatics have stumbled on to the heart of Christian reality and its power for life and ministry, so the Lord is honoring them with his blessing even if some of their vocabulary may lack theological preci-

sion. The renewal movement thus becomes a bell sounding in
the ears of the church, saying, "Hey, everyone, here's what it's
all about. Here's an emphasis you've forgotten!"

  *b. The view that Christian initiation has two stages: regeneration, then
baptism in the Spirit.* If evangelicals and others must look deeper at
what the renewal movement is all about and why it is producing
dramatic new life across the world, then Pentecostals and charismatics must likewise pause to hear what evangelicals and the
church down the ages have to say. Is baptism in the Spirit indeed
the correct term to describe the new release or fullness of the
Spirit which has come to so many through the renewal movement? Some humble give-and-take on both sides is in order so
that the truth both are looking at from different perspectives
may become clearer to all. The two groups, evangelicals and
charismatics, are not simply cousins; they are brothers. They
are certainly not opponents and they must not relate as such.

  For myself, I must admit that the term "baptism in the
Spirit" is problematic to describe my own Milner Park experience. As noted earlier, in none of the seemingly two-stage situations—the Samaritans (Acts 8), Saul (Acts 9), or the Ephesians
(Acts 19)—does the term "baptism in the Spirit" appear. Where
it *is* used (with Cornelius's household, Acts 10), the situation
reflects all the ingredients of human and divine initiation coming together at once. That makes the Cornelius story an uncon-
vincing basis for any two-stage concept.

  Thus the case for the two-stage idea (and for some charismatic vocabulary) does seem to rest rather fully on the disciples'
experience at Pentecost. Much depends on one's understanding
of John 20:22, where the risen Jesus breathed on them and said,
"Receive the Holy Spirit." Were they born again *then*, as David
du Plessis believes? Or was that a promise of something still to
come, as John Wesley believed? Or did "one-volume John,"
who did not write a second volume (like the book of Acts by
Luke), conflate the post-resurrection and Pentecost teachings
into one climactic account?

  In the continuing discussion of this question, we must all be careful not to erect our castles on one text. Castles should stand on converging conglomerates of exegetical data. I am not persuaded that we can claim such a convergence for the two-stage concept in the same way we can for the idea of the "infilling of the Spirit." As I see it, the "infilling" concept does cover the data of both charismatic experience and Pentecostal phenomena as we see them in our time.

With regard to Acts 1 and 2, we do have to recognize that when Jesus told the disciples to "wait for the promise of the Father" (Acts 1:4), which he seems to equate with "being baptized in the Holy Spirit" (1:5) and with the power of the Holy Spirit coming upon them (1:8), he was surely alluding to Old Testament promises. Those promises were that the Spirit would not simply come upon a few "giants" like Moses, Gideon, Samson, Isaiah, Jeremiah, or Ezekiel, but would be available to indwell all. The Lord had spoken through Ezekiel: "A new heart I will give you and a new spirit I will put within you... I will put my Spirit within you, and cause you to walk in my statutes" (Ezek. 36:26–27). The promise through Jeremiah of a new covenant had at its heart the Lord's promise that "I will put my law within them" (Jer. 31:33). The Joel prophecy, which Peter saw fulfilled in the day of Pentecost, focused on the pouring out of the Spirit "on all flesh" (Joel 2:28).

In other words, Pentecost (especially Acts 1:4–8) seems to bring together the two ideas of the Spirit coming "into" the believer (which all would agree is initiatory) and the Spirit being poured out "upon" the believer, which many charismatics see as a second stage. But in Acts 1 the Spirit *upon* is in fact equated with the Spirit being received *into* the believer (or is in extremely close association with it) in the initiatory process.

Perhaps, therefore, like the situation in Cornelius's household, Pentecost reflects a "package" happening, first for the disciples, who had heard Jesus' own teaching, and then for other hearers who, like Cornelius's household, had the "package" teaching correctly presented to them. Looking at what happened in Acts 2, we see the whole package: the Good News of

Jesus (2:23,32), including his death (2:23), resurrection (2:32), exaltation (2:33); the Father's promise of the Holy Spirit (2:33); the challenge to repent (2:38a); the dual offer of forgiveness, dealing with the past (2:38a), plus the gift of the Holy Spirit, empowering for the future (2:38b); reception of the word and immediate public baptism (2:41); effective followup with teaching, fellowship, sacraments, and prayer (2:42).

To my mind, as intimated earlier, many of our problems come from mistaken processes of preaching and teaching that separate, in presentation and in time, biblical concepts and spiritual experiences that belong together.

Conceivably, Philip made the same sort of mistake in Samaria. Or, alternatively, we could take the view of Acts 8 that God was preventing a spillover into the church of the Jewish/Samaritan split. Thus he may have withheld the Holy Spirit from the Samaritan believers until senior Jewish leaders from Jerusalem (people from whom they would have been tempted to dissociate) had come in love and solidarity and had been instrumental in introducing them to the Holy Spirit. What witness could there have been to the world of that time if a scandalous and long-standing division had not been healed, or if believers from the Jews and believers from the Samaritans had found a common blessing but not found each other? Perhaps we have Acts 8 not as a norm but to show the prevention of a catastrophe and to warn against an eccentricity—namely, believing without receiving the Holy Spirit.

To reject both of those alternatives is to land in the exegetically precarious position of building a two-stage theology on what is clearly an exception rather than a rule (thereby also stepping out of line with the teaching of the Epistles), or to ascribe the Acts 8 happenings to the mystery of the Spirit doing his own thing, as it were, baffling all our attempts to categorize them.

At that point, regardless of the stance to which our spirits are finally drawn, perhaps we can embrace the conviction of John Taylor, that:

the whole weight of New Testament evidence endorses the central affirmation of the Pentecostalists that the gift of the Holy Spirit transforms and intensifies the quality of human life and that this is a fact of experience in the lives of Christians. The longing of thousands of Christians to recover what they feel instinctively their faith promises them is what underlies the whole movement.[95]

A similar conviction is expressed by Michael Harper:

The basic theological position of the charismatic renewal, with some variations, is that the God who invaded our world in the person of Jesus Christ nearly two thousand years ago, and will come again "in like manner" sometime in the future, still actively moves among his people, and the effects of that real presence are to be expected and experienced in our own lives.[96]

c. The view that accepts charismatic experience but questions charismatic terminology. Given my comments on the first two views, it will come as no surprise that my own inclination is in the direction of the third view. My feeling is that the term "filling" or "infilling" of the Holy Spirit best fits both the exegetical data of the New Testament and the facts of Christian and especially charismatic experience in the twentieth century. Apart from any other consideration, the desirability of being "filled with the Holy Spirit" is shared by both "camps." The concept is one that both can embrace even if their understanding of the timing and mechanics varies somewhat. The term therefore has the advantage of being widely serviceable without being divisive.

Of course, some will still insist on using the term "baptism in the Spirit," one group applying it to the initial experience, another to a subsequent second-stage experience. Perhaps for them some resolution can come from the dual meaning of the Greek word *baptizo*. It meant both being "initiated into something" (which would speak of a *status*) and being "overwhelmed by something" (which speaks of an *experience*). (See Chapter 4.)

As David Watson has suggested, uncertainty and confusion come when either meaning is overstressed at the expense of the other. Watson says

> it is possible to think of the overwhelming of the Spirit as something entirely separate from Christian initiation, whereas the two, ideally and potentially, though not necessarily experientially, are one. On the other hand, it is possible so to stress that the Christian has "got it all" by being baptized into Christ that the overwhelming of the Spirit is never experienced. This is a danger many evangelicals can fall into.[97]

Many who are looking into this subject recognize that New Testament initiation, symbolized and sealed by water baptism, is basically a single work of God with many facets. Together those facets constitute what David Watson calls "a cluster of overlapping spiritual realities." That cluster includes:

proclamation of the gospel
faith
repentance
forgiveness
justification
adoption
conversion
regeneration and new birth
baptism in the spirit
baptism in water
new life in the spirit

Admittedly the church is not always agreed on the relationship between those realities or on how they should be taught or proclaimed in an evangelistic setting. Most Christians could probably agree on two points, however. First, even though such spiritual truths and experiences may have to be intellectually separated for teaching purposes, they actually belong together theologically and spiritually. Together they express the single full reality of the believer's incorporation into Christ, which leads to discipleship and power for living and serving in the Christian life.

Second, the initiatory cluster of experiences is understood and to some extent entered upon by different individuals in different ways and in different time scales, often according to what they were taught by Christian pastors, evangelists, and theologians.

I believe more work and reflection is needed by all who preach the gospel or teach young disciples. The Pentecost and Cornelius stories seem to call us to bring together the whole didactic package, so that we preach not only repentance and faith in the evangelistic setting, but reception of and baptism in the Spirit as well. People should leave evangelistic meetings knowing new theological truths and having new spiritual commitments. But they should also be aware of the Spirit of God by whom they have been indwelt and in whom they have been baptized by Jesus, the Baptizer in the Spirit.

Having said all the above, one must still recognize that there are incredibly capable scholars and men and women of deep spirituality who argue very convincingly for different positions. Perhaps part of the problem comes from the fact that we are seeking to systematize the work of the Holy Spirit who, because he "blows where he wills," is unsystematic and unpredictable—and therefore the bugbear of systematic theologians.

The fact is that in Acts there are no theologically tidy schemes of Christian initiation. Reception of the Holy Spirit followed baptism, as in the Pentecostal proclamation of Acts 2:38. It preceded baptism, as in the experience of Cornelius and his household (Acts 10:44–48). And elsewhere a man named Simon was baptized who had no part in the Christian gospel and whose heart was still "not right before God" (Acts 8:21).

So it is in modern times. The Spirit is blowing where he wills. He is falling on "little old ladies" and filling theologically untutored businessmen. He is coming on bishops and archbishops at the most odd moments. He is invading high schools and meeting with countless housewives as they prayerfully study the

Scriptures in their living rooms. He is sending this one out to preach renewal. He is sending that one out to evangelize. He is sending the next one out to bring justice in society. And he is sending a few eccentrics out to do all three at once.

That situation creates frantic problems of unpredictability for theological minds. Yet I believe it is hazardous to try to stereotype or straitjacket the work of the Holy Spirit or the experience of individual Christians. John Taylor says, "The authenticity of the book of Acts is gloriously apparent in the inconsistency of the various incidents of the Spirit's intervention from the day of Pentecost onwards. The Holy Spirit does not appear to have read the rubrics. He will not and cannot be bound."[98] Michael Green concludes that, "There is no tidy doctrine of the Spirit to be found in Acts or for that matter in the whole New Testament."[99] It is rigidity which divides God's people; but it is the nature of truth to set us free.

Gospel and Spirit

For a summary of the whole question we turn to a remarkable little document called *Gospel and Spirit*, which emerged from a dialogue in England between the charismatically oriented Fountain Trust and the more traditional Church of England Evangelical Council. Their debate in a spirit of love and openness produced the following affirmation, which is an extract out of the whole statement:

> We are agreed that every Christian is indwelt by the Holy Spirit (Rom. 8:9). It is impossible for anyone to acknowledge sin, confess Christ, experience new birth, enjoy the Savior's fellowship, be assured of sonship, grow in holiness, and fulfill any true service or ministry without the Spirit. The Christian life is life in the Spirit. We all thank God for this gift.
>
> In recent years there has been a fresh enrichment in many Christians' Spirit-given experience of Christ and in many cases they have called it "baptism in the Holy Spirit." Some

of these people have seen their experience as similar to that of the disciples on the day of Pentecost and other comparable events in Acts. Despite the observable parallels, however, there are problems attaching to the use of this term to describe an experience separated often by a long period of time from the person's initial conversion to Christ.

In the first place this usage suggests that what is subnormal in the New Testament should be regarded as normal today; namely that a long interval should elapse between new birth and any conscious realization or reception of the Spirit's power.

In the second place, the New Testament use of the words "baptize" and especially "baptize into" stresses their initiatory content and context and therefore refers to Christian initiation, rather than to a later enrichment of Christian experience.

However, we see that it may be hard to change a usage which has become very widespread, although we all agree in recognizing its dangers. We would all emphasize that it must not be employed in a way which would question the reality of the work of the Spirit in regeneration and the real difference that this brings in experience from the outset. On that we are unanimous. Some who speak of a post-conversion "Baptism in the Holy Spirit" think of it mainly in terms of an empowering for service similar to the disciples' experience at Pentecost, though all are agreed that we should not isolate this side of the Spirit's work from His other ministries to and in the believer.

Some, stressing the experiential content of the term "baptism in the Spirit" value it as having played a unique part in awakening Christians out of spiritual lethargy and bondage and regard it as still having such a role in the future. Others, concentrating rather upon its initiatory implications, prefer to use it only to describe one aspect of new birth.

None of us wishes to deny the possibility or reality of subsequent experiences of the grace of God which have deep and transforming significance. We all affirm that a constant hunger and thirst after God should characterize every Christian rather than any complacent claim to have arrived. We urge one another and all our fellow Christians to press on to know the Lord better, and thus to enter into the fullness of our inheritance in Christ.[100]

Appendix C

Spiritual Gifts

1. Prophecy: The gift of prophecy is the special ability that God gives to certain members of the body of Christ to receive and communicate an immediate message of God to his people through a divinely anointed utterance.

2. Service: The gift of service is the special ability that God gives to certain members of the body of Christ to identify the unmet needs in a task related to God's work, and to make use of available resources to meet those needs and help accomplish the desired goals.

3. Teaching: The gift of teaching is the special ability that God gives to certain members of the body of Christ to communicate information relevant to the health and ministry of the body and its members in such a way that others will learn.

4. *Exhortation:* The gift of exhortation is the special ability that God gives to certain members of the body of Christ to minister words of comfort, consolation, encouragement, and counsel to other members of the body in such a way that they feel helped and healed.

5. *Giving:* The gift of giving is the special ability that God gives to certain members of the body of Christ to contribute their material resources to the work of the Lord with liberality and cheerfulness.

6. *Leadership:* The gift of leadership is the special ability that God gives to certain members of the body of Christ to set goals for others in such a way that they voluntarily and harmoniously work together to accomplish those goals for the glory of God.

7. *Mercy:* The gift of mercy is the special ability that God gives to certain members of the body of Christ to feel genuine empathy and compassion for individuals, both Christian and non-Christian, who suffer distressing physical, mental, or emotional problems, and to translate that compassion into cheerfully done deeds that reflect Christ's love and alleviate the suffering.

8. *Wisdom:* The gift of wisdom is the special ability that God gives to certain members of the body of Christ to know the mind of the Holy Spirit in such a way as to receive insight into how given knowledge may best be applied to specific needs arising in the body of Christ.

9. *Knowledge:* The gift of knowledge is the special ability that God gives to certain members of the body of Christ to discover, accumulate, analyze, and clarify information and ideas that are pertinent to the growth and well-being of the body.

10. *Faith:* The gift of faith is the special ability that God gives to certain members of the body of Christ to discern with extraordinary confidence the will and purposes of God for the future of his work.

11. *Healing:* The gift of healing is the special ability that God gives to certain members of the body of Christ to serve as human intermediaries through whom it pleases God to cure illness and restore health apart from the use of natural means.

12. *Miracles:* The gift of miracles is the special ability that God gives to certain members of the body of Christ to serve as human intermediaries through whom it pleases God to perform powerful acts that are perceived by observers to have altered the ordinary course of nature.

13. *Discerning of spirits:* The gift of discerning of spirits is the special ability that God gives to certain members of the body of Christ to know with assurance whether certain behavior purported to be of God is in reality divine, human, or satanic.

14. *Tongues:* The gift of tongues is the special ability that God gives to certain members of the body of Christ (a) to speak to God in a language they have never learned and/or (b) to receive and communicate an immediate message of God to his people through a divinely anointed utterance in a language they have never learned.

15. *Interpretation:* The gift of interpretation is the special ability that God gives to certain members of the body of Christ to make known in the vernacular the message of one who speaks in tongues.

16. *Apostleship:* The gift of apostleship is the special ability that God gives to certain members of the body of Christ to assume and exercise general leadership over a number of churches with an extraordinary authority in spiritual matters that is spontaneously recognized and appreciated by those churches.

17. *Helps:* The gift of helps is the special ability that God gives to certain members of the body of Christ to invest the talents they have in the life and ministry of other members of the body, thus enabling the person helped to increase the effectiveness of his or her spiritual gifts.

18. *Administration:* The gift of administration is the special ability that God gives to certain members of the body of Christ to understand clearly the immediate and long-range goals of a particular unit of the body of Christ and to devise and execute effective plans for the accomplishment of those goals.

19. *Evangelism:* The gift of evangelism is the special ability that God gives to certain members of the body of Christ to share the gospel with unbelievers in such a way that men and women become Jesus' disciples and responsible members of the body of Christ.

20. *Pastoring:* The gift of pastoring is the special ability that God gives to certain members of the body of Christ to assume a long-term personal responsibility for the spiritual welfare of a group of believers.

21. *Celibacy:* The gift of celibacy is the special ability that God gives to certain members of the body of Christ to remain single and enjoy it; to be unmarried and not suffer undue sexual temptations.

22. *Voluntary poverty:* The gift of voluntary poverty is the special ability that God gives to certain members of the body of Christ to renounce material comfort and luxury and adopt a personal lifestyle equivalent to those living at the poverty level in a given society in order to serve God more effectively.

23. *Martyrdom:* The gift of martyrdom is the special ability that God gives to certain members of the body of Christ to undergo suffering for the faith even to death while consistently displaying a joyous and victorious attitude that brings glory to God.

24. *Hospitality:* The gift of hospitality is the special ability that God gives to certain members of the body of Christ to provide open house and warm welcome for those in need of food and lodging.

25. *Missionary service:* The gift of missionary service is the special ability that God gives to certain members of the body of Christ to minister whatever other spiritual gifts they have in a second culture.

26. *Intercession:* The gift of intercession is the special ability that God gives to certain members of the body of Christ to pray for extended periods of time on a regular basis and see frequent and specific answers to their prayers to a degree much greater than that which is expected of the average Christian.

27. *Exorcism:* The gift of exorcism is the special ability that God gives to certain members of the body of Christ to cast out demons and evil spirits.

This list of spiritual gift definitions is adapted by permission from Your Spiritual Gifts Can Help Your Church Grow © *1979 by C. Peter Wagner (Ventura, CA/USA: Regal Books, a Division of G/L Publications).*

Appendix D

Gifts of the Holy Spirit

I.	*Ministry Gifts*	Acts 6:4; 21:8. Rom. 12:7. 1 Cor. 12:28. Eph. 4:11, 12. Col. 4:17. 1 Tim. 1:12. 2 Tim. 4:5, 11. Apostles Prophets Evangelists Pastors Teachers
II.	*Knowledge Gifts* (Knowing)	(i) *Word of wisdom* 1 Cor. 12:8. (ii) *Word of knowledge* 1 Cor. 12:8; 13:8; 14:6.

III.	*Gifts of* *Power* (Doing)	(i) *Faith* 1 Cor. 12:9, (Acts 3:16). (ii) *Healing* 1 Cor. 12:9, 28. (iii) *Working of miracles* 1 Cor. 12:10, 28, 29. (iv) *Discerning of spirits* 1 Cor. 12:10.
IV.	*Gifts of* *Utterance* (Saying)	(i) *Prophecy* Acts 2:17, 18; 19:6; 21:9. Rom. 12:6. 1 Cor. 11:4, 5; 12:10; 13:2, 8, 9; 14:1, 3–6, 22, 24, 31, 39. 1 Tim. 1:18; 4:14. (ii) *Various kinds of tongues* Mark 16:17. Acts 2:4, 11; 10:46; 19:6. 1 Cor. 12:10, 28, 30; 13:1, 8; 14:2, 4–6, 13, 14, 18, 19, 22, 23, 26, 27, 39. (iii) *Interpretation of tongues* 1 Cor. 12:10, 30; 14:5, 13, 26–28.
V.	*Other Gifts*	(i) *Helps* 1 Cor. 12:28. (ii) *Administration* 1 Cor. 12:28. (iii) *Service* Rom. 12:7. 2 Cor. 8:4; 9:1. 1 Pet. 4:11. (iv) *Exhortation* Acts 13:15. Rom. 12:8. 1 Cor. 14:3. 1 Tim. 4:13. Heb. 13:22. (v) *Giving* Rom. 12:8. 2 Cor. 9:7. Phil. 4:15. (vi) *Leading* Rom. 12:8. 1 Tim. 5:17. Heb. 13:7, 17, 24. (vii) *Showing mercy* Rom. 12:8. (viii) *Revelation* 1 Cor. 14:6, 26. 2 Cor. 12:1, 7. Gal. 2:2.

Notes

1. Francis Schaeffer, "The Practice of Truth," *One Race, One Gospel, One Task* (Minneapolis: World Wide Publications, 1967), p. 453.
2. Charles Hummel, *Fire in the Fire Place* (Downers Grove, Ill.: InterVarsity Press, 1978), p. 25.
3. Ibid., p. 26.
4. Ibid., p. 27.
5. Peter Wagner, *Look Out, the Pentecostals Are Coming* (Carol Stream, Ill.: Creation House, 1973), p. 152.
6. Ibid., p. 153.
7. Ibid.
8. David Howard, *Hammered as Gold* (New York: Harper & Row, 1969), p. 146.
9. Wagner, p. 159.
10. Rodman Williams, *Era of the Spirit* (Plainfield, N.J.: Logos Publishing House), p. 23.
11. Ibid.
12. Karl Barth, *Church Dogmatics* (Edinburgh: T. & T. Clark, 1962), p. 828.
13. Emil Brunner, *The Misunderstanding of the Church* (London: Lutterworth Press, 1952), p. 48.
14. Ibid., pp. 47-49, 52.
15. Clark Pinnock, "The New Pentecostalism: Reflection by a Well Wisher," *Christianity Today,* September 14, 1973.
16. Charles Williams, *The Descent of the Dove* (London and Glasgow: Collins—The Fontana Library, 1939), p. 17.
17. John V. Taylor, *The Go-Between*

God (London: S.C.M. Press, 1972), p. 199.

18. Richard Lovelace, *Dynamics of Spiritual Life* (Downers Grove, Ill.: InterVarsity Press, 1979), p. 16.
19. Ibid., pp. 16-17.
20. Ibid., pp. 20-21.
21. The full story is chronicled in Michael Cassidy, *Prisoners of Hope,* (Pietermaritzburg: African Enterprise, 1974).
22. Ibid., p. 146.
23. Ibid., p. 147.
24. Ibid., pp. 151-152.
25. David Watson, *I Believe in the Church* (Grand Rapids, Mich.: Eerdmans, 1979).
26. David Watson, *One in the Spirit* (London: Hodder & Stoughton, 1973), p. 15.
27. Kenneth S. Kantzer, "The Charismatics Among Us," *Christianity Today,* February 22, 1980, p. 25.
28. Ibid., p. 28.
29. Ibid.
30. James Packer, "Theological Reflections on the Charismatic Movement," *The Churchman* 94 (1980): 119.
31. Ralph Martin, "A Catholic Assesses the Charismatic Renewal in His Church," *Christianity Today,* March 7, 1980, p. 18.
32. Ibid., p. 19.
33. Ibid.
34. Michael Harper, *This Is the Day* (London: Hodder & Stoughton, 1979), p. 106.
35. John C. King, *The Evangelicals* (London: Hodder & Stoughton, 1969), p. 68.
36. Ibid., pp. 70-71.
37. "Critics Corner—Aggressions and Charismatics," *The Christian Ministry,* September 1977, pp. 81-83.
38. Ibid.
39. Michael Griffiths, "The Power of the Holy Spirit," in *The New*

Face of Evangelicalism, ed. Rene Padilla (London: Hodder & Stoughton, 1975), p. 245.
40. Richard Quebedeaux, *The New Charismatics* (New York: Doubleday, 1976), p. 127.
41. Lovelace, pp. 262-63.
42. Edwyn Hoskyns, *The Fourth Gospel,* ed. F. N. Davey (London: Faber & Faber, 1940).
43. Packer, p. 104.
44. David du Plessis, *A Man Called Mr. Pentecost* (Plainfield, N.J.: Logos International, 1977), p. 78.
45. Ibid.
46. John Stott, *God's New Society* (London: Inter-Varsity Press, 1970), p. 52.
47. Ibid., pp. 53-54.
48. A. W. Tozer, *How to Be Filled with the Holy Spirit* (Harrisburg, Pa.: Christian Publications, Inc.).
49. Michael Griffiths, "The Power of the Holy Spirit," in *The New Face of Evangelicalism,* ed. Rene Padilla (London: Hodder & Stoughton, 1975), p. 251.
50. Harper, p. 47.
51. Karl Barth, "Gifts in the Community," *Church Dogmatics* (Edinburgh: T. & T. Clark, 1936-39), p. 828.
52. C. Peter Wagner, *Your Spiritual Gifts* (Glendale, Calif.: Regal, 1979), p. 32.
53. Ibid., pp. 49-50.
54. Ibid.
55. Michael Green, *I Believe in the Holy Spirit* (London: Hodder and Stoughton, 1975), pp. 155-56.
56. Festo Kivengere, *When God Moves* (Pasadena: African Enterprise, 1973), p. 11.
57. Roy Hession, *The Calvary Road* (London: Christian Literature Crusade, 1950), p. 16.
58. Ibid., pp. 52-53.
59. Ibid., p. 53.
60. Ibid., p. 54.

61. E. Stanley Jones, *The Way* (London: Hodder & Stoughton, 1947), p. 9.

62. E. M. Howse, *Saints in Politics* (London: George Allen and Unwin., 1953; reprint ed., 1971), p. 7.

63. Ibid.

64. George Carey, *I Believe in Man* (London: Hodder & Stoughton, 1977), p. 110.

65. John Stott, *Christian Mission in the Modern World* (London: Falcon, 1975), p. 32.

66. *Rand Daily Mail*, Johannesburg, 22 August 1981.

67. Ibid.

68. Ron Sider, *Rich Christians in an Age of Hunger* (London: Hodder & Stoughton, 1977), p. 120.

69. David Lyon, *Karl Marx* (England: Lion Publishing, 1979).

70. Ibid., p. 50.

71. Edgar H. Brookes, *Power, Law, Right and Love* (Durham, N.C.: Duke University Press, 1963), p. 36.

72. Ibid., pp. 39-40, 42.

73. Michael Cassidy, *Together in One Place* (Nairobi: Evangel Press, 1978), pp. 215-216.

74. Max Warren, *I Believe in the Great Commission* (London: Hodder & Stoughton, 1976), p. 31.

75. David Bryant, *In the Gap* (Madison, Wisc.: InterVarsity Missions Press, 1979), pp. 71-74.

76. W. B. Hocking, *Rethinking Missions* (New York: Harper & Bros., 1932).

77. Hendrik Kraemer, *The Christian Message in a Non-Christian World* (Grand Rapids, Mich.: Kregel, 1938).

78. Will Durant, *Story of Philosophy* (New York: Simon & Schuster, 1959), p. 1.

79. Richard Foster, *Celebration of Discipline* (London: Hodder & Stoughton, 1980), p. 23.

80. Lovelace, pp. 305-306.

81. Jonathan Edwards, "Thoughts on the Revival in New England," *The Great Awakening*, ed. C. C. Goen (New Haven: Yale University Press, 1972), p. 418.

82. Lovelace, p. 246.

83. Edwards, pp. 421-422.

84. Ibid., p. 422.

85. Bob Slosser, *Miracle in Darien* (Plainfield, N.J.: Logos International, 1979), pp. 177-180.

86. Ibid., p. 180.

87. Michael Green, *I Believe in the Holy Spirit* (London: Hodder & Stoughton, 1975), p. 39.

88. John Stott, *The Baptism & Fullness of the Holy Spirit* (London: Inter-Varsity Press, 1964), p. 19.

89. Ibid., p. 15.

90. David Watson, *One in the Spirit* (London: Hodder & Stoughton, 1973), p. 67.

91. Leon Cardinal Joseph Suenens, *A New Pentecost* (New York: Seabury Press, 1974).

92. Green, p. 39.

93. Derek Crumpton, personal letter to the author (15 Oct. 1981).

94. Ibid.

95. John V. Taylor, *The Go-Between God* (London: S.C.M. Press, 1972), p. 199.

96. Michael Harper, *This Is the Day* (London: Hodder & Stoughton, 1979), p. 57.

97. Watson, *One in the Spirit*, p. 69.

98. Taylor, p. 120.

99. Green, p. 65.

100. *Gospel & Spirit* (London: The Fountain Trust and the Church of England Evangelical Council, 1977).